BRUNO KREISKY FORUM
FÜR INTERNATIONALEN DIALOG

Gertraud S. Auer · Tove Raiby · Margit Schmidt (Ed./Hg.)

Crossing Borders

Grenzen überschreiten

GERTRAUD S. AUER · TOVE RAIBY · MARGIT SCHMIDT (HG./*ED.*)

CROSSING BORDERS

TOWARDS A CULTURE OF PEACE
THE MIDDLE EAST YOUTH PEACE FORUM

GRENZEN ÜBERSCHREITEN

FÜR EINE KULTUR DES FRIEDENS
DAS NAHOST-JUGEND-FRIEDENSFORUM

PICUS VERLAG WIEN

Die Deutsche Bibliothek – CIP-Einheitsaufnahme

Crossing borders : towards a culture of peace = Grenzen überschreiten / The Middle East Youth Peace Forum. Gertraud S. Auer ... (Hg). – Wien: Picus Verl., 1999
ISBN 3-85452-433-1

Grafische Gestaltung: Dorothea Löcker, Wien
Druck und Verarbeitung: Druckerei Theiss GmbH, Wolfsberg
ISBN 3-85452-433-1

CONTENT
INHALT

In lieu of a preface

I have the hope that both peoples – the Israelis and the Palestinians – will be able to coexist, not just living next to each other but also with each other. Even if these people have little material resources and no petroleum they are rich in terms of intellectual talent. There is an unusually large number of intellectuals and academics among Palestinians. The intellectual and human qualities of the Israelis and Palestinians could be used to create a prosperous region – maybe not as rich as oil-producing countries but certainly more productive and creative.

Bruno Kreisky
("France Soir", October 22, 1979)

Anstelle eines Vorwortes

Ich hoffe, daß beide Völker – die Israelis und die Palästinenser – ein Zusammenleben schaffen werden, nicht nur ein Nebeneinander, sondern ein Miteinander. Auch wenn sie arm an Rohstoffen sind und keine Erdölvorkommen haben, so sind sie doch reich an geistigen Talenten. Unter den Palästinensern gibt es eine große Anzahl von Intellektuellen und Akademikern. Die geistigen und menschlichen Qualitäten von Israelis und Palästinensern sollten zur Entwicklung einer blühenden Region genutzt werden – die vielleicht nicht so reich sein wird wie die erdölproduzierenden Länder, aber sicher produktiver und kreativer.

Bruno Kreisky
(»France Soir«, 22. Oktober 1979)

TOWARDS A CULTURE OF PEACE

The history of humankind is a chronology of conquests and of the feats of war heroes, filled with stories of continuous sorrow and destruction. The transition from a "culture of war and violence" to a "culture of peace" in which human rights are respected, wars prevented and dialogue recognised as a means of securing peace depends on our common commitment.

It can only be reached through a social development, which is based on participation, dialogue and non-violence. Peace agreements are negotiated by experts and signed by statesmen, but to implement them – to live peace – is the difficult task of the individual. In wars and warlike situations the death toll has mounted and so have hatred, fear and mistrust. Finding a way out of this vicious circle and abandoning one's prejudices requires great courage and tremendous effort.

The Bruno Kreisky Forum is committed to a dialogue based on intercultural understanding and religious tolerance as a means of promoting constructive relations between different groups and fostering co-operation between different regions. One of its key tasks is to observe the peace process in the Middle East and to support it by the institution of confidence-building measures between the parties in conflict.

We felt our target group had to be youth, the generation of tomorrow, because we are convinced that youth is an important factor in the future development of democratic societies, and the very example of youth co-operation promotes the message of peace. The needs and the preparedness of youth to co-operate are an important dimension of a new global ethic that improves prospects for a positive future. Youth are a force to be reckoned with and a key partner in the development of North-South relationships.

In 1993, under the influence of the Declaration of Principles subsequent to the Oslo talks, the idea of the Middle East Youth Peace Forum was born and the groundwork was laid for a series of encounters which have since contributed to cross-border peace education. The ongoing process, which led from coexistence and tolerance to co-operation and friendship within this international youth group is very encouraging. The outcome of the cross-cultural dialogue reached far out from the level of participants to the level of the accompanying delegation leaders and educators and last but not least to the families and friends in their home countries. The Austrian members of the "New Generation" – a name the multinational group has chosen as a corporate identity – have taken their catalytic role very seriously and acquired strategies for overcoming stereotypes, prejudices and racism. Cultural diversities have been perceived as an enriching factor. Equipped with practical political training and the tools for peace education, they become an important element of civil society and help to strengthen democracy.

The United Nations will proclaim the year 2000 "International Year for the Culture of Peace". Based on its experience with the promotion of youth dialogue, the Bruno Kreisky Forum actively seeks to support and enhance the role of young people in the promotion of change. The "New Generation" team of the Middle East Youth Peace Forum has proved that they are prepared to contribute with personal commitment and courage.

The Editors

FÜR EINE KULTUR DES FRIEDENS

Geschichte ist ein Kalendarium von Eroberungen und Kriegshelden, eine Chronologie des Leidens und der Zerstörung. Um von dieser »Kriegs- und Gewaltkultur« zu einer »Kultur des Friedens« zu gelangen, in der Menschenrechte beachtet und Kriege verhindert werden und in der der Dialog als Mittel der Friedenssicherung anerkannt wird, bedarf es des Engagements von uns allen.
Das Fundament dieser Kultur des Friedens ist eine Gesellschaft, in der Zivilcourage, Dialogfähigkeit und Gewaltverzicht vorherrschen. Kriege und kriegsähnliche Zeiten fordern ihren Blutzoll und sind Nährboden für Haß, Angst und Mißtrauen. Um aus diesem Teufelskreis auszubrechen und Vorurteile abzubauen, bedarf es großen Mutes und persönlicher Anstrengung. Friedensverträge werden von Experten ausgehandelt und von Staatsmännern unterzeichnet, aber sie umzusetzen – das heißt mit Leben zu füllen – ist die schwierige Aufgabe der Menschen vor Ort.
Das Bruno Kreisky Forum hat sich einem Dialog verpflichtet, in dem kulturelle Verschiedenheit und religiöse Toleranz die Bausteine für neue Beziehungen und Wegweiser für Zusammenarbeit und Koexistenz sind. Eines der Schwerpunktthemen ist daher die Beobachtung des Friedensprozesses im Nahen Osten und die Unterstützung von vertrauensbildenden Maßnahmen zwischen den Konfliktparteien.
Wir wußten, daß unsere Zielgruppe die Jugend, die Generation von morgen sein muß, weil wir überzeugt sind, daß junge Menschen voll an der Entwicklung und dem Fortschritt unserer Gesellschaft teilhaben. Mit ihrer beispielhaften Zusammenarbeit können junge Menschen wahre Friedensbotschafter werden. Ihre Bedürfnisse und ihre Bereitschaft, auf den anderen zuzugehen, können zum Schlußstein für eine neue globale Ethik und damit für ein zukunftsgerichtetes Engagement im Nord-Süd-Dialog werden.
Unter dem Eindruck der Oslo-Gespräche und der Prinzipienerklärung zwischen Israel und der PLO wurde 1993 die Idee eines Nahost-Jugend-Friedensforums geboren und damit die Grundlage für eine lange Reihe von Begegnungen geschaffen. Diese haben seither einen Beitrag zu grenzüberschreitender Friedenserziehung geleistet. Der kontinuierliche Prozeß innerhalb dieser internationalen Gruppe, der über Koexistenz und Toleranz zu Zusammenarbeit und Freundschaft führt, ist sehr ermutigend. Der entstandene interkulturelle Dialog reicht weit über die Grenzen der TeilnehmerInnen hinaus, umfaßt die Ebene der begleitenden DelegationsleiterInnen und PädagogInnen und integriert die Familien und den Freundeskreis in den jeweiligen Heimatländern.
Die österreichischen Mitglieder der »Neuen Generation« – so nennt sich die multinationale Gruppe – haben ihre Rolle als Katalysatoren bisher sehr ernst genommen und gelernt, mit Berührungsängsten, Vorurteilen und Rassismus umzugehen. Kulturelle Verschiedenheit wird von ihnen als Bereicherung wahrgenommen.
Ausgestattet mit praktischem, politischem Training und mit Werkzeugen zur Friedenserziehung werden sie ein wichtiger Teil der zivilen Gesellschaft und Garanten für demokratisches Handeln.
Das Jahr 2000 wird von den Vereinten Nationen zum »Internationalen Jahr für die Kultur des Friedens« ausgerufen. Das Bruno Kreisky Forum, mit seiner Erfahrung im Dialog mit der Jugend, fördert die Rolle der jungen Menschen beim Aufbau dieser Friedenskultur. Die Mitglieder der »Neuen Generation« des Nahost-Jugend-Friedensforums haben bewiesen, daß sie bereit sind, mit Engagement und Mut mitzuarbeiten.

Die Herausgeberinnen

THE MIDDLE EAST YOUTH PEACE FORUM
DAS NAHOST-JUGEND-FRIEDENSFORUM

Chronology
Chronologie

1992
December/Dezember
Federal Minister Rudolf Scholten starts the initiative of a peace programme for youth in the Middle East.
Bundesminister Rudolf Scholten initiiert die Idee eines Friedensprogrammes für junge Menschen im Nahen Osten.

1993
September
Signing of the Oslo Agreement in Washington
Unterzeichnung des Oslo-Abkommens in Washington

Invitation to the Bruno Kreisky Forum to carry out a Middle East Youth Peace Forum
Einladung an das Bruno Kreisky Forum zur Durchführung eines Nahost-Jugend-Friedensforums

1994
January/Jänner 16–18
Pre-conference of the delegation leaders in Vienna to plan the first Middle East Youth Peace Forum
Vorbereitungskonferenz der DelegationsleiterInnen in Wien zur Planung des ersten Nahost-Jugend-Friedensforums

July/Juli 10–21
The Middle East Youth Peace Forum inaugural meeting in Vienna and Tyrol, "Building bridges"
Gründungstreffen des Nahost-Jugend-Friedensforums in Wien und Tirol unter dem Motto »Brücken bauen«

November 13–16
Austrian participants accompany Austrian Federal President Thomas Klestil on a state visit to Israel and meet with their Israeli and Palestinian peers.
Österreichische TeilnehmerInnen begleiten Bundespräsident Thomas Klestil auf dem Staatsbesuch nach Israel und treffen mit ihren israelischen und palästinensischen Freunden zusammen.

1995
May/Mai 11–15
The Bruno Kreisky Forum organises an encounter for 400 Austrian and Israeli youth in Jerusalem to commemorate the 50th anniversary of the end of World War 2. Some of them are participants of the Middle East Youth Peace Forum and take the opportunity to see again their Israeli and Palestinian friends.
Das Bruno Kreisky Forum organisiert eine Begegnung von 400 österreichischen und israelischen Jugendlichen in Jerusalem zum 50. Jahrestag des Endes des Zweiten Weltkriegs. Unter den Jugendlichen sind auch TeilnehmerInnen des Nahost-Jugend-Friedensforums, die die Gelegenheit zum Wiedersehen mit ihren Freunden nützen.

August 9–15
The second Middle East Youth Peace Forum takes place in Lindabrunn/Austria under the motto: "From Co-existence and Tolerance to Co-operation and Friendship".
Das zweite Nahost-Jugend-Friedensforum findet in Lindabrunn/Österreich unter dem Motto: »Von Koexistenz und Toleranz zu Zusammenarbeit und Freundschaft« statt.

November 4
Assassination of the Israeli Prime Minister Yitzak Rabin
Ermordung des israelischen Ministerpräsidenten Yitzak Rabin

November 11
Austrian Federal Chancellor Franz Vranitzky, President of the Bruno Kreisky Forum, receives the J. William Fulbright Prize for International Understanding in Washington D.C. and donates its $ 50.000 award to the Middle East Youth Peace Forum for the project "Crossing Borders".
Der österreichische Bundeskanzler und Vorsitzende des Bruno Kreisky Forums, Dr. Franz Vranitzky, erhält in Washington D.C. den mit $ 50.000 dotierten J. William Fulbright Prize for International Understanding und stiftet den gesamten Betrag dem Nahost-Jugend-Friedensforum für das Projekt »Crossing Borders«.

1996

February/Februar
Margit Schmidt and Gertraud Auer on a fact finding tour in the Middle East to prepare the "Crossing Borders" project
Reise von Margit Schmidt und Gertraud Auer in den Nahen Osten zur Vorbereitung des »Crossing-Borders«-Projekts

June/Juni 16–18
Preparatory conference of the delegation leaders for "Crossing Borders" in Aqaba/ Jordan
Vorbereitungskonferenz der DelegationsleiterInnen für »Crossing Borders« in Aqaba/ Jordanien

September 1–10
The third Middle East Youth Peace Forum "Crossing Borders" in Israel, Jordan and the Palestinian Territories
Das dritte Nahost-Jugend-Friedensforum unter dem Motto »Crossing Borders« in Israel, Jordanien und den palästinensischen Gebieten

Autumn/Herbst
Weekend video seminar with wien xtra.
Wochenend-Videoseminar mit wien xtra.

November 28–December/Dezember 3
Delegation leaders' conference at the Kreisky Forum/Vienna to evaluate the "Crossing Borders" project and planning session for 1997 and 1998; meeting with the Austrian participants; report about ongoing projects: video and slide show about "Crossing Borders" for delegation leaders and special guests
Konferenz der DelegationsleiterInnen im Wiener Bruno Kreisky Forum zur Evaluierung des »Crossing-Borders«-Programms und zur Planung von 1997 und 1998; Treffen mit den österreichischen TeilnehmerInnen; Berichte über die laufenden Projekte; Präsentation von »Crossing Borders« mit Video- und Diaprojektion für geladene Gäste

December/Dezember 18
President Arafat visits the Bruno Kreisky Forum during his stay in Vienna and is updated about the Middle East Youth Peace Forum in general and the "Crossing Borders" project in particular.
Präsident Arafat besucht das Bruno Kreisky Forum während seines Wienaufenthaltes und wird über das Nahost-Jugend-Friedensforum im allgemeinen und »Crossing Borders« im besonderen informiert.

1997

February/Februar 17–19
Meeting of educators and leading team in Vienna to plan the programme for the "Youth Leader Training Project"
Konferenz der PädagogInnen und des Leitungsteams in Wien zur Vorbereitung des »JugendleiterInnen-Trainingsprogramms«

April 19
Meeting of the Austrian delegation in Vienna
Treffen der österreichischen Delegation in Wien

May/Mai 29–June/Juni 2
Meeting of the delegation leaders and the youth delegates in Rome
Konferenz der DelegationsleiterInnen und Jugenddelegierten in Rom

September 21–28
First seminar of the Youth Leader Training in Söchau/Austria
Erstes Seminar des JugendleiterInnen-Trainings in Söchau/Österreich

September 97–February/Februar 98
Field work on the ongoing projects in the Middle East
Praktikum an den laufenden Projekten im Nahen Osten

November 1997
Video workshop for the Austrian participants with Sylvain Biegeleisen
Wochenend-Videokurs für die österreichischen TeilnehmerInnen, mit Sylvain Biegeleisen

December/Dezember 9–14
Meeting of the educators in Jerusalem
Konferenz der PädagogInnen in Jerusalem

December/Dezember 11–14
Conference of the delegation leaders, organisers and educators in Jerusalem
Konferenz der DelegationsleiterInnen, des Leitungsteams und der PädagogInnen in Jerusalem

1998
January/Jänner
Institute for Conflict Research: Case Study on the Middle East Youth Peace Forum – evaluation, results
Institut für Konfliktforschung in Wien: Fallstudie über das Nahost-Jugend-Friedensforum – Evaluierung, Ergebnisse

February/Februar 5–15
Second seminar of the Youth Leader Training in Schlaining/Austria and Intercultural Workshop with youth of Austrian minority groups
Zweites Seminar des JugendleiterInnentrainings in Burg Schlaining/Österreich und interkultureller Workshop mit VertreterInnen österreichischer Minderheiten

May/Mai 27–31
Workshop with youth leaders, educators and leading team to plan the Bruno Kreisky Peace Forum 98
Arbeitstreffen der JugendleiterInnen, PädagogInnen und des Leitungsteams zur Vorbereitung des Bruno-Kreisky-Jugend-Friedensforums 98

August 11–19
Bruno Kreisky Youth Peace Forum – Creative Diversity – Looking for Common Ground in the Mediterranean in Helenental near Baden/Austria, youth leaders as partners.
Bruno-Kreisky-Jugend-Friedensforum – Kreativität in der Verschiedenheit – Auf der Suche nach Gemeinsamkeiten im Mittelmeerraum im Helenental bei Baden/Österreich, JugendleiterInnen als Partner

At the UN-City / In der UNO-City
Working group / Arbeitsgruppe
Opening at the Bruno Kreisky Forum –
Franz Vranitzky, Margit Schmidt
Eröffnung im Bruno Kreisky Forum
On the way to Innsbruck
Auf dem Weg nach Innsbruck

1994

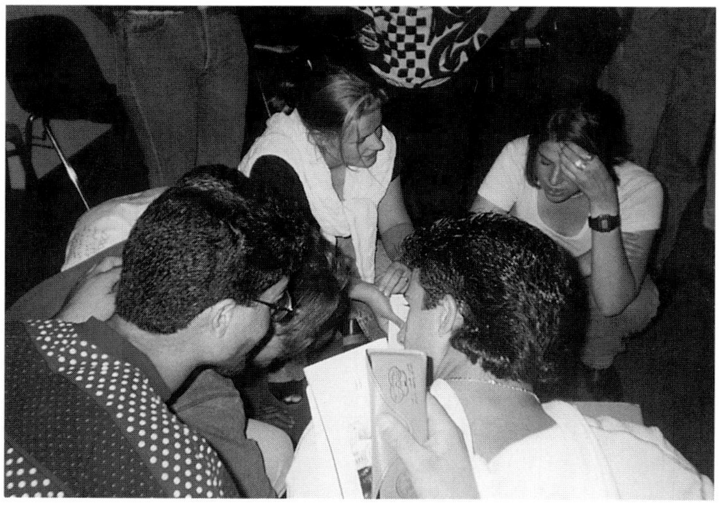

Excursion to the Lake Neusiedl
Ausflug zum Neusiedlersee
Working group / **Arbeitsgruppe**

1995

Dabka dancing / Beim Dabka-Tanzen
Tree planting in Eilat, Israel
Bäumepflanzen in Eilat, Israel
Petra, Jordan / Petra, Jordanien

1996

Plenary
Plenum
Contest for prince and princess of the seminar
Wahl zum Seminarprinzen und zur Seminarprinzessin

1997

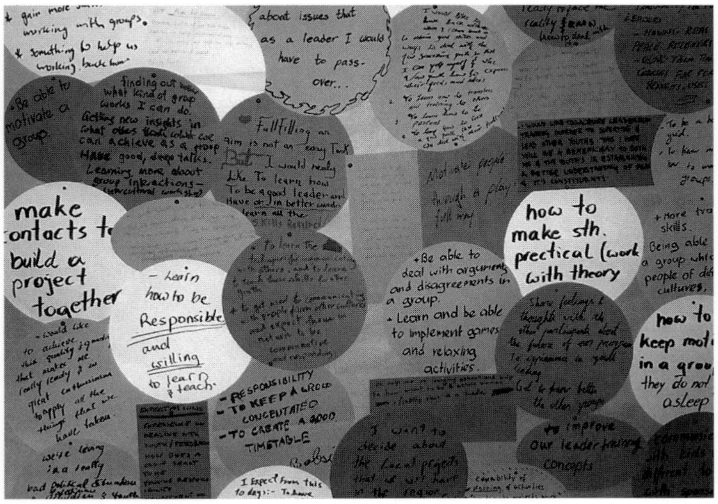

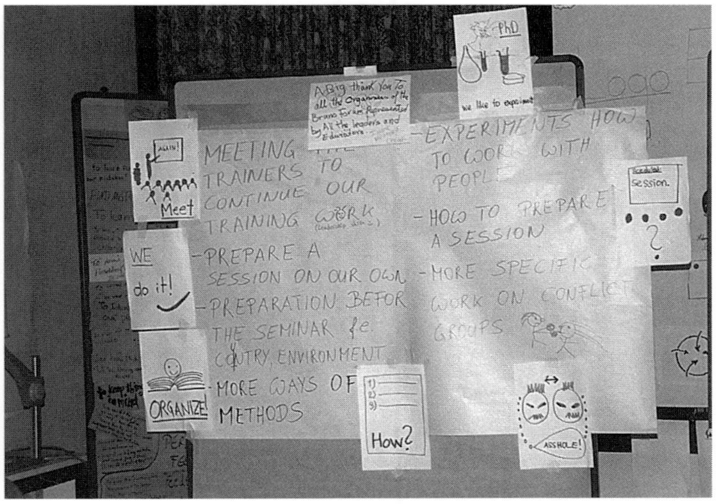

1998

Intercultural workshop
Interkultureller Workshop

Chancellor Viktor Klima and delegation leaders
Bundeskanzler Viktor Klima und Delegationsleiter
Discussion with the chancellor
Diskussion mit dem Bundeskanzler
Helenental, Austria / Österreich

1998

PURSUING PEACE TOGETHER
GEMEINSAME WEGE ZUM FRIEDEN

Background

Austria has always shown great interest in developments in the Middle East and in efforts to achieve peace there. The Middle East Youth Peace Forum is a contribution of the Austrian Federal Government and the Bruno Kreisky Forum for International Dialogue to promote the idea of peace in the Middle East.
The initiative of then Federal Minister of Education and the Arts Rudolf Scholten and invitations by the Bruno Kreisky Forum for International Dialogue led to the establishment of the Middle East Youth Peace Forum in Vienna in July 1994: an initial meeting of 64 young Israelis, Palestinians, Egyptians, Jordanians and Austrians was organised by the Bruno Kreisky Forum in co-operation with the Federal Chancellery, the Ministry of Foreign Affairs, the Ministry of Environment, Family and Youth Affairs, the Ministry of Education and the Arts, the Federal Youth Council, the Intercultural Centre and the Division of Youth Affairs in Tyrol.
The objective of this meeting was to bring youth together from the conflict parties in the region and to bridge the psychological gaps existing among them. Multinational groups articulated confidence building projects and continued to work on them between the meetings of the Middle East Youth Peace Forum. These projects include, for example, the publication of a jointly edited Israeli-Palestinian Youth Newsletter, the creation of a web page in the Internet, the organisation of joint conferences in schools and youth centres, regular work on the projects and contacts with the media to promote the ideas of the Middle East Youth Peace Forum.
Continuity is one of the unique characteristics of the Forum. In contrast to youth camps that are singular events or youth exchange programmes, it places special emphasis on continuity over an extended period of time as well as on continuity in terms of participation. The majority of the young adults involved in the Middle East Youth Peace Forum participated in its inaugural meeting in 1994 and are organising meetings on a regular basis in their respective communities to continue work on the projects since then. The Austrian students have become conscious of contemporary history and learned how to resist today's climate of xenophobia, racism and intolerance. The programme is meant to be an active contribution to an education for peace, giving the Austrians an important role as "catalysts" and neutral partners in a deep conflict.
The Bruno Kreisky Forum for International Dialogue in Vienna is responsible for the planning and co-ordination of the Middle East Youth Peace Forum. The direct collaboration between the Israeli, Jordanian and Palestinian delegation leaders is the guarantee for the programme's continuity. Thanks to our partners at the Unit for Democracy and Coexistence of the Israeli Ministry of Education, the Arab Studies Society in East Jerusalem and the Al-Hassan Youth Award in Jordan, it has been possible to master even very difficult situations.

Getting to know each other
Einander kennenlernen

Einleitung

Österreich hat stets starken Anteil an den Entwicklungen und Friedensbemühungen im Nahen Osten genommen. Das Jugend-Friedensforum ist ein Beitrag der Bundesregierung und des Bruno Kreisky Forums für Internationalen Dialog, die friedensstiftende Tradition Österreichs im Nahen Osten aufrechtzuerhalten.
Die Initiative von Bundesminister Rudolf Scholten und Einladungen des Bruno Kreisky Forums führten im Juli 1994 zum ersten Treffen von 64 jungen Israelis, PalästinenserInnen, ÄgypterInnen, JordanierInnen und ÖsterreicherInnen in Wien und zur Gründung des Nahost-Jugend-Friedensforums. Das Projekt wurde vom Bruno Kreisky Forum in Zusammenarbeit mit dem Büro des Bundeskanzlers, dem Bundesministerium für Auswärtige Angelegenheiten, dem Bundesministerium für Umwelt, Jugend und Familie, dem Bundesministerium für Unterricht und Kunst, dem Bundesjugendring, dem Interkulturellen Zentrum und dem Jugendreferat des Landes Tirol organisiert.
Ziel war es, Jugendliche der Konfliktparteien miteinander in Verbindung zu bringen und zu helfen, die psychologische Kluft zwischen ihnen zu überbrücken. Seither werden in multinationalen Gruppen vertrauensbildende Projekte erarbeitet, an denen auch zwischen den Forumsveranstaltungen weitergearbeitet wird. Beispiele dafür sind die Publikation eines multinationalen Jugend-Newsletters, die Einrichtung einer Homepage im Internet, gemeinsame Vorträge in Schulen, Projekte mit Jugendzentren und Kontakte mit Medien, um das Nahost-Jugend-Friedensforum einer größeren Öffentlichkeit nahezubringen.
Im Unterschied zu einmaligen Friedenscamps und Jugendaustauschprogrammen, wie sie auch von anderen Ländern organisiert werden, legt das Nahost-Jugend-Friedensforum besonderen Wert auf zeitliche und personelle Kontinuität. Ein Großteil der Jugendlichen ist seit 1994 dabei und organisiert auch in der Heimat regelmäßig Treffen. Die österreichische studentische Jugend ist mit diesem Vorhaben in ein direktes Erleben internationaler Zeitgeschichte eingebunden und erlernt damit die Fähigkeit, Phänomenen wie Fremdenhaß, Rassismus und Intoleranz zu widerstehen und dagegen anzukämpfen. Indem die österreichischen TeilnehmerInnen die wesentliche Rolle eines »Katalysators« zur Objektivierung des Konfliktes übernehmen, wird ein aktiver Beitrag zur Friedenserziehung geleistet.
Die organisatorische Betreuung des Nahost-Jugend-Friedensforums ging von Anfang an vom Wiener Bruno Kreisky Forum aus. Die enge Zusammenarbeit mit den israelischen, jordanischen und palästinensischen DelegationsleiterInnen garantiert den Erfolg dieser Initiative, besonders in sensiblen politischen Situationen.
Dank der MitarbeiterInnen der Unit for Democracy and Coexistence im israelischen Erziehungsministerium, der Arab Studies Society in Jerusalem und des Al-Hassan Award in Jordanien kann die Kontinuität des Nahost-Jugend-Friedensforums gewährleistet werden.

PARTICIPANTS
TEILNEHMER/INNEN

Excursion to the Hohe Wand, 1995
on the right Mousa
Ausflug zur Hohen Wand, 1995
rechts Mousa

ABBASI, MOUSA
1995, 1996

*8.5.1979
Jerusalem
Student at Bir Zeit University, member of the International Youth Service Palestinian delegation

ABD EL-QUADER, ALI
1996

*16.11.1978
Tulkarem
High school graduate, president of the cultural committee of his school
Palestinian delegation

Party at the youth hostel
on the right Ali
Party in der Jugendherberge
rechts Ali

Moriah and Kareem

ABDUL HADI, KAREEM
1994, 1996, 1997, 1998

*10.1.1978
Ramallah
Bir Zeit University, Science College, working on various peace keeping and political initiatives, very committed to the continuation of the Middle East Youth Peace Forum
Palestinian delegation

The Palestinian Youth Delegation is an idea for a big thing that I and a couple of friends had in mind, a kind of youth foundation with outside connections, i.e. the "New Generation", the Bruno Kreisky Forum, the Young Leaders Forum in Italy. I think that the beginning of this kind of work will create the motivation and capacity to work hard in youth projects.

Einige Freunde und ich hatten die Idee, eine palästinensische Jugenddelegation aufzubauen, eine Art Jugendstiftung mit Verbindung zu anderen Organisationen, wie z. B. die »Neue Generation«, das Kreisky Forum, das Young-Leaders-Forum in Italien. Diese Initiative könnte Motivation und Engagement für unsere Jugendprojekte fördern.

ABDULLAH, NISREEN
1995

*3.6.1975
Beit Hanina/Jerusalem
Bethlehem University
Palestinian delegation

Rabin's Assassination
The two bullets which put an end to the life of the late Prime Minister Yitzhak Rabin and which were made and sent out by an Israeli from Bar-Ilan University created a dilemma and chaos among the Israeli people. From the point of view of a Palestinian, the Arabs almost forgot all the harm caused by Rabin during the Intifada when he tried to oppress it with very austere measures, ordering the killing of demonstrators against the occupation and stone throwers. They almost forgot that he was leading the Six Day War, which resulted in the occupation of Gaza, the West Bank, the Golan Heights, and Sinai. Instead, the Arabs only remembered the good deeds he performed lastly, and that was the implementation of the peace process. He nearly performed a miracle, because who could believe that one day Arabs and Jews would live together in harmony after nearly thirty years of hatred and bloodshed.
Hopefully, Peres will continue in Rabin's footsteps and will expedite the implementation of the peace process, as he was motivated and encouraged to do so by all heads of state and governments who participated in Rabin's funeral.

Rabins Ermordung
Die zwei Kugeln, die dem Leben von Ministerpräsident Yitzhak Rabin ein Ende setzten, kamen von einem israelischen Studenten der Bar-Ilan-Universität und versetzten das israelische Volk in ein Chaos und ein Dilemma.
Für eine Palästinenserin stellt es sich aber auch so dar, daß die arabische Welt alles Unrecht vergessen hat, das ihr Rabin während der Intifada angetan hat, als er mit drastischen Mitteln vorging, Demonstranten und steinewerfende Jugendliche niederschießen ließ. Sie vergaßen fast, daß er den Sechstagekrieg kommandiert hatte, der zur Besetzung von Gaza, der Westbank, den Golanhöhen und des Sinai führte. Die arabische Welt erinnert sich nur an seine guten Taten, die er zuletzt vollbrachte, und das war die Umsetzung des Friedensprozesses. Er vollbrachte ein Wunder, denn niemand hätte geglaubt, daß eines Tages

Araber und Juden nach fast 30 Jahren des Hasses und des Blutvergießens in Harmonie zusammenleben könnten.
Peres wird hoffentlich diesen Weg fortsetzen und den Friedensprozeß, wie er von allen Staatsoberhäuptern anläßlich des Begräbnisses von Rabin unterstützt und eingefordert wurde, weiterführen.

ABU EIN, ALA'

1995, 1996, 1997, 1998

*3.1.1975
Ramallah
Bir Zeit University, engineering, youth co-ordinator of Palestinian Youth for Peace, Fateh Youth Mouvement, married, Palestinian delegation

After the last trip to Vienna in 1995, we tried hard to go ahead with the projects we took responsibilities for. The newsletter project ("The New Generation") is almost ready and it is supposed to be in printing. We prepared the proposals of the radio programme project, but we didn't get the chance to follow it up. The closure of the West Bank and the far distances between the members of the team made the continuity of these projects hard.

Nach unserem Aufenthalt in Wien 1995 versuchten wir, die Projekte weiterzuführen. Der Newsletter ist fast fertig und geht bald in Druck. Wir haben Vorschläge für das Radioprogramm ausgearbeitet, haben aber keine Möglichkeit, sie umsetzen. Die Sperre der Westbank und die weiten Distanzen zwischen den Mitgliedern des Teams machen die Fortführung des Projekts sehr schwierig.

Discussion with Chancellor Franz Vranitzky
Diskussion mit Bundeskanzler Franz Vranitzky

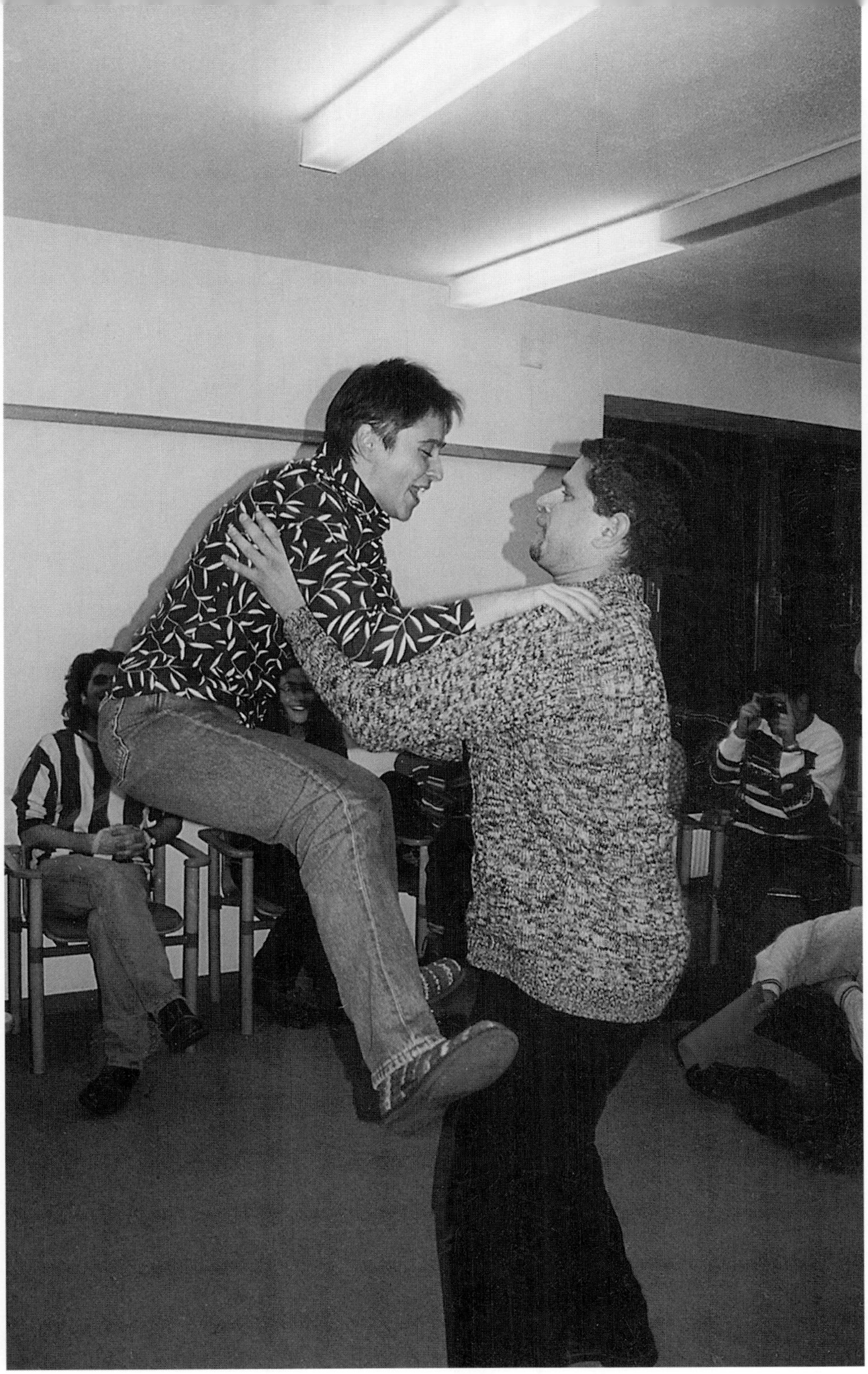

Simone, Anas

ABU KARAKI ANAS
1998

Technical engineer, currently working in
Saudi Arabia
Jordanian delegation

I want to tell you that I am going to Saudi Arabia in a few weeks time to work there. But that does not mean the end to our friendship with you and the Bruno Kreisky Forum. I hope that you are going to be in touch with me. I will support all our projects.
Please keep in touch, bye.

Ich möchte euch wissen lassen, daß ich in einigen Wochen nach Saudiarabien gehen werde, um dort zu arbeiten. Aber das bedeutet nicht das Ende der Freundschaft mit euch und dem Bruno Kreisky Forum. Ich hoffe, wir bleiben in Kontakt. Ich werde alle Projekte unterstützen. Bitte laßt von euch hören.

Farewell Party 1994
Abschiedsparty 1994

ABU-NEMEH, NANCY
1994

*29.5.1972
Battir (Bethlehem)
Graduate from Bethlehem University, married, one daughter, lives in Abu Dhabi
Palestinian delegation

Selected poems
Ausgewählte Gedichte

Where is Justice
There are thousands of children who pass away
Because of hunger and war, they die every day
While others live in a luxurious life
And have their food with silver fork and knife
This is because there is no justice or fair
And disappearance of equal air.

A New Dress for the Feast
That morning as the sun rose
Announcing the coming of the feast
She began crying
She's just a child wanting a new dress
But her dad in prison could only give her a kiss
"For next feast bring me a new dress
I want it red" she said
On her way home a bullet found refuge in her head
She gained a new red dress, but she's dead

Dreams better than life
I want to hold fast to my dreams
I don't want to live in a world full of crimes, wars and diseases.
In which death becomes better than life. And children grow up to hold a knife

Life
Life is divided into three terms:
That which was, which is and which will be.
Let us learn from the past
To forget by the present
To live better for the future.
I'm not afraid of Tomorrow,
Because I've seen Yesterday
And I love Today.

ABU SNINEH, SAMI
1994, 1995

*17.12.1977
Hebron
Palestinian delegation

On the move with Mozart
Mit Mozart unterwegs

ABU ZAYYAD, NISREEN
1995, 1996, 1997, 1998

*29.9.1974
Jerusalem
Hebrew University, philosophy and history,
Journalist, Political talk shows
Middle East Youth Peace Forum scholar 1998
Palestinian delegation

Ten Days of Freedom
1996
I was so glad when I got the letter from the Bruno Kreisky Forum telling us that the Austrian Federal Chancellor, Dr. Franz Vranitzky, the President of the Bruno Kreisky Forum, had donated his Fulbright Award prize ($ 50.000) to the "New Generation" for the "Crossing Borders" trip, which was one of the projects suggested in our 1995 meeting. I waited anxiously for it. But the situation in the country did not help us to keep our spirits up. It was very difficult to think about this project and continue working on the other projects in a time that the opposition on both sides, Palestinian and Israeli, managed to bring the peace process to a dead end. I had the opportunity to talk to Palestinian youth who thought that we were crazy, still believing that there was a chance, a hope to make a difference, and to tell you the truth, I had my own doubts too. To participate in a crossing borders trip to reach Eilat, while I know I cannot do that in my daily life. This trip was contradictious to our normal life. To reach the borders of Jordan passing easily, no questioning – not to mention to cross the Allenby bridge in half an hour – Wow!!! What a life, we, the Palestinians, are missing. We have to cross the checkpoints inside the country going from one city to the other, and we are used to get troubles passing borders and all of a sudden we reached Eilat and Aqaba with no difficulties.
What was so special about this trip is that it happened in the area in a time when it seemed that there was no hope in continuing to work for the peace process.
As for me, I believe that we can change, but we should believe more in ourselves and in the strength that we have to convince other young people to participate in this programme. We should not be afraid of the unfamiliar, the unknown, and should work together for our future toward deeper understanding, mutual cultural and political respect. We seemed to some people unrealistic, flying against the wind, but we did it, we sure did cross borders, psychological and political, inside our minds and that is the issue of the whole project. At the end, I would like to thank all the hands visible and invisible who made it possible and gave us ten days of freedom.

Zehn Tage Freiheit
1996
Ich war überglücklich, als ich den Brief vom Bruno Kreisky Forum mit der Nachricht erhielt, daß der österreichische Bundeskanzler Dr. Franz Vranitzky den Fulbright Preis ($ 50.000) der »New Generation« für ihr »Crossing-Borders«-Projekt gespendet hatte. Ich hatte gehofft, daß dieses Projekt, das wir bei unserem Treffen 1995 besprochen hatten, wahr werden könnte, denn die Situation im Land gab uns dazu keinen Anlaß. Es war schwierig, an dieses Projekt zu glauben und an den anderen zu arbeiten in einer Zeit, da die Gegner auf beiden Seiten – Palästinenser und Israelis – den Friedensprozeß zum Stillstand gebracht hatten.
Ich hatte die Gelegenheit, mit Jugendlichen zu sprechen, die uns für verrückt erklärten, weil wir an unseren Hoffnungen und unserem Glauben festhielten; und um euch die Wahrheit zu sagen, auch ich hatte meine Zweifel. An einer grenzüberschreitenden Reise nach Eilat teilzunehmen, wissend, daß ich das in meinem täglichen Leben nie tun könnte. Diese Reise barg so viele Widersprüche zu unserem Leben: die Grenzen zu Jordanien leicht zu erreichen, ohne Fragen, ganz zu schweigen von der Allenby-Brücke, die wir in einer halben Stunde überquerten – Wow!!! Was für ein Leben, das uns Palästinensern da entgeht. Wir müssen in unserem Land, um von einer Stadt zur anderen zu gelangen, Grenzposten passieren, wir sind an Ärger beim Passieren von Grenzen gewöhnt, und dann auf einmal kommen wir ganz problemlos nach Eilat und Aqaba.
Das Besondere an dieser Reise war, daß sie zu einer Zeit in unserer Region stattgefunden hat, als jede Hoffnung auf den Friedensprozeß verloren schien.
Ich bin überzeugt, daß wir uns ändern können, aber wir sollten mehr an uns glauben, an unsere Stärke, um andere junge Menschen von unserem Programm zu überzeugen. Wir sollten uns vor Ungewohntem und Unbekanntem nicht fürchten, zusammenarbeiten für ein tieferes Verständnis, für gegenseitigen Respekt in kultureller und politischer Hinsicht. Manche Menschen halten uns für unrealistische Träumer, die gegen den Strom schwimmen, aber wir haben es geschafft, wir haben sie überquert,

unsere psychischen und politischen Grenzen, in unseren Köpfen – und das ist das Wesentliche des ganzen Projektes. Am Ende möchte ich allen sichtbaren und unsichtbaren Händen danken, die das möglich gemacht und uns zehn Tage Freiheit gegeben haben.

1998
I hosted my first TV show, a three hour live talkshow. We hosted Hanan Ashrawi and other political figures. It was a success. I had only two days to work on it; I had no idea before of what it means to present a live talkshow or any programme on TV.

1998
Ich hatte meine erste dreistündige Live-Talkshow mit Hanan Ashrawi und anderen Politikern. Ich hatte so etwas noch nie gemacht und wenig Vorbereitungszeit, aber es war ein Erfolg.

AL-ABABNEH, ALI
1994, 1996, 1997, 1998

*1.4.1975
Sal Irbid University/engineering
Jordanian delegation

Ali and Emad in traditional dresses
Ali und Emad in traditionellen Gewändern

AL-FUGAHA, EMAD

1994, 1996, 1997, 1998

*22.3.1978
Madaba University graduate, very active in student's council, plans postgraduate studies abroad
Jordanian delegation

I began with this project when I was in school; now I am going to graduate, so I grew up for the real life with Bruno Kreisky Forum projects. From my diary I chose these notes:
1. When I heard about the Middle East Youth Peace Forum 1994, I was happy, especially because we should meet in Vienna. I felt that as a support to us.
2. I think people start to get to know each other, and it is really fun to see friendship grow across genders, nationality and age.
3. 1998 I believe it was a long, long road to the Middle East Youth Peace Forum 1998 with its achievements and problems.
God could have created one race, one thought, but he created many. I am a Muslim, love and understanding ...

The last thing that I wrote in my diary: It was a great feeling standing there together with a lot of new friends singing "Another Brick in the Wall" by Pink Floyd, joining hands and having a really good time. This forum will have a special place in my heart. About the future plans: I am going to marry one of the girls in the forum to have some kids as a proof of the fruit of peace!!!

Ich begann dieses Projekt, als ich noch zur Schule ging; jetzt bin ich mit meinem Studium fast fertig. Ich bin also mit dem Bruno Kreisky Forum aufgewachsen.
Einige Aufzeichnungen aus meinem Tagebuch:
1. Als ich vom Nahost-Jugend-Friedensforum 94 hörte, freute ich mich, vor allem weil wir uns in Wien treffen sollten. Es schien mir ein Zeichen der Unterstützung von der Außenwelt.
2. Es ist wunderbar zu sehen, wie Freundschaften entstehen, ungeachtet des Geschlechts, der Nationalität und des Alters. Gott hätte auch nur eine Rasse, ein Bewußtsein schaffen können, aber er hat viele gewollt. Ich bin Moslem ...

Die letzte Aufzeichnung in meinem Tagebuch:
Es war wunderbar, mit allen Freunden da zu stehen und das Pink-Floyd-Lied »Another Brick in the Wall« zu singen, einander die Hände zu reichen und Spaß zu haben. Dieses Forum wird immer einen besonderen Platz in meinem Herzen haben. Meine Zukunftspläne: Ich werde ein Mädchen aus dem Forum heiraten und viele Kinder als Beweis für die Früchte des Friedens haben!!!

AL-MASHAT, RANIA
1994

*20.6.1975
Cairo
American University of Cairo, graduate of economics, member of the Arab Culture Association
Egyptian delegation

I believe that all of the participants in this project know and do more than I, and that I am the one who can learn from them, not vice versa. Austrian history, particularly recent history, has shown us how clichés greatly influence the way people perceive each other, and to which abyss this kind of thinking can lead. We can observe how this way of thinking became reality, first in words and then in deeds, to the bitter end which, today, we find impossible to comprehend.
As a descendent of this generation, that was not to blame as a whole, but to a large degree, at least partially, I feel in addition to horror, which has been transformed into extreme aversion towards the perpetrators, shame.
And of course, I ask myself how I would have reacted in a time when division was in the foreground. It was not enough in those days to have only protested silently, to avoid having been an accomplice, it would have been necessary to set an example, to show resistance.
What you produce is the most gentle and caring form of resistance to this dividing fanaticism: searching for things which unite and taking part in the adventure of coming together, instead of believing clichés and worshipping prejudices.

Gerhard Roth

Ich glaube, daß alle an dem Projekt Beteiligten mehr wissen und tun als ich, und ich bin der, der von ihnen lernen kann, nicht umgekehrt. Aus der österreichischen Geschichte, besonders aus der jüngeren wissen wir, wie sehr Klischeevorstellungen von anderen Menschen das Denken beeinflussen können und zu welchem Abgrund so ein Denken führt. Wir konnten sehen, daß dieses Denken Wirklichkeit wurde, zuerst Wort und dann Tat, bis zu jenem unerbittlichen Ende, das wir heute letztendlich nicht nachvollziehen können.
Als Nachkomme dieser Generation, die nicht im gesamten, aber zu einem guten Teil dafür verantwortlich und mitverantwortlich war, empfinde ich außer Entsetzen, das sich in tiefe Abneigung gegen die Täter gewandelt hat, Scham.
Und selbstverständlich stellt sich mir die Frage: Wie hätte ich mich damals verhalten, in einer Zeit, in der das Trennende im Vordergrund stand. Es hat damals nicht genügt, nur in seinem Herzen dagegen Partei zu nehmen, um nicht mitschuldig zu werden, sondern es war notwendig, Zeichen zu setzen, Widerstand zu leisten.
Was Sie tun, ist der sanfteste und liebevollste Widerstand gegen trennenden Fanatismus: sich auf die Suche nach dem Gemeinsamen zu begeben und sich auf das Abenteuer der Begegnung einzulassen, statt an Klischees zu glauben und Vorurteile nachzubeten.

Gerhard Roth

AL-NIMRI, JUMAN
1994, 1996, 1997

*27.6.1974
Zarqa
Fine Arts graduate from Yarmuck University, pottery and ceramics, works at the Jordanian Association of Plastic Art
Jordanian delegation

In my point of view, signing a peace treaty is not a big deal, it's just a paper. The most important thing is trust.
We must build bridges of trust between the two cousins. They must believe in each other, like they did before, and they must transfer this trust to their future generations.

Vor langer Zeit lebten zwei Cousins friedlich auf dem selben Flecken Erde. Eines Tages aber begannen sie um das Land zu streiten, auf dem sie lebten, und wurden zu erbitterten Feinden. Sie weiteten ihren Krieg auf ihre Söhne und Töchter aus, bis der Moment kam, da ihre Nachbarn dem Töten eine Ende setzen wollten.
Es begannen Verhandlungen, die viele Jahre dauerten. Einer der beiden war so mächtig geworden, daß er das ganze Land sein eigen nennen wollte und den anderen verjagte, der nun verarmt durch die Welt zog.
Aber nach vielen Jahren gelang es den Freunden der beiden, den Traum vom Frieden wahrzumachen. Die Cousins unterzeichneten ein Friedensabkommen, und der schwächere der beiden bekam einen Teil seines Landes zurück.
Meiner Ansicht nach sind Friedensabkommen alleine nicht viel wert, bloß ein Stück Papier. Das wichtigste ist, einander vertrauen zu lernen. Wir müssen Brücken des Vertrauens zwischen den beiden Cousins bauen. Sie müssen einander glauben, wie früher, und sie müssen diesen Glauben an die zukünftigen Generationen weitergeben.

Fida and Shirley

AL-SHEIKH, FIDA
1994, 1995, 1996

*9.7.1975
Jerusalem – Silwan
Graduate of Amman Private University, pharmacy, works in his father's pharmacy
Palestinian delegation

Once upon a time, two cousins lived together in peace, sharing everything, dreaming together of a more peaceful life.
But one day, they started fighting for the land they owned, until they became enemies. They reached a level of hatred that cannot be described. War was their only solution in that moment, and it extended to their sons and daughters. Their "neighbours" and friends decided that there must be an end to this situation. Negotiations started between the two sides for many years. But, in that moment, one of the cousins was so powerful that he claimed all the land his own, and the other one was expelled out of it, wandering all around the world, powerless. Actually, after many years, their friends had succeeded in making the dream come true. The cousins signed a peace treaty and the powerless cousin retained few hectares of his stolen land.

AMIN IBSAIS, HANA'A
1996

*14.2.1978
Nablus
Studies in the USA, singer and actress, member of Palestinian Youth for Peace
Palestinian delegation

A New Attitude with the "New Generation"
On September 10, 1996 the four delegations that participated in the Peace Forum tour separated. Each member carried in his heart feelings of happiness, hope and determination to make our dream come true. For myself, it was the first time to live with Israeli youngsters for ten days. I was really surprised after that experience that something has changed in my attitude and beliefs. At this moment I feel that we, the youngsters, are able to build a real new generation which will break the psychological and physical borders. I did not expect that someday I will have Israeli friends. I never imagined that my tears would fall because I have to leave these friends. That experience contributed in opening a whole world in front of my eyes when I was told about the project. I was puzzled. How can I live with Israelis who kill our friends and torment my neighbours? How can I cross all those borders, while I cannot move from one city to another in my country?
Crossing the borders, which is also the name of the project, was my dream. I did not expect that someday it would come true. At the first day of the camp, I felt like a stranger who does not know how to get over his fears of being in a new world without even knowing what was happening. At the second day I felt that some of those walls and rocks were destroyed and the picture of the soldier began to fade away, the ice which occupied my heart started to melt.
Those Israeli youngsters are not guilty of the whole situation. They are victims as well as we are. They have dreams and the imagination of living peacefully on this sacred land. These thoughts started to enter my mind and I discovered that we, the Palestinian youngsters, do have the same hopes. Now I believe that working together is the best solution. Who knows, we may solve the problems that the governments were not able to solve. Those tight relationships which were formed in those ten days cannot be broken easily. Our new generation will do its best to build a prosperous future for both, Israelis and Palestinians.

Building a New Future From the Past
The young who survived the hard days of the last decade should be "The New Generation" which will build the future. But the question now is how. I believe that step by step we can break the walls and rebuild what has been destroyed. I still remember those days when we saw our friends suffering and aching from losing their parents and homes. I imagined that all the Israelis were soldiers who enjoyed killing the innocent. As the years went by, I realised that carrying those feelings of hatred toward the Israelis would give us a miserable life. This was the beginning of my new experience which created the motive to improve our conditions through the hard circumstances. Talking with the Israelis provides us with relief, we learn from the past that continuing the killing and the war is of no use. If both sides open their hearts and minds to each other they will be able to get over their problems. Working together hand in hand, building our new state is the greatest success. This state will symbolise our determination to have a peaceful life. Not only do we need peaceful lives but we also believe that neither of us can ignore the existence of the other, so we should plan our projects together.
The power is in our hands. We – the youngest – are able to create new systems of thoughts and feelings which will help us to have fruitful results in the years to come. I think if we take advantage of it and do our best to understand each other, we will spare the next generation a lot of suffering.

Eine neue Haltung mit einer neuen Generation
Am 10. September 1996 trennten sich die vier Delegationen, die am Friedensforum teilgenommen hatten. Jeder von uns hatte das Herz voll mit Gefühlen, Hoffnung und Entschlossenheit, unseren Traum wahrzumachen. Für mich war es das erste Mal gewesen, daß ich zehn Tage lang mit Israelis zusammenlebte. Ich war überrascht, daß sich nach dieser Erfahrung wirklich etwas in mir verändert hatte. Ich fühle in diesem Augenblick, daß wir, die Jungen, fähig sind, eine neue Generation aufzubauen, die psychische und physische Grenzen niederreißen kann. Ich hätte nicht erwartet, eines Tages israelische Freunde zu haben. Ich hätte mir nie gedacht, daß ich weinen könnte, weil ich sie verlassen muß. Diese Erfahrung hat mir eine Welt aufgetan, die ich nicht erahnt habe, als ich von dem Projekt hörte. Ich war verwirrt. Wie kann ich mit

Israelis leben, wo sie doch meine Freunde töten und meine Nachbarn quälen? Wie kann ich all die Grenzen überqueren, wenn ich doch in meinem Land nicht einmal von einer Stadt in eine andere gehen kann?
Grenzen zu überschreiten, wie das Projekt heißt, war immer mein Traum. Ich hätte nie gedacht, daß er eines Tages wahr werden könnte. Am ersten Tag fühlte ich mich wie eine Fremde, die nicht wußte, wie sie mit ihren Ängsten in einer Welt, die sie nicht kannte, umgehen sollte. Am zweiten Tag spürte ich, wie Mauern und Barrikaden einbrachen und das Bild von Soldaten zu verschwimmen begann. Das Eis, das mein Herz umgab, begann zu schmelzen.
Diese israelischen Jugendlichen haben keine Schuld an der ganzen Situation. Sie sind Opfer wie wir. Sie haben Träume und Vorstellungen von einem Leben in diesem heiligen Land. Diese Gedanken begannen mich zu beschäftigen, und ich entdeckte, daß wir, die palästinensischen Jugendlichen, dieselben Hoffnungen haben.
Ich bin jetzt überzeugt, daß zusammenzuarbeiten die beste Lösung ist. Wer weiß, vielleicht werden wir Probleme lösen, die die Regierungen nicht in der Lage waren zu lösen. Diese enge Beziehung, die in den zehn Tagen zwischen uns entstanden ist, kann nicht mehr so ohne weiteres zerstört werden.
Unsere Generation wird alles tun, um sowohl für Israelis als auch für Palästinenser eine blühende Zukunft zu bauen.

Aus der Vergangenheit die Zukunft bauen
Die Jugendlichen, die die schweren Tage der letzten zehn Jahre überlebt haben, werden die »Neue Generation« sein, die die Zukunft bauen wird. Die Frage ist, wie. Ich glaube, daß wir schrittweise die Mauern niederbrechen können und das wiederaufbauen, was zerstört worden ist. Ich erinnere mich an die Freunde, die unter dem Verlust ihrer Eltern litten. Ich dachte, alle Israelis wären Soldaten, die gerne Unschuldige töten.
Mit den Jahren erkannte ich, daß diese Gefühle des Hasses gegen die Israelis uns ein elendes Leben bereiten. Das war der Beginn einer neuen Erfahrung für mich, die meinen Wunsch motivierte, unsere schwierige Lebenssituation zu verbessern. Mit Israelis zu sprechen, erleichtert uns. Wir lernen aus der Vergangenheit, daß Töten und Krieg zu nichts führen.
Daß wir zusammenarbeiten, Hand in Hand unseren neuen Staat aufbauen, ist unser größter Erfolg. Dieser Staat wird Symbol sein für unsere Entschlossenheit, friedlich miteinander zu leben. Nicht nur, daß wir ein friedliches Leben brauchen, wir glauben auch, daß keiner von uns die Existenz des anderen ignorieren kann, und sollten daher unsere Projekte gemeinsam planen. Wir haben die Kraft, wir, die Jüngsten, sind fähig, neue Gedanken und Gefühle zu entwickeln, die uns in den kommenden Jahren reiche Ernte bringen werden. Wenn es uns gelingt, die Chance zu nutzen und einander Verständnis entgegenzubringen, werden wir der nächsten Generation eine Menge Leid ersparen.

AMRAM, SIMA
1994, 1995

*4.8.1977
Kiryat Gat (Negev)
Lives in a kibbutz
Israeli delegation

Eran and Sima at the Peace Conference 1994
Eran und Sima bei der Friedenskonferenz 1994

Rawan in a Bedouin tent at Wadi Rum
Rawan in einem Beduinenzelt in Wadi Rum

ANANI, RAWAN
1996

*2.4.1978
Ramallah
Trainee of Ramallah Women Training Centre RWTC, works at PECDAR, member of a youth group for peace
Palestinian delegation

ASAF, ZAFRIR
1996, 1997, 1998

*22.11.1978
Kibbutz Ein Hamifratz
Currently doing his army service, member of Hashomer Hatzair and active in various peace groups
Israeli delegation

This is how to make peace, for sure!

The bus has entered Bet-Lehem at a late evening hour. Military vehicle in front of it, military vehicle at the back. Palestinian policemen were standing on the roofs of the houses along the road. Even the weak anxiety has turned into a great moment. This is only one of many great moments in two years of encounters and constant contact with a Palestinian, Jordanian, Austrian and Israeli group, to which I belong.
It all started in summer 1994. The Austrian Bruno Kreisky Forum organized an encounter for youth from the Middle East in order to promote the dialogue and understanding between the different peoples. The encounter took the shape of a peace conference, and despite many tense moments, it was declared a success.
That success has led to a second encounter in Austria in summer 1995, which included more social aspects and contributed to enforcing personal relationships among the participants.
In September 1996 the third encounter took place – the "Crossing Borders" trip, in which I joined the group. That meeting was different from the previous ones, in a way that the four delegations (Israeli, Jordanian, Palestinian, Austrian) met for the first time in their "Home Court", trying to overcome psychological and physical borders by traveling together in Eilat, Aqaba, and Bethlehem. Strong friendships emerged during that trip, that helped us in our joint work (that is still ongoing) or several projects such as the cookery book, Internet site, newsletter and lectures in schools.
In order to encourage our independent work on the projects, the Bruno Kreisky Forum organized two leading seminars (September 97 and February 98) in Austria, in which we discussed and practised leading groups in a state of conflict.
This is the history, however, even more important is what was going on in our hearts and heads as a result of those meetings. First of all, it was the first time I met the individuals behind the title "Palestinian", "Jordanian". Many stereotypes I had, and probably you still have, have broken up in that direct encounter. Eating together, sleeping in the same room or shopping in Vienna are the best ways to get to know a person.
I became familiar with the real situation in the West Bank and Gaza Strip, with how we look like in the eyes of Jordanians and Austrians, with similarities and differences between the people, with their way of thinking and with their mentality. I was forced to examine my "lefty" opinions, my attitude toward military service and my points of view about the Israeli society. At the same time, I had asked my friends the hardest questions and received answers.
The gaps are still large, as well as the disinformation and the fear, yet it is interesting to discover how we and our neighbours are similar – in dress style, fields of interest, fears, love, ambitions.
You probably would say I'm young and innocent, but the meetings have forced my opinion that this region will experience periods of peace and quietness, for the simple reason that both our neighbours/ enemies and us seek quietness.
In August 98 we – 12 members of the "old" group (that is called the "New Generation") – led a new group – 60 members from ten Mediterranean nationalities. This article is

too short to describe that amazing experience. I was leading along with a Palestinian and a Jordanian an international group of 15 participants. We discussed a variety of different issues, and we tried to give our participants the thing which helped us so much: time to sit together, to share opinions, to travel, to play and to dance. We allowed them this time knowing that this is the way to bridge gaps, reach understanding and accept the other.
If you are interested in discovering the world we know only through that headlines, being through great, challenging and most of all important experiences, do not hesitate! Contact me and I would be glad to help you as much as I can.

So macht man Frieden!
Spät abends traf der Bus in Bethlehem ein. Militärfahrzeuge vor uns und hinter uns. Palästinensische Polizisten standen auf den Dächern der Häuser entlang der Straße. Die letzte leise Angst machte diesem großen Augenblick Platz.
Das ist nur einer der großen Momente in zwei Jahren des ständigen Kontakts und der Begegnungen in einer palästinensischen, jordanischen, österreichischen und israelischen Gruppe, zu der ich gehöre.
Alles begann im Sommer 1994, als das Bruno Kreisky Forum ein Treffen für Jugendliche aus dem Nahen Osten initiierte, das dem Dialog und dem besseren Verständnis zwischen den verschiedenen Völkern dienen sollte. Es begann mit einer Friedenskonferenz, die trotz vieler Spannungen ein Erfolg wurde. Dieser Erfolg führte zu einem zweiten Treffen im Sommer 1995; in diesem Seminar ging es vor allem um soziale Interaktion und persönliche Beziehungen zwischen den TeilnehmerInnen.
Im September 1996 fand das dritte Treffen statt – die »Crossing-Borders«-Reise, über die ich zur Gruppe kam. Dieses Mal war es anders als bisher, denn die vier Delegationen trafen einander zum ersten Mal »zu Hause«, um gemeinsam von Eilat über Aqaba nach Bethlehem reisend psychische und physische Grenzen zu überqueren. Enge Freundschaften entstanden auf dieser Reise, die uns bei der gemeinsamen Arbeit halfen, die weitergeht und Projekte entstehen ließ, wie ein Kochbuch, eine Homepage im Internet, einen Newsletter und Vorträge in Schulen.
Damit wir unsere Arbeit unabhängig durchführen konnten, organisierte das Bruno Kreisky Forum in Österreich zwei Trainingsseminare, in denen wir lernten, Konfliktgruppen zu leiten.
Das ist die Geschichte, doch das Wichtigere ist in unseren Herzen und Köpfen passiert. Ich habe zum ersten Mal Individuen kennengelernt, die hinter der Bezeichnung »Palästinenser« und »Jordanier« stecken. Viele Vorurteile, die ich hatte und die ihr vielleicht noch immer habt, sind bei der direkten Begegnung mit den Menschen in sich zusammengebrochen. Gemeinsam essen, im selben Zimmer schlafen und in Wien einkaufen gehen sind hervorragende Möglichkeiten, einander kennenzulernen. Ich habe viel über die wirkliche Situation in der Westbank und im Gazastreifen erfahren und darüber, wie Österreicher und Jordanier uns sehen, ich habe Unterschiede und Gemeinsamkeiten in der Art, zu denken und zu sein, entdeckt. Ich mußte meine »linken« Ansichten überdenken, meine Haltung zum Militär und meine Sicht der israelischen Gesellschaft. Gleichzeitig habe ich meinen Freunden unangenehme Fragen gestellt und Antworten bekommen. Die Kluft ist noch immer groß, wir sind falsch informiert und haben Angst, doch es ist spannend zu entdecken, wie ähnlich wir und unsere Nachbarn einander sind in der Art, uns zu kleiden, in unseren Interessen, Ängsten, darin, was Liebe und Sehnsüchte betrifft. Ihr werdet mich für jung und unerfahren halten, doch diese Treffen haben in mir die Überzeugung gefestigt, daß diese Region eine Zeit des Friedens und der Ruhe erfahren wird, und zwar aus dem einfachen Grund, weil sowohl wir als auch unsere Nachbarn/Feinde Ruhe suchen. Im August 98 haben wir – zwölf TeilnehmerInnen der »alten« Gruppe (die sich »New Generation« nennt) – mit 60 Jugendlichen aus zehn Mittelmeerländern gearbeitet. Ich habe zusammen mit einem Palästinenser und einem Jordanier eine internationale Gruppe von 15 jungen Menschen geleitet. Wir haben verschiedene Themen diskutiert und versucht, den TeilnehmerInnen das zu geben, was uns so sehr geholfen hat: zusammensitzen, Meinungen austauschen, reisen, spielen und tanzen. Wenn ihr die Welt entdecken wollt, die wir nur aus den Schlagzeilen kennen, und aufregende, aber vor allem wichtige Erfahrungen machen wollt, zögert nicht! Ruft mich an, ich freue mich, euch dabei behilflich zu sein.

ASKRIA-DABABNEH WAFA
1994, 1996, 1997, 1998

*24.11. 1973
Amman
Graduate from Amman University, B.A.
Public Administration and Political Science,
participates in many international seminars
Jordanian delegation

We have gone a long way since the 1994 meeting in Austria, and a lot has changed in our world, our lives and our thoughts. Before, we asked for peace, and now, we are learning to live it. We have encountered new developments, primarily in the signing of the peace treaty between Jordan and Israel. Borders have been defined, land and water reclaimed, and now, we, the generation of peace, are looking upon a future dawning with security and hope; a future full of happiness and joy for all.
Here we are again, shaking hands, crossing borders within our land of peace, with hearts full of hope, with eyes looking to have a bright future for all nations. Let's remember, God created and gave us this earth to coexist upon as brothers and sisters. We can learn from each other to preserve this land, to preserve our peace.
May peace be upon everyone.

Poem
There is a future, there is also a past,
but we are in the present,
which goes by very fast.
The past is just some memories far away,
waiting to be forgotten, by the running of each day.
The future is waiting, waiting for you,
so pray for tomorrow, that's all that you can do.
now we are in the present so live for today,
pray for tomorrow and let the past fade away.

At Deheisheh refugee camp
Im Flüchtlingslager Deheisheh

Wir sind einen weiten Weg gegangen seit unserem Treffen 1994, viele Veränderungen sind in der Welt, in unserem Leben und in unseren Gedanken passiert. Wir haben lange um Frieden gebetet, jetzt lernen wir, ihn zu leben. Neue Entwicklungen haben stattgefunden, an erster Stelle die Unterzeichnung des Friedensabkommens zwischen Israel und Jordanien. Grenzen wurden gezogen, Wasser und Land zurückgefordert, und nun schauen wir, die Friedensgeneration, voll Hoffnung und Zuversicht unserer Zukunft entgegen; einer Zukunft voll Freude und Glück. Da sind wir nun, händeschüttelnd, Grenzen querend in unserem Land des Friedens, mit hoffnungsvollen Herzen und leuchtenden Augen. Erinnert euch, daß Gott uns diese Erde gegeben hat, auf daß wir miteinander wie Brüder und Schwestern darauf leben. Wir können voneinander lernen, dieses Land und den Frieden zu erhalten.
Friede sei mit euch.

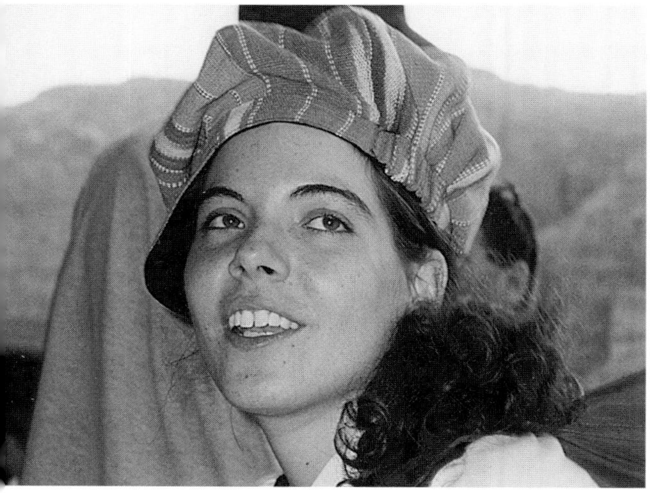

AVIDAN, SHIRLEY
1994, 1996

*21.3.1976
Rishon Lezion
Finished army service, studies, politically active in peace groups
Israeli delegation

I wish your youth project lasting success, because I find it exceptionally important. Maybe you are interested in what is happening in another part of the world in this respect – here are a few words about it. There were hardly any relations between Germany and Poland – two countries that have caused so much sorrow to each other. Through student exchange programmes and similar activities, this relationship has normalised to such an extent that the Poles, as a sign of reconciliation, have named one of their schools after me. This would have been unthinkable a few years ago.
Now I attend the graduation celebrations in Nikolajki every year and have to give a small address. In the first year (1995) I said this: Maybe you are asking what I feel to be the most important component of the intellectual spirit of the future. I think that, above all, you must try to be tolerant. Of course, you could make a long list but, no matter how long, tolerance has to be at the top. Those who are truly tolerant will not succumb to hate, and will therefore, not be tempted to resort to violence.
They will respect the opinions of others, even if they contradict their own, they will not discriminate against foreigners and ethnic minorities, and they will not – and this is most important – develop any new concepts of the enemy in order to slander their opponent.

Marion Gräfin Dönhoff

Ihrem Jugendprojekt wünsche ich bleibenden Erfolg, denn ich finde es außerordentlich wichtig. Vielleicht interessiert es Sie, was in einer ganz anderen Ecke der Welt in dieser Hinsicht vor sich geht – darum ein paar Worte dazu: Zwischen Deutschland und Polen – zwei Ländern, die einander unendlich viel Leid angetan haben – gab es so gut wie keine Beziehungen. Durch Schüleraustausch und ähnliche Maßnahmen hat sich das Verhältnis so normalisiert, daß die Polen im Zeichen der Versöhnung eine ihrer Schulen nach mir benannt haben, was noch vor ein paar Jahren undenkbar gewesen wäre.
Jetzt bin ich jedes Jahr zur Abiturfeier in Nikolajki und muß dort eine kleine Rede halten. Im ersten Jahr (1995) lautete diese:
»Vielleicht werden Sie fragen, was mir als geistige Einstellung für die Zukunft am wichtigsten erscheint. Ich denke, ihr müßt vor allem versuchen, tolerant zu sein. Gewiß, man könnte eine lange Liste aufstellen, aber wie lange sie auch sein mag, Toleranz muß jedenfalls ganz oben stehen, denn wer wirklich tolerant ist, der wird nicht in Haß verfallen und darum auch nicht versucht sein, Gewalt zu üben.
Er wird die Meinung des anderen respektieren, auch wenn sie seiner eigenen widerspricht, er wird den Ausländer und den ethnisch anderen nicht diskriminieren, und er wird – und das ist sehr wichtig – keine neuen Feindbilder erfinden, mit denen der Gegner verunglimpft wird.«

Marion Gräfin Dönhoff

AWEIDAH, MOHAMMAD
1995, 1996

*28.3.1978
Jerusalem
Bir Zeit University, graduate of business and economics, works in his uncle's hotel
Palestinian delegation

... yes indeed we are the new generation who represents only a very small minority of our people, and we may have a little influence on some of them. We have to make them believe in what we are believing. Camps and anything as such can contribute in making our dream come true ...

... ja, wir sind sie, die neue Generation, die nur eine kleine Minderheit unseres Volkes ist und wenig Einfluß auf andere hat. Wir müssen sie aber davon überzeugen, wovon wir überzeugt sind. Gemeinsame Treffen können das, können helfen, Träume wahr werden zu lassen ...

Tommy and Abir, excursion to the Hohe Wand, 1995
Tommy und Abir, Ausflug zur Hohen Wand, 1995

BARAKAT, ABIR
1995

*9.1.1978
Jerusalem
Amman University/political science
Palestinian delegation

BASHEER, BASHEER
1994, 1995, 1996, 1997, 1998

*15.4.1976
Sakhnin
Graduate of Hebrew University, Jerusalem, politics and sociology, worked at Van Leer Institute and in the Knesset, postgraduate student at London School of Economics
Israeli delegation

Some reflexions
For a long time, the youth education in the two sides of the conflict in the Middle East was based on a lack of information and disinformation about the other side, which created ethnocentricity problems, prejudices, stereotypes, ignorance of the other side. Those things and others destroyed all the bridges that can build a real confidence, coexistence and co-operation between the Palestinians (including the Palestinian Arabs in Israel) and Jews.
The peace process in the Middle East gave a big chance to the two sides to try to change the situation to a better one, but did they (Palestinians and Israelis) devote and invest enough time in doing so?
I think that they didn't take this chance and didn't invest enough energy for it. Unfortunately, also activities to build confidence, co-operation and coexistence between Palestinians and Israeli Jewish youth still are very few and we didn't see any changes in the contents of the syllabus (studying programmes) or lessons in the schools (in some places the situation got worse). We, "The New Generation" – Arabs and Jewish youth – recognised the importance of youth education as a basis to build confidence, co-operation and coexistence. I decided to work in a special project – that has been delayed due to the closure – organising visits to Palestinian and Israeli schools explaining our experiences and goals (coexistence between Arabs and Jews). The human history and experience teaches us that if peace is not built on co-operation, confidence and equality, respect of mutual interests and understanding of the other side, uprooting hatred, stereotypes, and prejudices through education, it will collapse. We therefore welcome and invite every school that would like to participate in this project to join us.

Einige Überlegungen
Lange Zeit war die Erziehung der Jugend auf beiden Seiten des Nahostkonflikts durch mangelnde oder falsche Information über die andere Seite gekennzeichnet. Dadurch entstanden viele ethnische Probleme, Vorurteile, Stereotype und Unwissen. Das und anderes hat dazu beigetragen, daß wirkliches Vertrauen, Zusammenleben und Zusammenarbeit zwischen Palästinensern (einschließlich der palästinensischen Araber in Israel) und Juden gestört war. Der Friedensprozeß im Nahen Osten ist eine große Chance für beide Seiten, die Situation zu verändern, aber haben sie (Palästinenser und Israelis) genug Zeit und Energie darauf verwendet? Ich glaube, sie haben die Chance nicht genützt. Unglücklicherweise gibt es heute noch immer sehr wenige vertrauensbildende Maßnahmen zwischen palästinensischen und israelisch-jüdischen Jugendlichen, und selbst in den Schulprogrammen hat sich wenig verbessert, manchmal sogar einiges verschlechtert. Wir, die »Neue Generation« – arabische und jüdische Jugendliche –, haben erkannt, wie wichtig Jugenderziehung ist als Basis für Vertrauen, Zusammenarbeit und Koexistenz. Ich habe beschlossen, bei einem besonderen Projekt mitzuarbeiten, das durch die Sperre leider behindert wurde, nämlich in israelischen und palästinensischen Schulen unsere Erfahrungen und Ziele des Zusammenlebens zwischen Juden und Arabern zu erklären.
Die menschliche Geschichte und Erfahrung lehrt uns, daß Frieden nur durch Zusammenarbeit, Vertrauen, Gleichberechtigung, gegenseitigen Respekt und Verständnis für die andere Seite erreicht und Phänomene wie Haß, Stereotype und Vorurteile abgebaut werden können. Daher lade ich jede interessierte Schule ein, an diesem Projekt teilzunehmen.

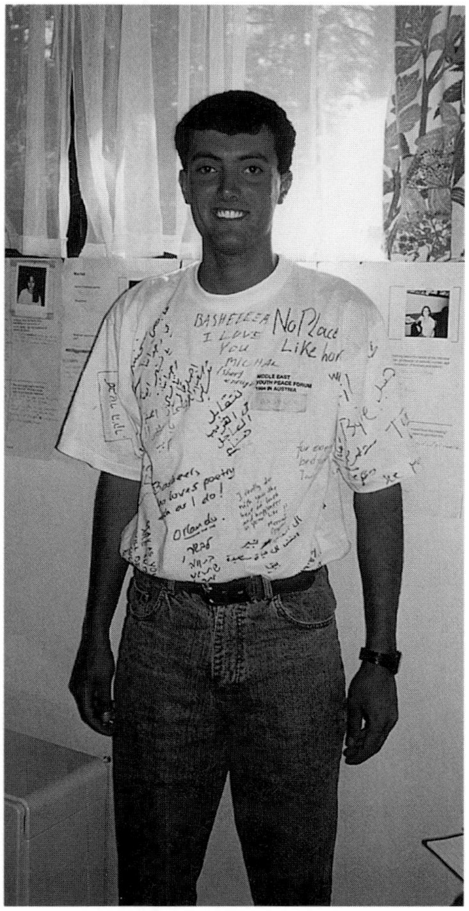

Orlando, Itamar

BEN-ET, ITAMAR
1994, 1995

*18.8.1976
Kibbutz Bet Ha' emek
Finished army service
Israeli delegation

BILIA, ITSIK
1994

*16.11. 1976
Nahariya
Israeli delegation

Farewell 1994. Second from right Itsik
Abschied 1994. Zweiter von rechts Itsik

CASPI, RAFFI
1994, 1995, 1998

*22.7.1976
Tel Aviv
Student
Israeli delegation

CESNOVAR, CHRISTOF
1994, 1995, 1996

*30.1.1976
Maria Rain
University of Vienna / Law Faculty
Freelance journalist in the KSSSD –
Slovenian Students' Club
Austrian delegation

Crossing Borders!

Being a part of the "Crossing Borders" project made me happy in many ways.
First of all, I was keen to see everyone who participated in the previous projects so far and of course to see new people who joined to experience the same things we have. The ones who joined us for the first time were quickly integrated and found many friends with whom they could share their feelings and thoughts about the problems in the Middle East.
For me personally, it is hard to describe what this unique experience really meant for me. Apart from getting to know many new people from different cultures, the personal benefit is tremendous. The things you learn out of these projects cannot be taught in any school or university. This is also the reason for the uniqueness of the project …

Crossing Borders!

Ein Teil von »Crossing Borders« zu sein hat mich in vielerlei Hinsicht glücklich gemacht. Erstens war ich froh, alle wiederzusehen, die an den vorangegangenen Veranstaltungen teilgenommen hatten, und neue kennenzulernen, die ähnliche Erfahrungen machen wollten wie wir. Die Neulinge waren schnell integriert und fanden Freunde, mit denen sie Gefühle und Gedanken in bezug auf den Nahen Osten teilen konnten. Mir selbst fällt es nicht leicht, diese einzigartige Erfahrung zu beschreiben. Außer den vielen neuen Menschen und Kulturen, die ich kennengelernt habe, ist der persönliche Gewinn besonders wichtig. Was wir hier gelernt haben, wird an keiner Schule oder Universität gelehrt. Das macht auch die Einzigartigkeit dieses Projektes aus …

COHEN, TAL
1996

*19.4.1979
Raanana
Political and social studies, army service, member of the Society for the Protection of Nature in Israel, counsellor of its hiking club
Israeli delegation

DAHER, SANA
1994, 1995

*28.8.1975
Beit Hanina – Jerusalem
English literature at Bethlehem University
Palestinian delegation

To tell you the truth the one in 1994 was and will continue to be one if not the most beneficial, unforgettable experience in my life … and I thank you again for giving me this opportunity …
I would like to send you a poem I wrote myself, which I like a lot.

Ehrlich gesagt war und ist die Erfahrung aus dem Jahr 1994 die nachhaltigste, unvergeßlichste, die ich in meinem Leben gemacht habe … Danke, daß ihr mir diese Möglichkeit gegeben habt … Hier ein Gedicht, das ich geschrieben habe und das ich sehr mag.

A homeless in Winter
My winter is different than yours
for my winter is terribly cold;
My fireplace has been destroyed;
and my precious wood has been sold.
No warm blankets have I
nor a comfortable bed to lie.
My cover is the SKY!
My bed lies in my sigh.

And how difficult it is.
When I see your great bliss:
Food, shelter, warmth and a kiss.
OH, what a cosy atmosphere I miss!

Ecstatic is your chimney smoke and restless,
spreading the tidings and the divine bliss,
telling the story of the great happiness,
and thanking the Lord for his gentleness.

Seeing it arises lots of desires,
yet, envy and grudge aren't my features.
Lonely and homeless are some creatures,
one of them is me, and many are others.

Working at the Bruno Kreisky Forum.
Second from right Sana
Arbeit im Bruno Kreisky Forum.
Zweite von rechts Sana

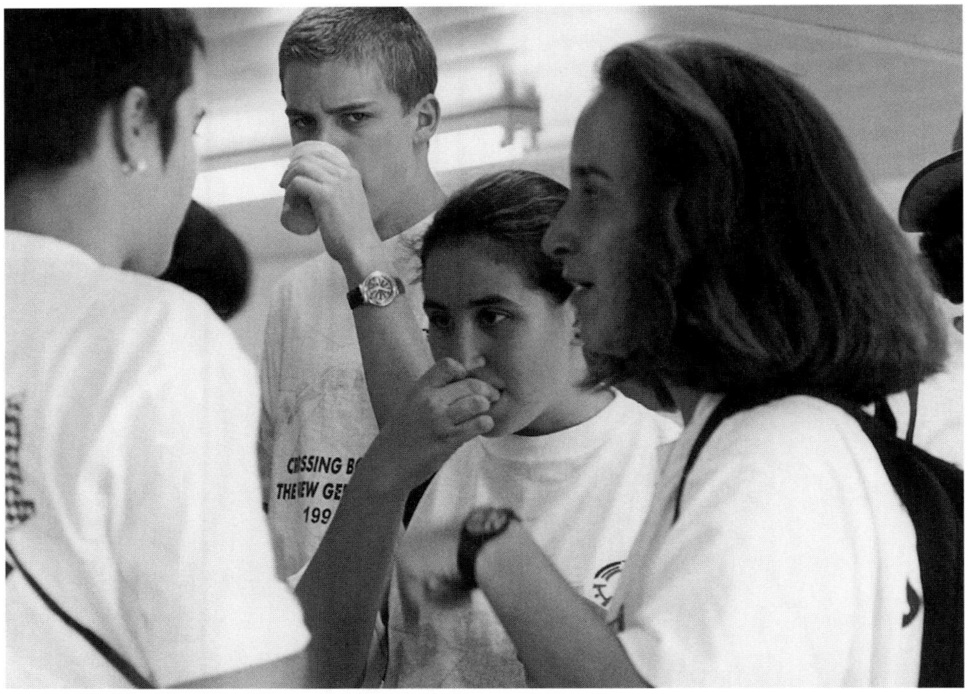

Yannic, Tal, Nataly

DAVIDAI, NATALY
1996, 1997

*8.11.1979
Kiriat Ono/Tel Aviv
Currently doing her army service, member of Bat Shalom, delegate of the dialogue group for peace with the Palestinians.
Her aim is to work for the UN after university.
Israeli delegation

The Middle East

Someone once told me that after the dark night comes always a shiny day. I kept thinking about this saying lately. I wondered if he was right! Because if he is right, we are probably living in the dark ages.
In the Middle East you cannot ignore what is going on around you. Wherever you are you hear the news, in schools, in parks, in your car, day and night, you cannot run away from it. And all I have been hearing lately is that: "A war is coming to the Middle East" or "the Middle East is on the edge of exploding".
People around me had long ago stopped asking if there would be a war.
Ironically though everyone agrees about one thing: After this war there will be peace. Basically what our leaders say is that the others are too stubborn to make peace, but we are willing to fight in order to make peace a reality. Thinking about it, fights and deeds are becoming a way in the Middle East to promote the peace process. Here when a dead end is reached, instead of finding a solution and compromising, the people of the Middle East reach for their guns and bombs, with the excuse that by these actions they would buy peace. People won't understand that this is not the solution. They prefer the easiest way, the way that doesn't force them to deal with their fears, with the differences between them or to deal with each other. In all this craziness there is one thing that keeps me going: "The New Generation".
It is good to know that there are people who want to try the other way, who are taking the hardest path to peace ...

Der Nahe Osten

Jemand sagte mir einmal, daß nach einer dunklen Nacht immer ein sonniger Tag kommt. Ich dachte vor kurzem wieder daran und fragte mich, ob das wohl stimmt. Wenn es nämlich stimmt, dann leben wir in den finsteren Zeiten. Im Nahen Osten kann man nicht ignorieren, was um einen herum passiert. Wo immer du bist, hörst du Nachrichten, in Schulen, in Parks, in deinem Auto, Tag und Nacht. Und was ich zuletzt hörte, war: »Ein Krieg kommt im Nahen Osten« oder »Der Nahe Osten steht kurz vor der Explosion«. Die Menschen um mich herum haben schon vor langem aufgehört zu fragen, ob es einen Krieg geben wird oder nicht. Ironischerweise ist aber jeder überzeugt, daß es nach diesem Krieg Frieden geben wird. Grundsätzlich sagen uns unsere politischen Führer, daß die anderen zu starrköpfig sind, um Frieden zu schließen, aber wir willens zu kämpfen, um Frieden zu schaffen. Kämpfe sind im Nahen Osten der Motor für den Friedensprozeß. Wenn wir hier an einen toten Punkt gelangen, wird anstatt nach Lösungen und Kompromissen nach Bomben und Gewehren gesucht, weil damit Frieden erreicht werden kann. Die Menschen verstehen nicht, daß das keine Lösung ist. Sie ziehen den leichteren Weg vor, den, der sie nicht zwingt, mit ihren Ängsten, mit ihrer Verschiedenheit, mit den anderen zurechtzukommen. Angesichts all dieser Verrücktheit macht mir eines Mut: »Die Neue Generation«.
Es ist gut zu wissen, daß es Menschen gibt, die den anderen Weg wählen, die den schwereren Weg zum Frieden gehen ...

DROR, ADI
1995, 1996, 1997

*27.12.1977
Kibbutz Dalia
Used to work at the factory of his kibbutz, currently doing his army service, guide of Hashomer Hatzair
Israeli delegation

Going to the army
Next month I'm going to the army, I have dreamt of that day since I was very young. Now I am also afraid of that day. To me that day symbolized the end of my childhood. I know I will experience new things during my service. I'll face a different reality than the one I know. Going to the army is to meet new friends, to see new places, to live in a different order.
I have been taking part in the "New Generation" for the past three years and probably I wont see most of you, friends, in the next three years. I learned a lot from the "New Generation" and I will never forget my experiences. I had good days and even better days. I hope that when you see a soldier on TV, or in life, you will think about me, about the person behind the uniform and the gun. Good-bye (for now).

His way – our way
I stood there and saw all the happy faces. Then it happened. Someone shot Yitzhak Rabin and with the same shot he hit me. I couldn't understand what actually happened, but I felt that it was something terrible. Perhaps I did not want to believe that Rabin was not with us anymore.
When I came home I was very angry. I felt that my hope for peace was gone.
The next day I woke up and the only thing in my mind was Rabin. I thought it was a bad dream, but it wasn't.
In the afternoon, I went to Jerusalem to say good-bye for the last time to Rabin. When I stood in line for the Knesset, Israel's Parliament, I saw young men holding a sign which said: "Isra-Hell" – for people who murdered their hope for peace. I think that the young men were right. I did not shoot Rabin, but I didn't do enough to show my support for him. Rabin was my hope for peace and I believed in him. He was a man of war who became a man of peace. He was the greatest leader I have ever known. Rabin showed us the way to peace and left. Now each one of us should give his or her best for the peace process. Rabin started and we will finish the task.

Zum Militär
Nächsten Monat gehe ich zum Militär. Seit meiner Kindheit habe ich von diesem Tag geträumt. Jetzt fürchte ich mich auch davor. Dieser Tag symbolisiert für mich das Ende meiner Kindheit. Ich weiß, ich werde neue Erfahrungen machen und neue Wirklichkeiten kennenlernen. Zum Militär gehen heißt, neue Freunde finden, neue Orte kennenlernen, anders leben.
Seit drei Jahren bin ich ein Teil der »Neuen Generation«, und wahrscheinlich werde ich die meisten von euch, meine Freunde, in den nächsten drei Jahren nicht sehen. Ich habe von der »Neuen Generation« eine Menge gelernt, und meine Erfahrungen werden mich begleiten. Ich hatte eine schöne Zeit. Ich hoffe, daß ihr an mich denken werdet, wenn ihr im Fernsehen einen Soldaten seht, oder einem begegnet, an den Menschen hinter der Uniform und dem Gewehr.
Lebt wohl (einstweilen)

Sein Weg – unser Weg
Ich stand dort und sah all die glücklichen Gesichter. Dann geschah es. Jemand schoß auf Yitzhak Rabin und traf damit auch mich. Ich konnte nicht verstehen, was genau geschehen war, aber ich fühlte, daß es etwas Schreckliches sein mußte. Vielleicht wollte ich nicht glauben, daß Rabin nicht mehr unter uns war. Als ich nach Hause kam, war ich wütend. Ich hatte all meine Hoffnung auf Frieden verloren. Als ich am nächsten Morgen aufwachte, galt mein erster Gedanke Rabin. Ich dachte, ich hätte schlecht geträumt, aber es war nicht so. Am Nachmittag fuhr ich nach Jerusalem, um ihm ein letztes Lebewohl zu sagen. Als ich vor der Knesset, dem israelischen Parlament, Schlange stand, sah ich junge Männer mit einem Transparent, auf dem »Isra-Hell«, »Isra-Hölle«, stand, für ein Volk, das seine Hoffnung auf Frieden umgebracht hatte. Ich glaube, daß die jungen Männer recht hatten. Ich habe Rabin nicht erschossen, aber ich habe ihm auch nicht genug Unterstützung gegeben. Rabin war meine Hoffnung auf Frieden gewesen, und ich hatte ihm geglaubt. Er war ein Mann des Krieges gewesen, der ein Mann des Friedens wurde. Er war der größte Führer, den ich je gekannt habe. Rabin hat uns den Weg zum Frieden gezeigt und ist gegangen.
Jetzt muß jede und jeder von uns alles für den Friedensprozeß tun. Rabin hat begonnen, wir werden die Aufgabe zu Ende führen.

Adi, Shirley, Simone

Tommy, Karin, Hani, Simone

EGERER, THOMAS
1994, 1995, 1996, 1997, 1998

*9.8.1976
Wien
University of Vienna, political science and ethnology
Austrian delegation

Poem

The sun attacks with floods of light
and blinding brightness strikes our eyes.
For in this light the world is watching
everybody but oneself
But also moon spends lovely light
so penetrating we must say
The softness of this shining body
reveals the secrets banned by day
At night we find deserted place
where we hide our nakedness
And only there learn hands to touch
break inner walls of horridness
Spotlights in the conference hall:
we violate the microphone
At Stephansplatz the streetlamps show
we decide which streets to roam
Our vision seems to be
control for free imagination
but when the shadows disappear
then trust becomes our salvation

EL DIN NASRAT, AHMED NOUR
1994

*16.12.1973 in Sudan
Lived in Italy, Guatemala and Turkey,
graduate of the American University of
Cairo, mass communication
Egyptian delegation

Ahmed at the Peace Conference
Ahmed auf der Friedenskonferenz
Ahmed, Wafa

EL MIKURAD, HESHAM
1994

*4.8.1974
Cairo
Graduate of the American University of Cairo
Egyptian delegation

ELLOULOU, MAGED
1994, 1995

*8.7.1975
Gaza
Budapest University, Faculty of Law
Palestinian delegation

Mousa, Maged

At the UN-City
In der UNO-City

EL-RAZZAZ, RANIA
1994

*7.10.1974
Cairo
Graduate of the American University of Cairo, B.A. in international relations
Egyptian delegation

Many conflicts are only resolved when both parties display a certain fatigue. Not that he or she was right but they have had enough. The syndromes of fatigue in the Middle East are a blessing. I am not afraid of tired people in the Middle East, I am afraid of the tireless people among Palestinians, among Israeli settlers. I wish they would get tired.

Amos Oz

Viele Konflikte werden nur gelöst, wenn sich bei beiden Parteien eine gewisse Müdigkeit einstellt. Nicht, daß er oder sie recht hätte, aber sie haben einfach genug. Die Syndrome der Ermüdung im Nahen Osten sind ein Segen. Ich fürchte mich nicht vor den müden Menschen im Nahen Osten. Ich habe Angst vor den Unermüdlichen unter den Palästinensern und unter den israelischen Siedlern. Ich wünschte, sie würden müde werden.

Amos Oz

ERFAN, IHAB
1994

*25.1.1973
Cairo
Graduate from the American University of Cairo, engineering
Egyptian delegation

Ihab, Ramzi

Eyal, Wafa, Mahar, Kobi, Tal

NIV, EYAL
1996

*20.2.1980
Currently doing his army service, member of Maccabi Hatzair and the Hanoch fellowship/ Meretz youth
Israeli delegation

FEIDI, ADEL
1994

*5.7.1977
Studies medicine
Palestinian delegation

Doomed to live together

I went to Vienna carrying a load of thoughts and impressions about Israelis, usually known to me only as soldiers, occupants, and oppressors of the Palestinian people. As such, they represented our biggest enemy.
I was travelling all the way to Vienna with new people to meet with, discuss, get acquainted and make peace with each other. We spent eleven days together exchanging ideas and simply laughing together. I found out that the Israeli youngsters are not different from us; their hopes, aspirations and fears are similar to ours. We all want to live a happy, prosperous and peaceful life. I think these things are a good basis for coexistence. But to ensure the success of such endeavours toward peace, we also need on both sides, to learn how to accept and respect each other despite our differences. We seem to have been doomed to live on this land; so we'd better prove to be worthy of this most sacred spot on earth.

Zum Zusammenleben bestimmt

Ich trug eine Menge Gedanken und Eindrücke über Israelis mit mir herum, als ich nach Wien kam; ich kenne sie üblicherweise als Soldaten, Besatzer und als Unterdrücker des palästinensischen Volkes. Und daher als unseren größten Feind. Ich reiste mit unbekannten Menschen nach Wien, um sie kennenzulernen, mit ihnen zu diskutieren und Frieden zu schließen.
Wir verbrachten elf Tage zusammen, tauschten Gedanken aus oder hatten einfach gemeinsam Spaß. Ich entdeckte, daß israelische Jugendliche nicht anders sind als wir. Ihre Hoffnungen, Wünsche und Ängste sind unseren ähnlich. Wir wollen alle ein glückliches, friedvolles und erfülltes Leben. Ich denke, diese Gemeinsamkeiten stellen eine wichtige Basis für ein Zusammenleben dar. Aber wir müssen auch lernen, einander zu respektieren und zu akzeptieren, trotz aller Unterschiede, um unserem Vorhaben eine Chance zu geben. Wir scheinen dazu bestimmt zu sein, in diesem Land zu leben; daher sollten wir beweisen, daß wir diesen heiligen Flecken Erde auch wert sind.

Lisa, Simone, Basheer, Nisreen, Suha, Adi
Kirstin, Lisa, Katrin

FISCHER, LISA
1996, 1997, 1998

*10.6.1975
Wien
University of Vienna, Faculty of Medicine, studied at Copenhagen University and did an internship in Greenland
Austrian delegation

I am writing these lines in Denmark, where I am studying at the moment and I am happy to have the possibility to contribute to this book via e-mail, although I am geographically quite far away from the Middle East. It is technology of communication, which makes that possible and it was communication again, which was a key word in our Middle East Youth Peace Forum. Talking to each other makes people trust in one another and opens new perspectives and possiblities. For me it was one of the main points during the process of the Forum to see and feel how people get to talk and therefore also trust in each other. It was great to observe this process and to be involved in it. Personal contacts and experiences are essential for understanding and one of the reasons for the success of this project. I can say out of my own experience that my time with the Middle East Youth Peace Forum made me a lot more sensitive in judging other people's opinions and attitudes ... The fact that we managed to solve conflicts many times shows that there happened a lot in our minds and it was worth it to give it a try.
Thanks to everybody, who was involved in the Middle East Youth Peace Forum.

Ich schreibe diese Zeilen in Dänemark, wo ich zur Zeit studiere, und bin froh, via E-Mail einen Beitrag zu diesem Buch leisten zu können, auch wenn ich geografisch gesehen weit weg vom Nahen Osten bin. Dank der Technologie ist Kommunikation möglich, wie auch Kommunikation ein Schlüsselwort in unserem Nahost-Jugend-Friedensforum war. Wenn Menschen beginnen, miteinander zu sprechen, beginnen sie auch, einander zu vertrauen, und es öffnen sich neue Möglichkeiten und Perspektiven. Diesen Prozeß zu beobachten und ein Teil davon zu sein war für mich etwas sehr Zentrales bei dem Forum. Persönliche Kontakte und Erfahrungen sind wichtig für das gegenseitige Verstehen und machen den Erfolg des Programms aus. Ich persönlich kann sagen, daß mich das Nahost-Jugend-Friedensforum sensibler in der Beurteilung anderer gemacht hat ... Die Tatsache, daß wir so oft Konflikte gelöst haben, zeigt, daß viel mit uns passiert ist und daß es sich gelohnt hat, es zu versuchen. Danke allen, die dabei waren.

GERSHTEIN, INA
1995, 1996

*10.8.1978
Born in Russia, immigrated to Israel in 1990, works and lives in Kibbutz Yad Mordechai
Israeli delegation

GILBERT, JASON
1995

*16.2.1978
Member of a Likud youth group
Israeli delegation

There is no way the Israelis and the Palestinians can agree in the foreseeable future on who started it all and who is to blame for the job. There is no way that this sweet fantasy will materialise of the other getting down on their knees and saying, oh brother, I have sinned to you, will you ever forgive me. This is not going to happen. The Israeli-Palestinian conflict is a clash between right and right. It is a clash between two very convincing claims. As such we can deal with it through a certain sense of relativism, through the ability which novels and stories can educate us, the ability to live with two conflicting narratives.
If I had any leverage at all, any say at all in the peace talks, I would make a conspiracy not with the delegates but with the sound technicians. I would bribe the sound technicians into disconnecting the microphones each time any of the delegates or the politicians refers to the past. Those people are getting paid to deal with the present and especially with the future. The past, the diverse narratives ought to remain the business of the storytellers, the thinkers, the intellectuals.
Having said that the Israeli-Palestinian conflict is a tragedy and not a clash between right and wrong, tragedies traditionally can be resolved in one of two manners.
There is the Shakespeare tradition of resolving the tragedy by bloodshed and there is the other tradition, the Chekhov tradition. At the end of a Shakespeare tragedy the stage is cluttered with dead bodies and a justice of sorts prevails high above. In the conclusion of a tragedy by Chekhov in the end everybody is bitter, disillusioned, unhappy, melancholic, but alive. I have been working for many years to try to find a Chekhovian, not a Shakespeare resolution to the Israeli-Palestinian conflict. Let us all work in the spirit of Chekhov.

Amos Oz

Es besteht keine Aussicht darauf, daß sich Israelis und Palästinenser in absehbarer Zukunft darüber einig werden, wer mit dem Ganzen angefangen hat und wer die Schuld trägt. Es besteht keine Chance, daß sich einer niederkniet und sagt. »Oh Bruder, ich habe gesündigt, wirst du mir je verzeihen können.« Dies wird nicht passieren. Der israelisch-palästinensische Konflikt ist ein Aufeinanderprallen von Recht und Recht. Er ist das Aufeinanderprallen von zwei sehr überzeugenden Sichtweisen. Insofern können wir ihn mit einem gewissen Relativismus betrachten, jenem Relativismus, der es uns beim Lesen eines Romanes oder einer Erzählung ermöglicht, mit zwei gegensätzlichen Schilderungen einer Geschichte zurechtzukommen.
Wenn ich auch nur ein wenig Einfluß hätte, bei den Friedensgesprächen ein klein bißchen mitreden könnte, ich würde eine Verschwörung anstiften – nicht mit den Delegierten, sondern mit den Tontechnikern. Ich würde die Tontechniker bestechen, auf daß sie die Mikrofone abschalteten, sobald irgendeiner von den Delegierten oder Politikern anfinge, von der Vergangenheit zu reden. Diese Leute werden bezahlt, damit sie sich mit der Gegenwart und ganz besonders mit der Zukunft auseinandersetzen. Die Vergangenheit, die diversen Schilderungen sollten Sache der Geschichtenerzähler, der Denker bleiben.
Ausgehend davon, daß der israelisch-palästinensische Konflikt eine Tragödie und nicht einfach ein Aufeinandertreffen von Recht und Unrecht ist, bedenke man, daß Tragödien traditionell auf zwei verschiedene Arten gelöst werden. Es gibt die Shakespeare-Tradition, in der Tragödien in einem Blutbad gipfeln, und es gibt die andere Tradition, jene Tschechows. Am Schluß einer Tragödie von Shakespeare sind die Bretter mit Leichen übersät, und es herrscht eine Art Gerechtigkeit von oben. Bei Tschechow sind zum Schluß alle verbittert, ernüchtert, melancholisch, aber am Leben. Seit Jahren suche ich eine Lösung im Sinne Tschechows – nicht Shakespeares – zum israelisch-palästinensischen Konflikt. Laßt uns alle im Sinne Tschechows arbeiten.

Amos Oz

GLATZ, PHILIPPE
1994, 1995

*1.11.1977
Rußbach
Graduate of Lester B. Pearson United World College, civil service in Auschwitz and Yad Vashem, currently works as a teacher in Bolivia
Austrian delegation

Messages from Philippe during his stay in Israel
On Thursday, Israel commemorated the assassination of Yitzhak Rabin with an official ceremony at his grave, which was some hundred metres away from Yad Vashem. In the evening, in a different kind of event, two participants in the "Crossing Borders" project, Suha and Moriah, took part in a television show (CH2).

Last Thursday I spoke on the phone with Kareem, Nano, Moriah and Tali, and yesterday with Hani. Nano could not leave her house at this time because there was a shooting in front of it. Kareem and Firas were slightly wounded in a demonstration in Ramallah (luckily, only with rubber bullets). Moriah's settlement is of course quiet, though also only 15 minutes away from the shooting.

Today there should have been a meeting between the Israeli group and the Palestinians in the Orient House, and I wanted to go, too. Because of the tense situation, this plan has been postponed. I will keep you informed of the exact situation.

Am Donnerstag gedachte Israel der Ermordung Yitzhak Rabins, und einige hundert Meter von Yad Vashem entfernt fand eine offizielle Zeremonie an seinem Grab statt. Am Abend gab es unter anderem eine TV-Show (CH2), in der auch zwei Teilnehmerinnen des »Crossing-Borders«-Projekts auftraten, Suha und Moriah.

Letzten Donnerstag habe ich mit Kareem, Nano, Moriah und Tali telefoniert, gestern mit Hani. Nano konnte ihr Haus zu diesem Zeitpunkt nicht verlassen, da genau davor gerade geschossen wurde; Kareem und Firas wurden bei einer Demonstration in Ramallah leicht verletzt (Gott sei Dank nur durch Gummigeschosse). Moriahs Siedlung ist natürlich ruhig, wobei auch von dort nur 15 Minuten entfernt geschossen wurde.

Heute hätte eigentlich ein Treffen zwischen der Israelischen Gruppe und den Palästinensern im Orient House stattfinden sollen, ich wollte auch hingehen. Wegen der angespannten Lage ist es aber verschoben worden.

Karin, Philippe

GRIESSER, MARTIN

1996

*29.11.1978
Dornbirn
University of Innsbruck, physics and mathematics
Austrian delegation

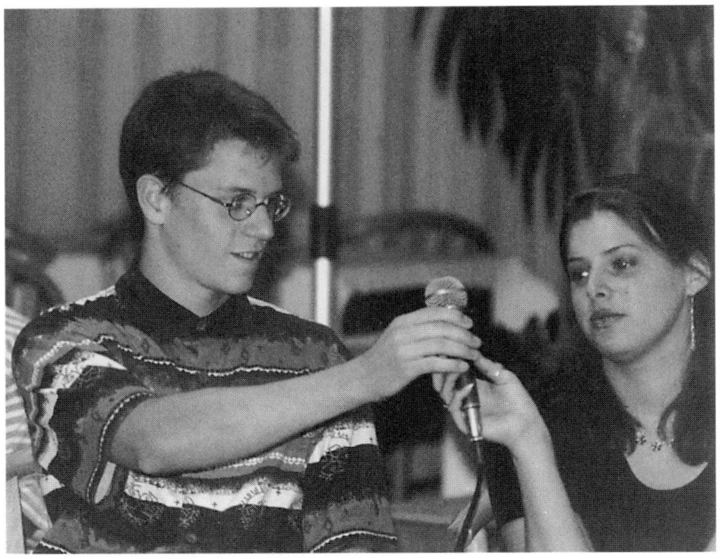

Martin, Ori
At the SOS Children's Village, Bethlehem
Im SOS-Kinderdorf, Bethlehem

HABASH, RAMZI
1996, 1997, 1998

*5.4.1976
Ramallah
Bir Zeit University, business and economics, works with his father, member of Youth for Peace in Ramallah
Palestinian delegation

Ramzi, Suha

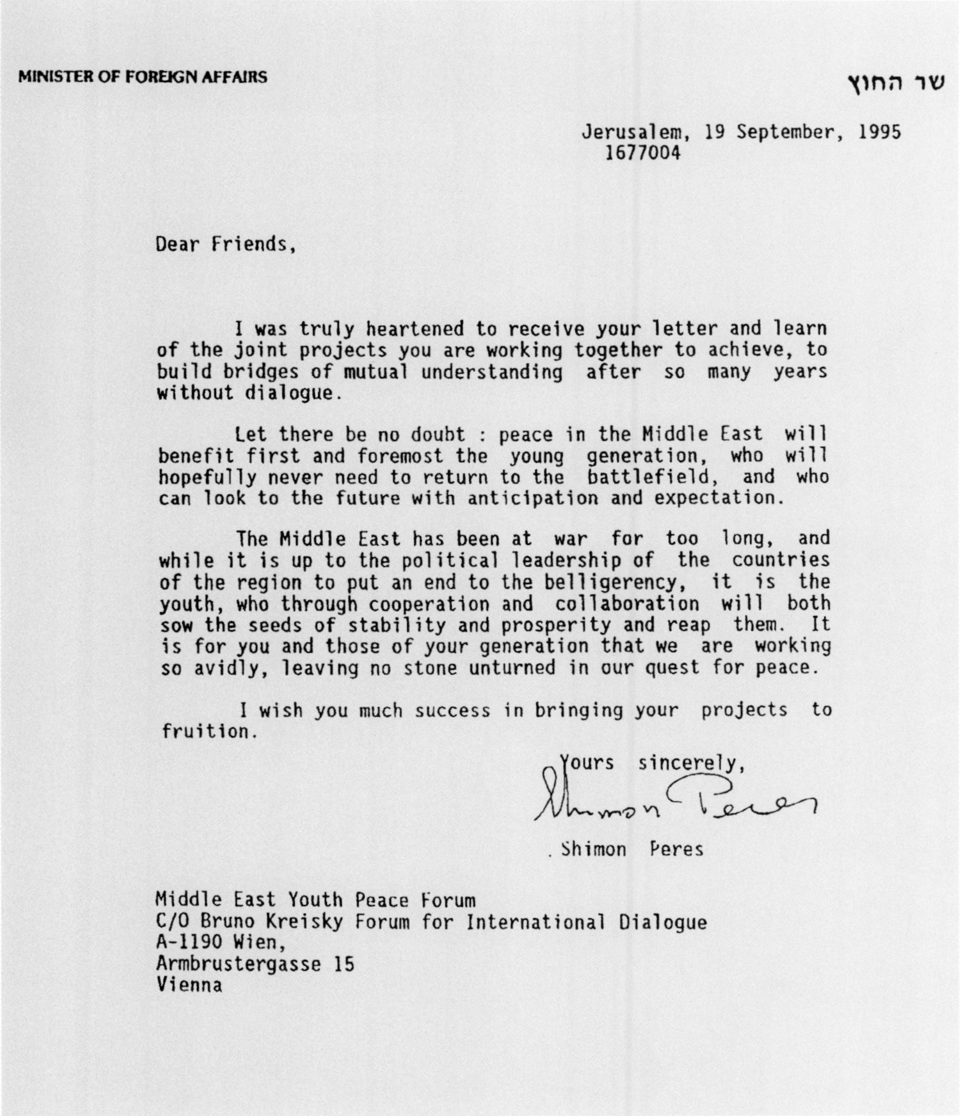

MINISTER OF FOREIGN AFFAIRS שר החוץ

Jerusalem, 19 September, 1995
1677004

Dear Friends,

I was truly heartened to receive your letter and learn of the joint projects you are working together to achieve, to build bridges of mutual understanding after so many years without dialogue.

Let there be no doubt : peace in the Middle East will benefit first and foremost the young generation, who will hopefully never need to return to the battlefield, and who can look to the future with anticipation and expectation.

The Middle East has been at war for too long, and while it is up to the political leadership of the countries of the region to put an end to the belligerency, it is the youth, who through cooperation and collaboration will both sow the seeds of stability and prosperity and reap them. It is for you and those of your generation that we are working so avidly, leaving no stone unturned in our quest for peace.

I wish you much success in bringing your projects to fruition.

Yours sincerely,

Shimon Peres

Middle East Youth Peace Forum
C/O Bruno Kreisky Forum for International Dialogue
A-1190 Wien,
Armbrustergasse 15
Vienna

Ihab, Ramzi
Ramzi, Oraib

HALABY, RAMZI
1994

*1977
Amman
Jordanian delegation

It was a valuable experience for my colleagues and me, as we set out to represent our cultures and heritages, to discuss our political beliefs openly and to shape our own common future. It presented us with an opportunity to break down some of the prejudices that have been inbred in all of our cultures – Israeli, Palestinian, and Jordanian since the beginning of the Arab-Israeli conflict.
I feel strongly that my attitude towards our counterparts has changed radically over the past few months. The success of the conference confirmed that regional peace is attainable. The hope of all the participants was strengthened visibly, and so was the commitment to the peace process and the future of the Middle East.

Es war eine wertvolle Erfahrung für mich und meine Freunde, unsere Kultur und unsere Geschichte zu präsentieren, politische Überzeugungen offen zu diskutieren und unsere gemeinsame Zukunft zu entwerfen. Es war eine Gelegenheit, mit unseren Vorurteilen, die wir seit Beginn des israelisch-arabischen Konfliktes in uns tragen, aufzuräumen. Ich fühle, daß sich meine Haltung gegenüber den anderen in den vergangenen Monaten radikal verändert hat. Der Erfolg der Konferenz beweist, daß Frieden in unserer Region möglich ist. Die Hoffnung aller TeilnehmerInnen war sichtbar gestärkt und dementsprechend auch unser Engagement für den Friedensprozeß und die Zukunft des Nahen Ostens.

HAMEED AL-HAJJ, AHMAD
1994, 1996

*21.8.1975
Amman
University of Amman, Faculty of Medicine,
finished his doctorate in June 1999
Jordanian delegation

... But I must say that you have changed a lot in our lives, mine at least ... if it wasn't for you, I would have never got a chance to meet "the other side", or propose my thoughts to a neutral side, so that I would get an objective response about them; not to forget the exchange of ideas and of course the fun we had together. And I had the opportunity to meet great people; like Hani, who provided me with the chance to visit my home land, a small ruined village in northern Palestine (Israel), that I would have never achieved without you ... I sincerely thank you from the bottom of my heart, and thank God that I had this opportunity in my life.

... Ich muß euch sagen, daß ihr eine Menge in unserem Leben verändert habt, zumindest in meinem ... Ohne euch hätte ich nie die Chance gehabt, »die andere Seite« kennenzulernen, einem neutralen Partner meine Gedanken mitzuteilen und eine objektive Antwort zu bekommen – den Gedankenaustausch und den gemeinsamen Spaß natürlich nicht zu vergessen. Und ich hatte die Gelegenheit, großartige Menschen kennenzulernen; wie Hani, der mir die Möglichkeit bot, meinen Heimatort zu besuchen, ein kleines Ruinendorf im nördlichen Palästina (Israel), das ich ohne dich, Hani, nie gesehen hätte ... Ich danke dir aus ganzem Herzen dafür und danke Gott für diese Chance in meinem Leben.

Eran, Ahmad
Juman, Ahmad, Hiba

Rania and Bassant in the garden of the Bruno Kreisky Forum
Rania und Bassant im Garten des Bruno Kreisky Forums

HELMI, BASSANT
1994

*25.7.1972
Cairo
Graduate of the American University of Cairo, mass communication and international relations
Egyptian delegation

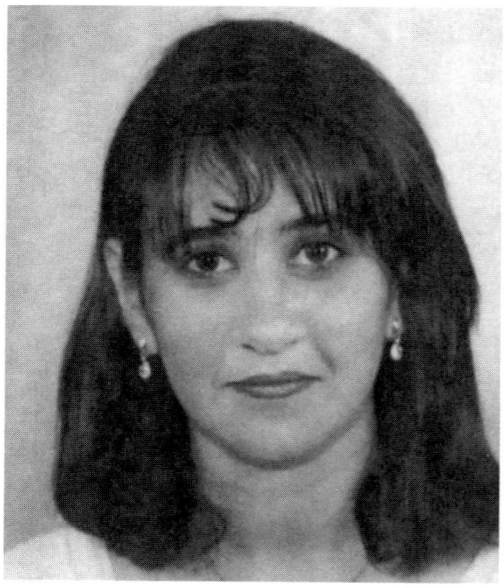

INMANN, KATRIN
1996

*23.10.1977
Salzburg
Studies biotechnology in Salzburg
Austrian delegation

... I went back (to Zimbabwe) in 1982 after the war which people have never really thought about, as seriously as I think they should. This war went on for well over a decade, and it was an extremely brutal war. It was very vicious, very savage on both sides. It was seen in some parts as a quite simple black-white conflict: blacks on one side, whites on the other. If it were as simple as that, it would be easy. There were black soldiers fighting on the white side who – as we all know when there is a war people do not behave nicely – behaved just as brutally as soldiers do, once they are soldiers, and so did the black armies on the other side. These armies were not united ... This was an extremely complicated scene, and it left behind very serious psychological scars. When a war is over – I think we all do this – we build war memorials. We set up ceremonials, but we do not really want to think about what the war was like because we cannot stand it. What we have learned about what human beings are like is so horrible, we don't want to think about it, so we build war memorials.

Doris Lessing

Katrin, Kirstin

1982, nach dem Krieg, über den die Menschen nie so ernsthaft nachgedacht hatten, wie sie es meiner Meinung nach hätten tun sollen, ging ich zurück (nach Simbabwe). Dieser Krieg dauerte weit über ein Jahrzehnt, und er war äußerst brutal. Er war sehr grausam, sehr hinterhältig von beiden Seiten. Teilweise wurde er als ein einfacher Rassenkonflikt zwischen Schwarzen und Weißen betrachtet – die Schwarzen auf der einen Seite, die Weißen auf der anderen. Wenn es so einfach wäre, wäre es leicht. Es gab schwarze Soldaten, die auf der Seite der Weißen kämpften und – wie wir alle wissen, wenn Krieg ist, benehmen sich die Menschen nicht sehr nett – sich genauso brutal aufführten wie Soldaten es tun, sobald sie Soldaten sind. Genauso verhielten sich die schwarzen Armeen auf der anderen Seite. Diese Armeen waren nicht verbündet ... Es war eine äußerst komplizierte Sache, die gravierende psychologische Narben hinterließ. Wenn ein Krieg vorbei ist – und in dieser Hinsicht, glaube ich, sind wir alle gleich – bauen wir Kriegerdenkmäler. Wir halten Feierlichkeiten ab, wollen aber eigentlich über den Krieg nicht nachdenken, weil wir das nicht aushalten. Das, was wir über die Menschen erfahren haben, ist so grauenvoll, daß wir darüber nicht nachdenken wollen, und daher errichten wir Kriegerdenkmäler.

Doris Lessing

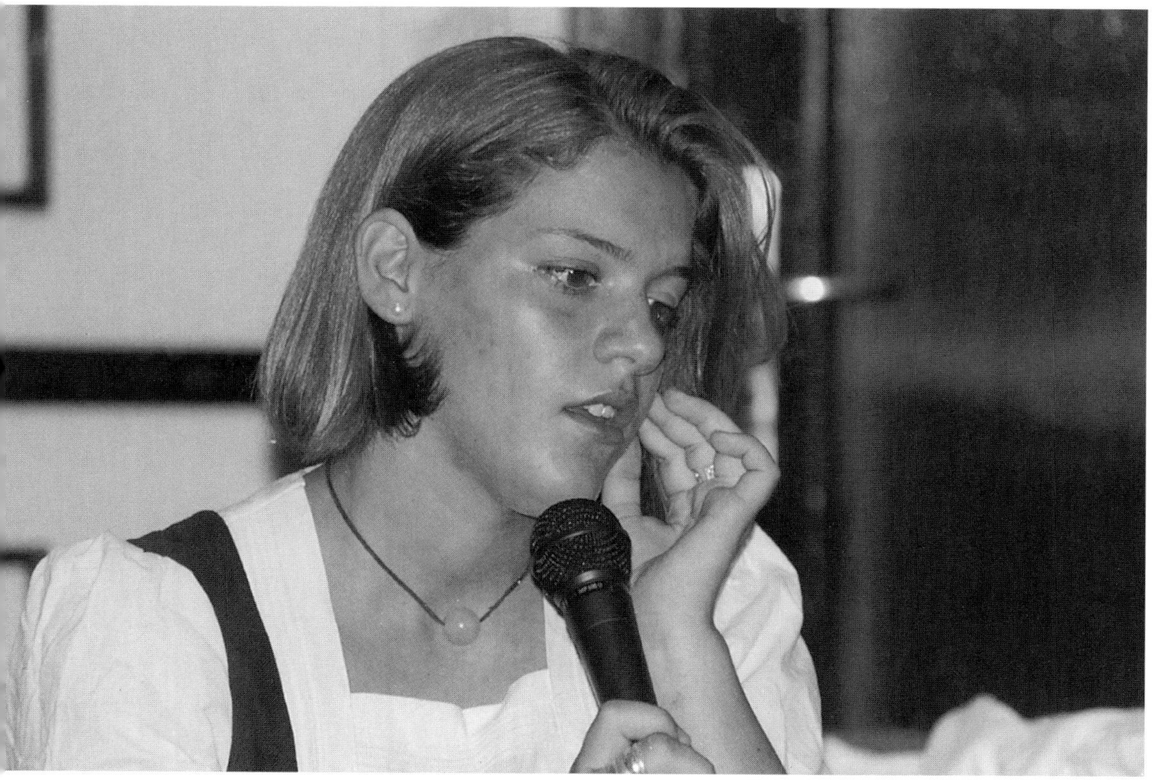

INMANN KIRSTIN
1996

*22.10.1977
Salzburg
Vienna University, commerce, worked in Nepal
Austrian delegation

... I have been familiar with the work of the Bruno Kreisky Forum for some years and wholeheartedly admire it. By now we all know that "we must love one another or die" (The poet, W.H. Auden). This forum performs brilliantly the task of getting people from all over the world, and from many different cultures, to talk to each other. This message comes with all the good wishes possible.

Doris Lessing

Ich bin seit einigen Jahren mit der Arbeit des Bruno Kreisky Forums vertraut und bewundere sie aus vollem Herzen. Heutzutage wissen wir alle: »Wir müssen einander lieben, oder sterben« (der Dichter W.H. Auden). Dieses Forum erfüllt in hervorragender Weise die Aufgabe, Menschen von überall auf der Welt und aus den verschiedensten Kulturen zusammenzubringen, damit sie miteinander reden können.
Diese Botschaft kommt mit allen erdenklich guten Wünschen.

Doris Lessing

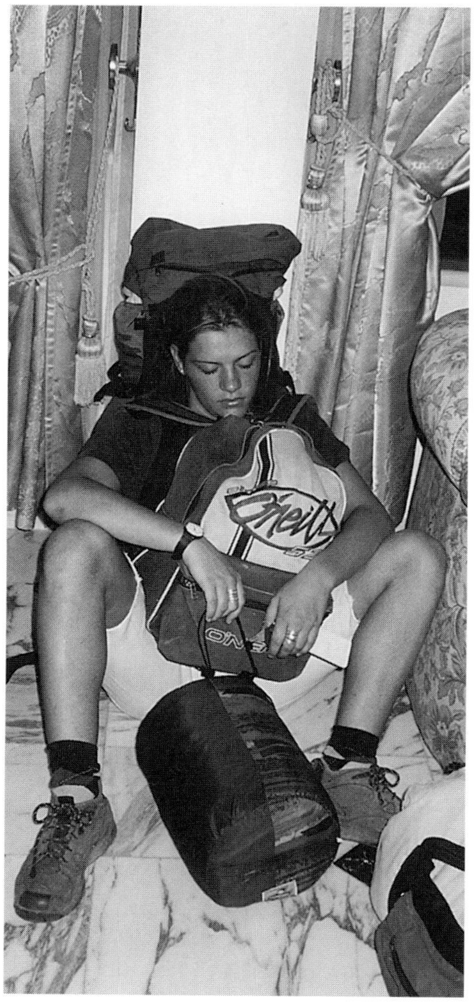

JALABNEH, HIBA
1996

*28.11.1975
Amman
B.A. in business administration, married, lives in Rome/Italy
Jordanian delegation

... Confused ... surprised ... these were the first feelings for me away from my country with different people from different countries, nations, with different cultures, thoughts and languages ... then day by day and year after another these emotions started to change in another way it took the way of understanding, tolerance and friendship.
I was really happy to participate with other youth for the benefit of all of us ... the group, then the society. Now I feel I am related to a big family ... everyone of it has a motive, a strong basis of confidence. Finally, I think I had taken with me ... love ... friendship ...
knowledge ... a memory of nice days.

Hiba, Mahar, Abeer, Wafa

... Verwirrt ... überrascht ... das waren meine ersten Gefühle, als ich außerhalb meines Landes auf neue Menschen traf, andere Länder – Kulturen – Gedanken – Sprachen ...
Dann mit der Zeit, Tag für Tag, Jahr um Jahr, veränderten sich diese Gefühle und wurden zu Verständnis – Toleranz – Freundschaft. Ich war glücklich, mit anderen Jugendlichen teilzunehmen, zu unser aller Wohl, unserer Gruppe ... unserer Gesellschaft. Jetzt weiß ich, daß ich einer großen Familie angehöre ... und jede/r von uns hat ein starkes Motiv, eine Basis des Vertrauens. Und letzten Endes habe ich ... Liebe ... Freundschaft ... Wissen ... eine Erinnerung an wunderbare Tage mitgenommen.

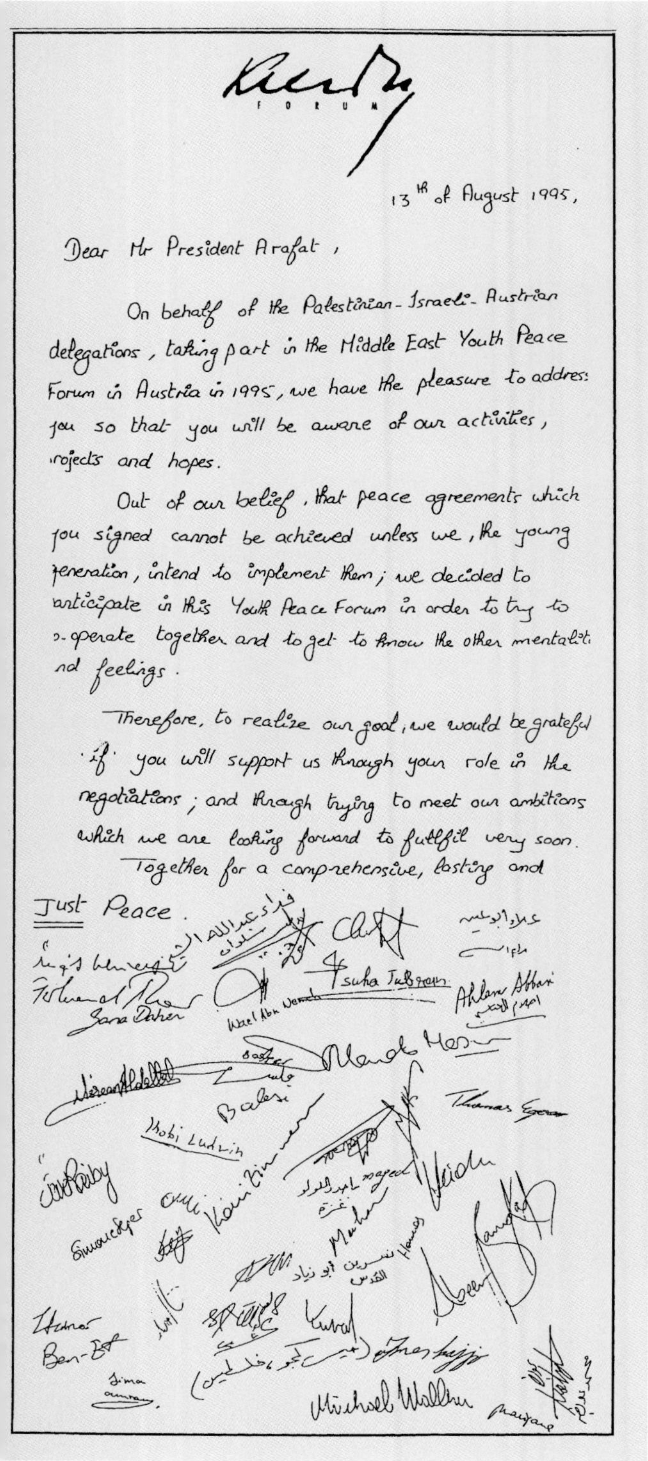
FORUM

13th of August 1995,

Dear Mr President Arafat,

On behalf of the Palestinian-Israeli-Austrian delegations, taking part in the Middle East Youth Peace Forum in Austria in 1995, we have the pleasure to address you so that you will be aware of our activities, rojects and hopes.

Out of our belief, that peace agreements which you signed cannot be achieved unless we, the young eneration, intend to implement them; we decided to articipate in this Youth Peace Forum in order to try to o-operate together and to get to know the other mentaliti nd feelings.

Therefore, to realize our goal, we would be grateful if you will support us through your role in the negotiations; and through trying to meet our ambitions which we are looking forward to fulfil very soon.

Together for a comprehensive, lasting and Just Peace.

Simone, Mahmoud, Reem
Zein, Reem, Suad

JARRAR, REEM
1996

*17.6.1977
Jennin
University of Nablus, science and computer
Palestinian delegation

JECH, BARBARA
1994, 1995, 1996, 1997, 1998

*28.4.1976
Bad Tatzmannsdorf
University of Vienna, Faculty of Medicine, active in the student branch of Médecins sans Frontières and in a group against nuclear weapons
Austrian delegation

Presenting gifts at the SOS Children's Village, Bethlehem
Geschenküberreichung im SOS-Kinderdorf Bethlehem

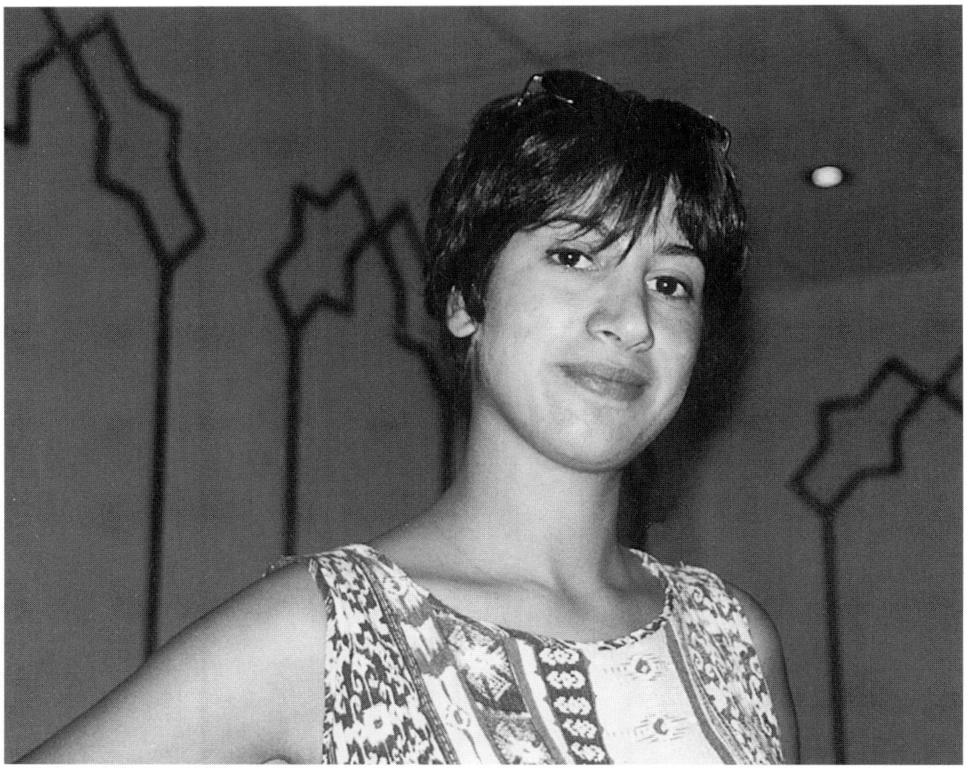

Demokratien leben von der öffentlichen Debatte. Sie leben von abweichenden Ansichten, und sie leben auch vom Aufeinanderprallen der politischen Meinungen, wie sie sich in den Medien widerspiegeln. Auf Dauer können sie politische Angriffe nicht unterbinden …

Freimut Duve

JUBRAN, SUHA
1994, 1995, 1996, 1997, 1998

*10.12.1976
Haifa
University of Haifa. psychology
Israeli delegation

… Any democracy needs freedom of expression for two reasons: the first is the great tradition of the struggle for human rights in which we all believe. The second reason is: we all have experienced what happens to societies and economies that do not allow for the necessary corrective function of public criticism … Democracies live on public debate. They live on divergent views and they also live on a clash of political opinion as reflected in the media. In the long run they cannot withstand political hostilities …

Freimut Duve

Jede Demokratie braucht Redefreiheit aus zwei Gründen: der erste ist die große Tradition des Kampfes für Menschenrechte, an die wir alle glauben. Der zweite Grund ist: Wir alle haben erlebt, was mit Gesellschaften und Wirtschaften passiert, die die notwendige korrigierende Funktion der öffentlichen Kritik nicht zulassen …

Mike, James, Elisabeth

JUHA, ELISABETH
1994

*9.4.1974
Bethlehem
Clerk in the Arab Bank
Palestinian delegation

… I must say that I think back, with some sadness, on our joint project, which was arduous but not without significant success. With sadness, because I have worked for the Near and Middle East with my heart and soul. But also because the situation as it is now and has been for a long time depresses me deeply … So there are only a few such as you, Mrs Schmidt, who keep the flag flying, which is more important today than ever.

Alexander Christiani,
Ambassador, The Hague
Former director of the Middle East desk at the Austrian Ministry of Foreign Affairs,
July 1998

… Ich muß sagen, daß ich mit ein wenig Wehmut an unser gemeinsames Projekt, das zwar mit Mühen, jedoch auch mit nicht unerheblichen Erfolgen verbunden war, zurückdenke.
Mit Wehmut deshalb, weil ich den Nahen und Mittleren Osten »mit Leib und Seele« bearbeitet habe. Aber auch deshalb, weil mich die Situation, wie sie sich seit längerer Zeit darstellt, zutiefst deprimiert …
Deshalb werden die wenigen, die wie Sie, liebe Frau Schmidt, das Fähnlein hochhalten, heute mehr benötigt denn je zuvor …

Alexander Christiani,
Botschafter, Den Haag.
ehemaliger Direktor der Nahostabteilung des österreichischen Außenministeriums,
Juli 1998

Dabka dancing
Beim Dabka-Tanzen

KAJJO, JAMES
1994, 1995, 1996,1997,1998

*21.10.1973
Jerusalem
Printer and graphic designer
Palestinian delegation

Words to consider
As a Palestinian I want to comment upon the assassination of Yitzhak Rabin. I'm sorry for what happened, even if it is difficult to forgive him that he gave the order to break the bones of us and to kill us for no reason. As he started the peace process, I and many other Palestinians were on the way to forgive and believe that he started to treat us as equal persons and to persuade his people to do so, too. The Israelis see most of us as terrorists. Now they see that there are bad and good persons in every society and every people. This might help to change their attitude towards us. We have to deal with each other in a better way, not at least because we are living in the same region. A terrorist is not necessarily a crazy person; he has to take the responsibility for what he is doing. Nevertheless, he is under pressure of others, e. g. his parents, the people he is dealing with or his friends and sometimes his leaders. Personally, I will put more effort on supporting the peace process, and I hope that all the people who believe in peace will do so.

For a better future
To those who believe or are interested in co-operation among different nations, I ask them to share it with the "New Generation". Share with us projects, ideas and friendship. Let us all work together to achieve our desired goals. Let us not take a negative step from the current status, the peace process is not moving, but we have to move, for all those peace lovers. Let us not worry about leaders, they have their own strategies, and let us put our own strategies and benefit from our friendship. If we wait for the peace process to take its full share then we will wait for a long time. Now it is the best time to begin. Let us follow this equation for a better life: Trust + Loyalty + Co-operation + hard work = a better future for us all.

Überlegungen
Ich möchte als Palästinenser über die Ermordung Yitzhak Rabins schreiben. Ich bin betroffen von dem, was passiert ist, auch wenn es mir schwerfällt, ihm zu verzeihen, daß er den Befehl gegeben hat, die Knochen unserer Leute zu brechen und uns ohne Grund zu töten. Aber er hat den Friedensprozeß begonnen, und für mich und viele andere Palästinenser war das der Grund, ihm zu verzeihen und daran zu glauben, daß er uns endlich als gleichwertige Menschen behandeln und sein Volk davon überzeugen würde, dies ebenso zu tun. Die Israelis sehen die meisten von uns als Terroristen. Jetzt begreifen sie, daß es in jeder Gesellschaft Gute und Böse gibt. Vielleicht ändern sie auch ihre Haltung uns gegenüber. Wir müssen einander besser behandeln, nicht zuletzt, weil wir in derselben Region leben. Ein Terrorist ist nicht unbedingt verrückt, er ist verantwortlich für das, was er tut. Dennoch, er steht unter dem Druck von außen, seiner Eltern, seiner Umgebung, seiner Freunde und seiner Führer. Ich persönlich möchte mich mehr für den Friedensprozeß einsetzen und hoffe, daß alle, die an Frieden glauben, es mir gleichtun werden.

Für eine bessere Zukunft
Alle, die an einer Zusammenarbeit zwischen den verschiedenen Nationen interessiert sind, sind aufgerufen, zur »Neuen Generation« zu kommen. Teilt mit uns Projekte, Ideen und Freundschaften. Laßt uns zusammenarbeiten, um unsere Ziele zu erreichen. Laßt euch nicht entmutigen durch den momentanen Stillstand des Friedensprozesses, setzen wir uns in Bewegung für alle friedensliebenden Menschen. Kümmert euch nicht um politische Führer, die haben ihre eigenen Strategien. Laßt uns unsere Strategien entwerfen und von unserer Freundschaft profitieren. Wenn wir auf den Frieden warten, warten wir lange. Jetzt ist der Moment zu beginnen. Laßt uns folgende Gleichung befolgen: Vertrauen + Loyalität + Zusammenarbeit + harte Arbeit = eine bessere Zukunft für uns alle.

KHALAF, FIRAS
1996, 1997, 1998

*11.5.1977
Ramallah
Bir Zeit University, business
Palestinian delegation

Thank you for the information concerning the Middle East Youth Peace Forum. Their work seems not only to be crossing literal boundaries, but figurative ones as well. The information is very inspiring for me and has left me feeling a part of a network of people worldwide, committed to building better relationships based on trust and friendship between Jewish and Muslim youth.

Elana Friedman,
European Palestine Israel Centre, London

Danke für die Information über das Nahost-Jugend-Friedensforum. Ihre Arbeit scheint mir nicht nur im Überwinden physischer Grenzen zu bestehen, sondern auch psychischer und intellektueller. Diese Vorstellung begeistert mich und gibt mir das Gefühl, Teil eines weltweiten Netzwerkes zu sein, das sich dem Aufbau von besseren Beziehungen zwischen Moslems und Juden widmet, die auf Freundschaft und Vertrauen beruhen.

Elana Friedman,
Europäisches Palästina-Israel-Zentrum, London

Nisreen, Margit, Firas

Natasha, Hana'a, Mahmoud, Kareem, Mahar, Khuloud

KHALIDI, NATASHA
1996

*3.9.1977
Ramallah
Bir Zeit University, language studies, active in a peace group
Palestinian delegation

After the "Crossing Borders" trip Natasha Khalidi and Tomer Shadmi were invited to a conference in Norway

Norway
Though my trip to Norway lasted only eleven days, I had a lot to learn from it. It was an experience not many people get to go through, to live with an Israeli, to have to discuss the issues that affect our lives and to tell all Norwegians about what the conflict in the Middle East was all about. I think Tomer and I learned a lot about each other and about Norway and its people …
We were dealing with citizens of one of the states on earth which has had peace and prosperity for the past two hundred years … where schools are well equipped and children educated and even universities are for free … Tomer and I decided to show them from which part of the world we came, we blamed our hot temper on the high temperature we have here in the Middle East … and we talked about our life, what we are going through every day … But by talking about the situation we faced dead ends, we had two versions of the same story. Both of us could not give up our version because we felt that we were both right about it. We tried not to forget the past because this is what we are, but we tried also to look at the present and the future. At some point I was furious at what Tomer was saying, about the closure, the suffering of the Palestinian people. When I brought the issue of refugee camps (about three million Palestinians

around the Arab world), her reaction was either to find a way to go around the subject or to find a reason for why Israel did what it had to do ...
I expected people to understand and recognize that what was done to the Palestinian people was wrong. As I found it as an obligation to say that Hamas was doing the wrong thing in killing people, which is something I believe in, I thought it is also logical from Tomer not to find Likud government the appropriate one, but this did not happen ... This trip made me realise that both the Palestinians and Israelis have a lot to learn about each other, and that they are very far from understanding each other. These long years of hatred need a long time to heal. And if we don't stop looking back on the past we will never get out of this circle. At some point after two or three days of our visit to Norway we made a decision to leave what was said in lectures aside. The political issues we will never agree on, so we decided to put more time in becoming friends and I think we did that to the same extent. There is only one thing that I just have to mention. One of the Norwegian teachers was telling Tomer that her capital was never Jerusalem, it was always Tel Aviv. Tomer tried to convince her that she was wrong, many times, and then Tomer could not take it any more and started crying. I just have a question: Put yourself in a Palestinian's situation and imagine someone telling you that this is not your land and you don't belong here.
I wonder how you would feel or how angry you might get?

Nach der »Crossing-Border«-Reise waren Natasha Khalidi und Tomer Shadmi (Israel) zu einer Konferenz in Norwegen eingeladen.

Norwegen
Obwohl die Reise nach Norwegen nur elf Tage dauerte, habe ich eine Menge daraus gelernt. Nicht viele meiner Mitmenschen machen die Erfahrung, was es heißt, mit einer Israelin zusammenzuleben, alles miteinander zu diskutieren, was unser Leben betrifft, und den Norwegern zu erzählen, worum es sich beim Nahostkonflikt dreht. Ich glaube, Tomer und ich haben viel übereinander gelernt, aber auch über Norwegen und seine Menschen ...
Wir hatten mit den Bewohnern eines Landes zu tun, das in den letzten zweihundert Jahren nur Wohlstand und Frieden kannte ... wo Schulen gut ausgestattet und Kinder gut erzogen werden und sogar Universitäten unentgeltlich sind ... Tomer und ich haben beschlossen, ihnen von dem Teil der Welt zu erzählen, aus dem wir kommen; unser hitziges Temperament brachten wir mit dem heißen Klima in Verbindung ... und wir sprachen über unser Leben, was wir täglich durchmachen ... Aber in diesen Gesprächen kamen wir immer an einen toten Punkt, wir hatten zwei Fassungen derselben Geschichte. Jede hielt an ihrer Version fest, weil sie glaubte, recht zu haben. Wir achteten darauf, die Vergangenheit miteinzubeziehen, weil sie uns zu dem gemacht hat, was wir sind, wollten aber auch die Gegenwart und die Zukunft besprechen. Manchmal war ich wütend über Tomer und die Art, wie sie über die Sperre, über das Leid des palästinensischen Volkes sprach. Wenn ich das Gespräch auf die Flüchtlingslager brachte (ca. drei Millionen Palästinenser in der gesamten arabischen Welt), redete sie entweder um das Thema herum oder fand Gründe, warum Israel so handle, wie es handeln müsse ... Ich erwartete mir Verständnis, die Anerkennung der Fakten und die Einsicht, daß das, was dem palästinensischen Volk angetan wurde, falsch war. So wie ich es als meine Verpflichtung empfand zu sagen, daß die Hamas im Unrecht ist, wenn sie unschuldige Menschen tötet, wovon ich überzeugt bin. Für mich war klar, daß auch Tomer die Likud-Regierung als nicht angemessen empfinden würde, aber das traf nicht zu ... Mir ist auf der Reise bewußt geworden, daß wir beide, Palästinenser und Israelis, noch eine Menge voneinander lernen müssen, daß wir vom gegenseitigen Verständnis noch weit entfernt sind. Diese langen Jahre des Hasses brauchen ihre Zeit der Heilung. Aber wenn wir nicht aufhören zurückzuschauen, werden wir nie aus dem Teufelskreis ausbrechen. An einem gewissen Punkt angelangt, haben wir beschlossen, diese Art der Diskussion sein zu lassen. Was politische Themen betrifft, würden wir uns nie einigen, also beschlossen wir, uns mehr darauf zu konzentrieren, Freundinnen zu werden. Und ich glaube, es ist uns gelungen. Eines möchte ich noch erwähnen. Eine norwegische Lehrerin sagte Tomer, daß die Hauptstadt Israels nie Jerusalem, sondern schon immer Tel Aviv gewesen sei. Tomer versuchte sie zu überzeugen, daß sie sich irrte, immer wieder, bis sie schließlich weinend aufgab. Ich möchte eine Frage stellen: Versetzt euch in die Situation der Palästinenser, denen immer wieder gesagt wird, daß das nicht ihr Land sei, daß sie nicht hierher gehörten. Wie würdet ihr euch fühlen, wie wütend wärt ihr?

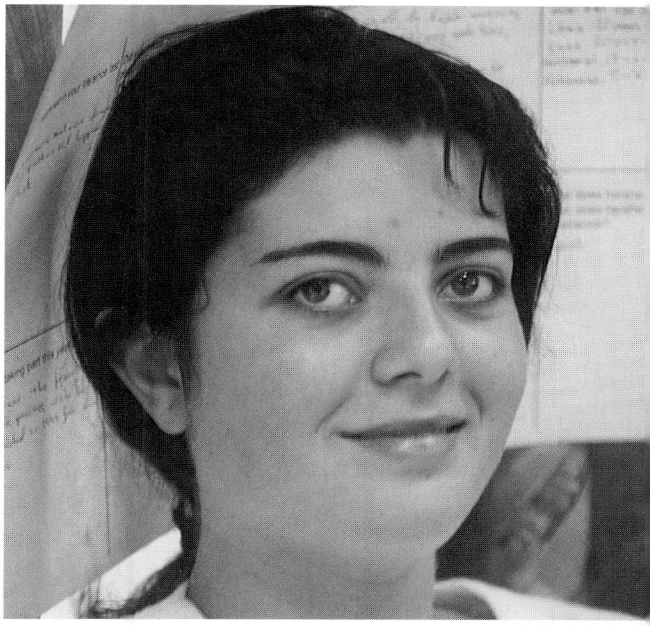

KHEIRALLAH, AMRO
1994

*23.7.1972
Cairo
Graduate of the American University of Cairo, political science
Egyptian delegation

In my own life it was clear to me that on the one hand I felt that I had the duty to become politicised and so I became involved in politics. And in becoming politicised I grew more and more alienated from my own work and my own thoughts. In fact, the language I used in my writing was very similar to political or ideological writing – writing that is instrumental to bringing about a political end. And there was more and more distance from the content. The question for us is do we leave politics and should we not leave politics to politicians and return to our original places, which are in fact ordinary situations, maybe unattractive for a politician but very satisfying for the people themselves. My answer is that there is a limit to what individuals can give to society. And the limit is self-preservation, the preservation of oneself as a person, not as a politician.
Sari Nusseibeh

In meinem eigenen Leben war es mir klar, daß es irgendwie meine Pflicht wäre, mich zu politisieren, und so ließ ich mich auf die Politik ein. Und dabei entfremdete ich mich mehr und mehr von meiner eigenen Arbeit und meinen eigenen Gedanken. Tatsächlich war die Sprache, die ich in meinem Werk verwendete, der Sprache der politischen oder ideologischen Schriften sehr ähnlich – ein Stil, der einem politischen Zweck dient. Und ich entfernte mich mehr und mehr vom Inhalt. Die Frage an uns lautet: Sollen wir uns von der Politik abwenden, und sollten wir die Politik nicht den Politikern überlassen und uns auf unsere Ausgangslage zurückziehen, die eigentlich einer ganz normalen Lebenssituation entspricht, vielleicht nicht sehr attraktiv für einen Politiker, aber sehr befriedigend für die Leute selber. Meine Antwort ist, daß dem, was die Einzelperson zur Gesellschaft beitragen kann, eine Grenze gesetzt ist. Und diese Grenze heißt Selbsterhaltung, die Erhaltung des Ich als Mensch, nicht als Politiker.
Sari Nusseibeh

KOHLER, BERNHARD
1996

*30.12.1976
Dornbirn
University of Innsbruck, medicine
Austrian delegation

Let me take you to a medieval Arabic fort, to an Arab thinker Ibn Tufayl who lived in North Africa and wrote a thought-provoking political allegory which he called Hayy Ibn Yaqthan. There are three main actors in the story, two young and inquisitive friends, who grew up together in a polis, and a wise old man who lives and has always lived on an island all by himself, a sort of Robinson Crusoe. Now the two young friends who lived in the city are dissatisfied with the present political situation. They both believe that there is something wrong with it, that there should be something beyond it. In other words, there should be some deeper significance to it, some value to it that has not yet been really noticed by their fellow citizens. Thus alienated from it, each seeks a way to deal with this problem. One of the two friends decides to seek the true significance of his political reality precisely by immersing himself into this reality. And the second person takes off in a boat and seeks seclusion on a nearby island. Truth can only be sought and appraised, this person probably thinks to himself, in total isolation from the distractions of political life. At this point Ibn Tufayl leaves behind the young activist in the polis and takes the reader along to the nearby island where the would-be ascetic happens upon the old wise man. Through the example of his new master, he discovers the truth about life and human affairs that suddenly reveal to him the significance and real value of political life. He is suddenly able to see the true shapes of things, objects, and not their pure images. Now, delighted with this discovery, a discovery which he feels will surely end the state of alienation of all mankind, he sometimes prevails upon his master to return with him to the city where he plans to face his fellow citizens with the truth, a truth which will lead his city to salvation. Now, on their return, the two sages are hospitably welcomed and their strange views are first listened to with a mixture of tolerance and amusement. However, not before long reactions become derisive and even hostile. Indeed, one assumes that the only reason why they are finally allowed to leave the city safely, without being beaten up, attacked, assassinated, to return to their seclusion is their impeccable contact in the city. The other dissident from the beginning of the story has by now ensconced himself as a ruler.

Sari Nusseibeh

Martin, Bernhard, Tommy

Laßt mich euch in eine mittelalterliche arabische Festung entführen, zum arabischen Denker Ibn Tufayl, der in Nordafrika lebte und eine nachdenklich stimende politische Allegorie – die er Hayy Ibn Yaqtan nannte – schrieb. Es gibt drei Hauptpersonen in der Geschichte, zwei junge neugierige Freunde, die gemeinsam in einer Polis aufwuchsen, und einen weisen alten Mann, der ganz alleine auf einer Insel lebt und immer dort gelebt hat, eine Art Robinson Crusoe. Die zwei jungen Freunde, die in der Polis leben, sind mit der politischen Lage nicht zufrieden. Beide glauben, daß einiges nicht in Ordnung sei, daß es da noch etwas geben müsse. Mit anderen Worten, daß das Dasein eine tiefere Bedeutung haben müsse, irgendeinen Wert, den die Mitbürger bis dahin nicht bemerkt hätten. In diesem Gefühl sucht jeder einen Weg, mit dem Problem fertigzuwerden. Einer der beiden Freunde beschließt, nach der wahren Bedeutung seiner politischen Wirklichkeit zu suchen, indem er in genau diese Wirklichkeit eintaucht. Der zweite segelt davon und sucht die Abgeschiedenheit auf einer nahen Insel. Man kann die Wahrheit nur in der totalen Isolierung vom politischen Leben suchen und bewerten, denkt dieser wahrscheinlich. Hier verläßt Abu Tufayl den jungen Aktivisten in der Polis und nimmt den Leser mit auf die nahe Insel, wo der Möchtegern-Asket zufällig einem alten, weisen Mann begegnet. Am Beispiel seines neuen Meisters entdeckt er die Wahrheit des Lebens und der menschlichen Natur, die ihm plötzlich die Bedeutung und die wirklichen Werte des politischen Lebens enthüllt. Plötzlich ist er fähig, die wirklichen Formen von Objekten zu sehen und nicht nur ihr Abbild. Begeistert von dieser Entdeckung, einer Entdeckung, die, so meint er, sicher die Entfremdung der Menschheit beenden wird, bringt er seinen Meister dazu, mit ihm zurück in die Stadt zu gehen, um die Bevölkerung mit dieser Wahrheit zu konfrontieren, einer Wahrheit, die die Stadt zur Erlösung führen wird. Bei ihrer Heimkehr werden die zwei Weisen freundlich empfangen, und ihre seltsamen Ansichten werden zuerst mit einer Mischung aus Toleranz und Belustigung angehört. Jedoch nach nicht allzu langer Zeit werden die Reaktionen höhnisch und sogar feindselig. Es heißt, der einzige Grund dafür, daß sie die Stadt am Ende verlassen und in ihre Abgeschiedenheit zurückkehren können, ohne zusammengschlagen, überfallen oder gar ermordet worden zu sein, liegt in ihren hervorragenden Beziehungen in der Stadt. Der andere Dissident vom Anfang der Geschichte hat sich inzwischen als Herrscher etabliert.

Sari Nusseibeh

Crossing borders
Grenzen überschreiten

KRENCHEL, MAR'IT
1996

*12.4.1980
Kibbutz Ramat-Hashofet
Studies Arabic and biology, member of Youth of Meretz
Israeli delegation

Most of my life, I have convinced myself, that it is possible, as we say in Arabic, to hold two melons in one hand. Our ancestors used to say "You cannot hold two melons in one hand." I convinced myself that I could hold the two melons in one hand, the melon of literature and the melon of daily political work. Until only recently – the end of my life – and out of my experience, and with the help of others, I nearly broke both melons. Now, I have decided to save one melon. It is the melon of literature …

Emile Habiby

Die meiste Zeit meines Lebens redete ich mir ein, daß es möglich ist – wie man auf arabisch sagt – zwei Melonen in einer Hand zu halten. Unsere Ahnen sagten einst: »Du kannst nicht zwei Melonen in einer Hand halten«. Aber ich redete mir ein, es zu können, die Melone der Literatur und die Melone der täglichen politischen Arbeit. Bis vor kurzem – nunmehr am Ende meines Lebens – hätte ich gemeinsam mit anderen beide Melonen fast zerbrochen. Jetzt habe ich mich entschlossen, eine Melone zu retten. Es ist die Melone der Literatur …

Emile Habiby

KROM, GUY
1994, 1996, 1998

*20.10.1976
Active in peace groups, former youth speaker of Peace Now
Israeli delegation

1994
I came to Austria with enormous hope about a better future. Is it a better future five years later? The answer to this question is not so simple, affected by the general situation, and this is what is important – isn't it???

1998
It was such an amazing and interesting experience to be part of the Middle East Youth Peace Forum; in the last four years, and especially this year, as a leader.
I could use many words and sheets of paper to try to explain my feeling, without getting the real change that happened to me.

The conditions for peace
More than once, we try to search in our head archives and in our traitor memory to understand how the Israeli-Palestinian conflict continues for more than thirty years, without seeing the end of it.
In the days of the Rabin and Peres government, we thought that the Israeli and the Palestinian people are taking off coat by coat the hostility and suspicion and march in confident and adamant step towards historical appeasement.
More than ever, in that time of renewed hope and realisation of old dreams, a not insignificant part of the Israeli and Palestinian people have done all they could to distinguish the cord of peace and to light the cord of fright and hate. On the Israeli side it was nasty and destructive incitement that led to Rabin's assassination, and on the Palestinian side it was fanatic and morbid preaching that caused heartless terror attacks.
The fanatic person (Israeli or Palestinian) will have absolute and radical political concepts and a deep and strong religious belief. The fanatic person generally will be from low social positions and narrow education. The only chance to give a push to the peace process is to break this overlapping.
The Israeli society and the Palestinian society must do all they can to stop the radical religious preachers from brainwashing innocent peoples' mind with fanatic ideas.
The leadership must do everything to abolish the gap between low and high social

standards and to make sure that more young students will finish high school and go to university.
I am sure that these three conditions realised, the day that we will live in peace will come faster than we think.
But if not ...

1994
Ich kam nach Österreich mit einer enormen Hoffnung auf eine bessere Zukunft. Ist sie jetzt, fünf Jahre später, besser? Die Antwort auf diese Frage ist nicht einfach, sie ist von der allgemeinen Situation bestimmt, und das ist es, was zählt – oder???

1998
Es war eine beeindruckende und interessante Erfahrung, Teil des Nahost-Jugend-Friedensforums zu sein, in den letzten vier Jahren und besonders in diesem, da ich als Jugendleiter dabei war. Ich müßte viele Seiten füllen, wollte ich mein Gefühl beschreiben, dennoch würde ich die wirkliche Veränderung in mir nicht treffen.

Bedingungen für einen Frieden
Mehr als einmal haben wir unser Gehirn zermartert und unsere Erinnerungen durchwühlt, um den israelisch-palästinensischen Konflikt, der nun schon mehr als 30 Jahre ohne absehbares Ende andauert, zu verstehen. In den Tagen von Rabin und Peres dachten wir, beide Völker würden Schicht um Schicht Feindseligkeit und Mißtrauen ablegen und vertrauensvoll gemeinsam einer historischen Befriedung entgegengehen.
Mehr denn je haben Israelis und Palästinenser in jenen Tagen neuer Hoffnung und alter Träume alles getan, um das Licht des Friedens zu löschen und Haß und Furcht zu entfachen. Auf der israelischen Seite war es diese eklige Hetze, die zur Ermordung von Rabin geführt hat, auf der palästinensischen Seite waren es die fanatischen Predigten, die in entsetzlichen Terroranschlägen endeten.
Fanatiker (Israeli oder Palästinenser) haben radikale politische Konzepte und tiefe religiöse Überzeugungen. Fanatiker kommen meistens aus niedrigen sozialen Schichten und haben einen niedrigen Bildungsgrad. Um dem Friedensprozeß eine Chance zu geben, müssen wir dieses Schema durchbrechen.
Die israelische und die palästinensische Gesellschaft müssen alles tun, um radikale religiöse Prediger mit ihren Gehirnwäschen

davon abzuhalten, unschuldige Menschen mit fanatischen Ideen zu verführen. Die politischen Führer müssen alles tun, um die Kluft zwischen sozialen Standards abzubauen und die Ausbildung junger Menschen zu forcieren.
Ich bin überzeugt, wenn diese drei Bedingungen erfüllt sind, wird der Tag, an dem wir in Frieden leben können, schneller kommen, als wir denken.
Doch wenn nicht ...

Mike, Fida, James
James, Yossi, Mike

KUDSIEH, MIKE
1994, 1996

*22.10.1977
Jerusalem
Palestinian delegation

Notes from a diary
When pupils from Deheishe Boys School come out to meet with our students, they start to talk and to ask questions; they are surprised to be able to discuss with Israelis. Our students are curious to know how the Palestinian children live, learn more about their hopes and fears. They begin to explain to the children the ideas of the Middle East Youth Peace Forum and their own experience.
... In the summing-up plenary, Mike from the Palestinian delegation recapitulated with these words: "Ten days of hopes, ten days of dreams, ten days of achievements: the biggest one is that we are all together here in Bethlehem."

Tagebuchnotizen
Als die Schüler der Deheishe Knabenschule mit unseren Studenten zusammentrafen, fingen sie an, Fragen zu stellen; sie waren überrascht, mit Israelis diskutieren zu können. Unsere Studenten waren neugierig, wie die palästinensischen Kinder leben, was ihre Hoffnungen und Ängste sind. Sie erklärten den Kindern das Nahost-Jugend-Friedensforum und ihre eigenen Erfahrungen.
... Im Abschlußplenum formulierte Mike von der palästinensischen Delegation folgende Zusammenfassung: »Zehn Tage Hoffnung, zehn Tage Träume, zehn Tage Erfolg: der größte ist, daß wir alle hier in Bethlehem sind.«

LEIBOVITZ, ORI
1995, 1996, 1997, 1998

*10.9.1977
Kibbutz Gaash
Currrently doing her army service, member of Hashomer Hatzair
Israeli delegation

How much we are alike
When I was asked to write about the seminar in Austria, I thought how can I describe in words all the feelings I had there. You would have to be there to really understand what I mean.
Starting with the fears and hopes before, through the good times during the seminar itself and ending with the sadness of the farewell. I have been on the left side of politics for all of my life, so it may be a bit difficult for you to understand that it was only after this seminar that I began to realise how much the Palestinians and the Israelis are alike. We both have feelings – fears, sadness, hate and love.
During that week in Austria, I got to know and to love everyone of the participants – Israelis, Austrians and Palestinians. I hope that more and more youngsters will be able to take part in this kind of seminars. You will never know how much it means, unless you have been there.

Wie ähnlich wir einander sind
Als ich gebeten wurde, einen Artikel über unser Treffen in Wien zu schreiben, wußte ich nicht, wie ich meine Gefühle in Worte fassen sollte.
Angst und Hoffnung vorher, wunderbare Tage während des Seminars und Tränen beim Abschied.
Ich war mein ganzes Leben eine Linke, daher ist es vielleicht verwunderlich, wenn ich sage, daß ich mir erst nach diesem Seminar der großen Ähnlichkeit zwischen uns Israelis und den Palästinensern bewußt wurde. Wir haben beide Gefühle der Angst, der Traurigkeit, des Hasses und der Liebe. Während meines Aufenthalts in Österreich habe ich jeden der Teilnehmer kennen- und lieben gelernt – Österreicher, Israelis und Palästinenser. Ich hoffe, immer mehr junge Menschen werden an diesen Seminaren teilnehmen. Ihr werdet erst dann wissen, was es bedeutet, wenn ihr einmal dabei gewesen seid.

Israeli delegation, disguise at a party
Israelische Delegation, bei einem Kostümfest

LEITL, MARKUS
1994

*18.12.1976
Kufstein
Austrian delegation

LEVINE, RONIT
1996

*2.7.1979
Rehovot
Member of the Society for Protection of Nature and of The International Federation of Young Musicians, member of the school students council and editor of the school's newspaper
Israeli delegation

... People have their own beloved clichés, writers and poets not excluded. For many years the kind of clichés which I and my colleagues have used in order to promote a two-state solution, a compromise between Israelis and Palestinians, have been regarded as unclean vocabulary, a treacherous vocabulary, a perverted vocabulary. The consensus, the middle-of-the-road Israelis and the leadership, they had a different vocabulary. It was not because of our words, but perhaps because of a harsh snap of reality, that after the change, suddenly those same people who objected to our views, our opinions and our vocabularies took up that very same vocabulary. And bits and pieces of my own clichés are now suddenly coming back to me from the most unexpected walks of life.

Amos Oz

... Die Menschen haben ihre eigenen geliebten Klischees; Schriftsteller und Dichter sind da keine Ausnahmen. Für viele Jahre wurden die Klischees, die ich und meine Kollegen verwendeten, um eine Zweistaaten-Lösung zu fördern, als dreckiger Wortschatz, gefährlicher Wortschatz, pervertierter Wortschatz angesehen. Die anderen, die Durschnitts-Israelis und die Politiker, sie hatten eine andere Sprache. Nicht auf Grund unserer Wörter, sondern vielleicht wegen eines brutalen Bruchs in der Wirklichkeit verwendeten die gleichen Menschen, die unsere Sichtweise abgelehnt hatten, nach der Wende plötzlich genau dieses Vokabular. Und jetzt kommen Fragmente meiner eigenen Klischees aus den unerwartetsten Richtungen zu mir zurück.

Amos Oz

Fida, Basheer, Yossi, Mike and Ronit with a piece of the mosaic
Fida, Basheer, Yossi, Mike und Ronit mit einem Stück des Mosaiks

LUDWIN, KOBI
1995, 1996

*6.5.1979
Natanya
Studies physics
Israeli delegation

... That I endorse the idea of a co-existence between Israel and Palestine as next-door neighbours not as a married couple, not as a honeymoon scenario, but perhaps as a semi-detached house scenario, did not come to me as a result of a special expertise on Middle Eastern affairs or a special understanding of strategy or a special professional conception, knowledge about the nature of this conflict. I got there because fairly early on in my life I was intrigued by the prospect of putting myself in Palestinian shoes or under a Palestinian skin. Not necessarily that I loved everything that I have seen under this skin, or felt, or imagined, not that I have ever felt I can identify 100 percent with the Palestinian complaint or with the Palestinian cause, not that I had ever become an admirer of the Palestinian national movement. I have not. But I have realised very early on that whether I like the Palestinian struggle for their cause or not, whether I appreciate the Palestinian leader or not (and I did not appreciate him very much) the basic cause, the basic complaint, the basic lamentation, the basic sense of loss is genuine and ought to be addressed seriously. What equipped me for this early realisation was the fact that I was in the business of writing stories. And I had to write a dialogue about a fight between husband and wife and I have to provide them both with very convincing arguments.

Amos Oz

Die Idee der Koexistenz zwischen Israel und Palästina als Nachbarn, nicht als ein Ehepaar, nicht als ein Flitterwochen-Szenario, sondern als Reihenhaus-Szenario zu unterstützen, ist mir nicht auf Grund irgendwelcher besonderer Sachkenntnisse über die Angelegenheiten im Nahen Osten, Strategiekenntnisse oder professionelles Wissen um die Natur dieses Konflikts in den Sinn gekommen. Es kam dazu, weil mich ziemlich früh in meinem Leben die Vorstellung faszinierte, mich selbst in den Schuhen eines Palästinensers – in seiner Haut zu sehen. Nicht unbedingt, weil ich alles liebte, was ich unter dieser Haut sah oder fühlte oder mir vorstellte. Nicht, daß ich mich jemals hundertprozentig mit der Klage der Palästinenser oder den palästinensischen Anliegen hätte identifizieren können, nicht, daß ich jemals ein Bewunderer der palästinensischen Nationalbewegung geworden wäre. So war es nicht. Aber ich habe sehr früh erkannt, daß, ob ich den Kampf der Palästinenser für ihr Anliegen mag oder nicht, ob ich den palästinensischen Führer schätze oder nicht (und ich habe ihn nicht sehr geschätzt), das Grundanliegen, die Grundbeschwerde, die Grundklage, der Grundgedanke des Verlusts echt ist und ernstgenommen werden sollte. Die Basis für diese frühe Erkenntnis war mein Beruf des Erzählers: Ich mußte einmal eine Geschichte schreiben über einen Streit zwischen einem Mann und seiner Frau, und ich mußte beide mit sehr überzeugenden Argumenten ausstatten.

Amos Oz

Shirley, Kobi

Yuval, Moriah, Simone, Kobi, Guy, James, Adi, Tomer, Mahar, Suad, Amir, Wa'el

MAIER, HEIDRUN LISELOTTE
1994, 1995, 1996, 1997, 1998

*24.2.1975
Hetzendorf
University of Vienna, political science, history and law
Middle East Youth Peace Forum scholar in 1998
Austrian delegation

Song created by the Austrian delegation in 1996
Ein österreichisches Volkslied mit neuem Text

We started in sunny Eilat,
diving, swimming and more,
met some cows, cheese and mangoes,
lots of fish at the shore.

Diria, hollarediria, hollarekuku ...

Crossed the border to Aqaba,
spent ten hours on a bus,
air condition is luxury,
but it couldn't stop us.

Diria ...

The last crossing to Bethlehem
for some days was in doubt.
But we'll get there eventually,
and once there, we'll shout loud.

Diria ...

I grew up in the mountains of Styria, one of the Austrian provinces and it was a rural childhood. I remember myself that I always tried to be stronger than the boys, and sometimes I won, sometimes I did not. You must know, that the Styrian mountains were a little bit too narrow for me and I was glad to leave the narrow valley. Now I love it to go back home and to enjoy the rural surroundings at home.

Ich bin in den steirischen Bergen aufgewachsen und verbrachte meine Jugend auf dem Land. Ich wollte immer stärker als die Buben sein, manchmal gelang es mir, manchmal nicht. Ihr müßt aber wissen, daß die steirischen Bergen mir zu eng wurden und ich froh war, das kleine Tal zu verlassen. Jetzt erst wieder schätze ich es, nach Hause zu kommen und das Landleben zu genießen.

Sima, Heidi, Mike

Gegner, mit dem Eroberer zu kämpfen – aber nicht mit dem Innersten, mit dem Innersten des Volkes, mit dem Innersten des Individuums.
Die Pflicht eines Schriftstellers hingegen ist es, ein Künstler zu sein, sich mit dem Innersten zu befassen, mit dem Innersten des Volkes, mit dem Innersten des menschlichen Gewissens …

Emile Habiby

MAROM, NIV
1996

*30.8.1978
Kfar Saba
Currently doing his army service
Israeli delegation

There is a difference between the sphere of activity of a politician and the sphere of activity of a writer. The sphere of activity of a politician is to discuss problems and fight problems with the other, with the enemy, with the conqueror but not the inside, the inside of your people, the inside of the individual. While the duty of a writer is to be an artist, to deal with the inside, the inside of his people, the inside of the human conscience …

Emile Habiby

Es gibt einen Unterschied zwischen dem Wirkungsbereich eines Politikers und jenem eines Schriftstellers. Der Wirkungsbereich eines Politikers ist, Probleme zu diskutieren und wegen der Probleme mit dem anderen, mit dem

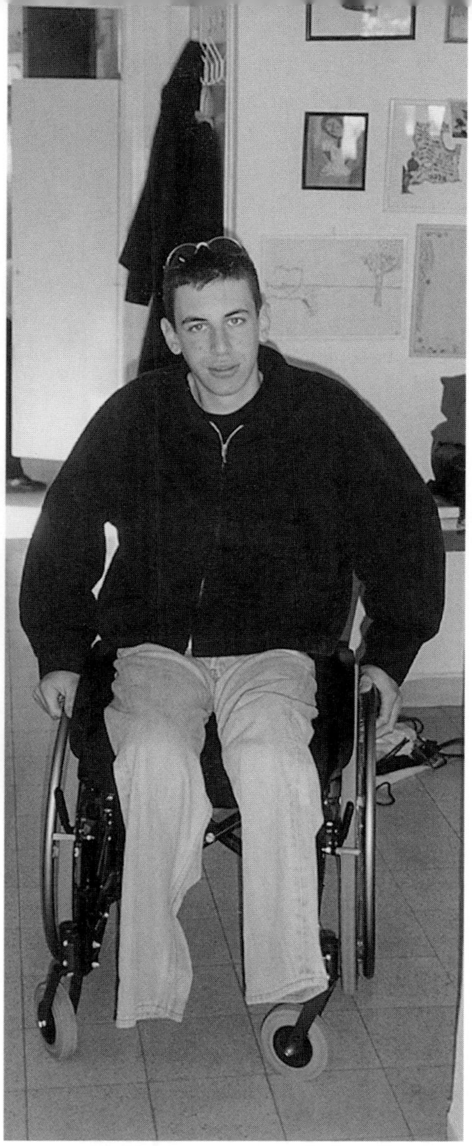

Ali, Ori, Yaron

MARX, YARON
1997

*4.10.1980
Ramat Hasharon
Currently doing his army service, member of the youth council of Ramat Hasharon
Israeli delegation

I was first offered to join the Israeli delegation on the "Crossing Borders" journey in the Middle East in September 1996, but I couldn't participate. Meanwhile I started building the website.
On July 1997 I was offered to join the Israeli delegation to the Youth Leader Seminar that was supposed to take place in September 1997 in Austria. This time I decided to attend the seminar and become a youth trainer. As a consequence of an accident which has occurred during the stay, I lost both my legs.
Today, after a rehabilitation process I have volunteered to the Israeli Defense Forces just like any other teenager in Israel who is obligated to serve in the army at the age of 18. My struggle to make people more aware of their surroundings and the big importance of peace in our region, became a different struggle – a very private one, to try and keep the life I had before the accident and to try and get over the everyday struggle and the great pain I suffer.

1996 wurde mir zum ersten Mal angeboten, mit der israelischen Delegation am »Crossing-Borders«-Projekt teilzunehmen, aber ich konnte nicht. In der Zwischenzeit begann ich an der Homepage der »Neuen Generation« zu arbeiten.
Im Juli 1997 wurde mir von der israelischen Delegation die Teilnahme am JugendleiterInnen-Training angeboten, und ich beschloß, dieses Seminar zu besuchen. Als Folge eines Unfalls während dieser Zeit verlor ich beide Beine.
Heute, nach Monaten der Rehabilitation, mache ich freiwillig meinen Militärdienst wie jeder andere israelische Teenager. Mein Engagement, die Menschen wachsamer zu machen gegenüber ihrem Umfeld und der großen Bedeutung des Friedens in unserer Region, wurde zu einem anderen Kampf – einer sehr persönlichen Anstrengung, das Leben, das ich vor dem Unfall hatte, weiterzuführen und die täglichen Schwierigkeiten und Schmerzen zu überwinden.

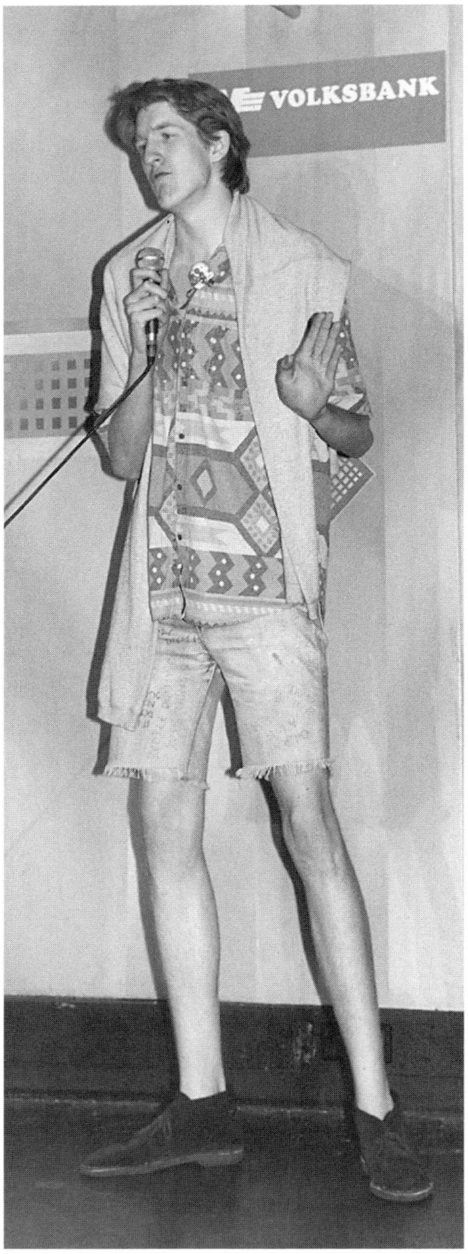

MASON, ORLANDO
1994, 1995, 1996

*23.5.1976
Linz
University of St. Andrews/Scotland, graduate, international relations and philosophy; actor and singer, member of the Scottish labour students (publicity officer)
Scholar in 1997
Austrian delegation

It would not be an exaggeration to say that my contact with the Bruno Kreisky Forum has changed my life considerably over the past four years.
The intense excitement of the first Middle East Youth Peace Forum solved the confusion I was in over what to study at university (and I have never even thought of switching from international relations to anything else since) ... I remember the first morning in July 1994, when we first met the other delegations in the basement of the youth hostel, and the flood of faces and unpronounceable names seemed almost overwhelming. Thinking back, I never would have guessed at the beginning of those first ten days what close friendships we would build up over the coming days and years, the kind of friendships that would allow us to feel the same affection and understanding after not seeing one another from one year's end to the next.
Ultimately, the success of the venture will not be measured by whether I as a member of the Austrian delegation am a better person, but to what extent it has contributed to the lives of those involved in the conflict. As we have seen, the formal peace process flourishes, fades and almost flounders over the past four years, the value of the Middle East Youth Peace Forum project has become more and more apparent. In these volatile times the lasting personal friendships have remained constant. This alone has been a great achievement, and should not be forgotten when we consider how much more there is to do. For when that final, formal peace deal is struck, be it in five years, ten years, or 25 years, it will only be the first step in a far longer, more painful peace process than we can imagine. Gaining another's trust, learning how to trust, and recognising what can be gained from co-operation is such a vulnerable process and so dependent on outside forces that the organisers must at times feel like Sisyphus, continually gaining ground only to lose it again. But unlike Sisyphus, they persist not in the recognition of the futility of their efforts but in the knowledge that their work does make a difference, and that the work must continue if we are to build on what has already been achieved.

Ich übertreibe nicht, wenn ich sage, daß der Kontakt mit dem Bruno Kreisky Forum mein Leben in den letzten vier Jahren verändert hat. Die intensive Auseinandersetzung mit dem Nahost-Jugend-Friedensforum hat meine Verwirrung und Unentschlossenheit bezüglich meines Studiums beseitigt (und seither habe ich nie mehr über einen Studienwechsel nachgedacht) ... Ich erinnere mich an jenen Morgen im Juli 1994, als wir im Erdgeschoß der Jugendherberge einander zum ersten Mal sahen, diese vielen neuen Gesichter und diese vielen unaussprechbaren Namen wirkten geradezu überwältigend. Wenn ich zurückdenke, hätte ich mir nie träumen lassen, was für tiefe Freundschaften da entstehen würden, die über die Jahre dieselben Gefühle bewahren, auch wenn wir uns wenig sehen. Der Erfolg dieses Unternehmens wird sicher nicht daran gemessen werden, ob ich als österreichisches Delegationsmitglied ein besserer Mensch bin, sondern wieweit es das Leben der Betroffenen bereichert hat. Der Stellenwert des Nahost-Jugend-Friedensforums wird aber umso deutlicher, als der politische Friedensprozeß nach seinem Aufblühen in den vergangenen vier Jahren Phasen des Stillstands und des Rückschlags erlebt hat. Die persönlichen Freundschaften blieben aber konstant. Das allein ist schon eine wichtige Errungenschaft. In fünf, zehn oder 25 Jahren, wenn vielleicht der formale Friedensprozeß abgeschlossen sein wird, wird sie einen ersten Schritt darstellen in einem noch viel mühevolleren Friedensprozeß. Vertrauen herzustellen und zu erkennen, was den Wert von Zusammenarbeit ausmacht, sind so sensible Vorgänge, daß sich die Verantwortlichen manchmal wie Sisyphus fühlen müssen: Terrain gewinnen, um es immer wieder zu verlieren. Aber im Unterschied zu Sisyphus merken sie, daß ihre Anstrengungen nicht umsonst sind, sondern verändern, und daß diese Arbeit weitergehen muß, um auf dem aufzubauen, was bereits erreicht worden ist.

MEIR, HAGIT
1996

*26.11.1978
Haifa
National service, apprentice of Ben Akiva
Israeli delegation

Hagit playing with a Bedouin child in Petra
Hagit beim Spiel mit einem Beduinenkind in Petra
Tomer, Hagit, Kobi
Shirley, Hagit, Ahmad

MELICHAR, THOMAS
1994, 1995, 1996, 1997,

*10.5.1977
Wien
Studies at the Vienna University of Applied Arts, civil service at a Jewish home for old people, created the logo of the "New Generation" and does the layout work, produced the cookery book
Austrian delegation

Moriah, Ori, Thomas

MITWALLI, SUAD
1996, 1997, 1998

*29.7.1974
Jerusalem
Bir Zeit University graduate, psychology, psychologist for children, active with Palestinian women
Palestinian delegation

Dima, Mahar, Suad

For more than ten years Palestinian and Israeli women have been working together to find ways out of the conflict. For this reason, we founded the peace project "The Jerusalem Link". "Women Make Peace" is a joint project. We attempt to learn, to listen to each other, and to respect the other's opinion. To learn to accept the other as he or she is. To learn that "being different" or "acting differently" is not the same as "being wrong" or "acting wrongly".
This co-operation was not always easy. In particular, the beginning, when we met for the first time during the Intifada, was difficult. We were politically active Israeli and Palestinian women. We had never learned to talk to each other, even though as women we felt a kind of solidarity. However, after the initial friendly greeting, prejudices and accusations soon arose. We were indignant and upset, but persevered for many long hours. There was – and still is – so much mistrust, hate and ignorance in both societies. That all had to be articulated. When we had finished, we were bound by a common feeling of misgiving and depression. But, it was a beginning and soon we were proud of our joint work, which we used in peace education during the Intifada.
In August 1996 we adopted our charter of principles: "We Palestinian and Israeli women, united in our engagement for a just and lasting peace between our peoples, affirm our desire to co-operate within the framework of the Jerusalem Link ..."
We women renounce violence and are committed to democracy and a civil society. In a period when the peace process has come to a halt, an ambitious project, like ours, must reckon with setbacks. We hear repeatedly from women: "We refuse to speak to the others! We protest and resist." But, we also must understand and respect those feelings. In critical situations we organise, if feasible, special meetings so that, in spite of everything, we continue to talk to each other. Sometimes, when it seems that nothing is possible between Israel and Palestine, it is also good to share our depression. Both sides, the Israelis and the Palestinians, have fears which must be addressed and overcome – and, if possible, transformed into trust. Together, we have to analyse our own – as well as the other's – history and politics. This is only possible through rethinking and the courage to take action. The survival of the one side is closely intertwined with the survival of the other. Peace and security can only be guaranteed, when they are valid for both sides. For this reason, the international community must commit itself to a just peace. We appeal particularly to people in Europe, because Europe is partly responsible for our situation.
Help us to believe in hope because we cannot afford the luxury of hopelessness.
Sumaya Farhat-Nasr

Seit nunmehr zehn Jahren arbeiten palästinensische und israelische Frauen zusammen, um Wege aus dem Konflikt zu finden. Dazu haben wir das Friedensprojekt »The Jerusalem Link« gegründet. »Frauen machen Frieden« ist ein gemeinsames Projekt. Wir versuchen zu lernen, einander zuzuhören und die Meinung der anderen zu respektieren. Zu lernen, die anderen anzunehmen, wie sie sind. Zu lernen, daß »anders sein« und »anders handeln« nicht »falsch sein« oder »falsch handeln« bedeuten muß.
Die Zusammenarbeit war nicht immer

Suad, Reem

leicht. Besonders der Anfang war schwer, als wir uns 1988 während der Intifada das erstemal trafen. Wir, das waren politisch engagierte Israelinnen und Palästinenserinnen. Nie hatten wir gelernt, miteinander zu sprechen, auch wenn wir uns als Frauen irgendwie solidarisch fühlten. Nach freundlichen Begrüßungsworten kamen bald Vorurteile und Anschuldigungen zum Tragen. Wir waren empört und betroffen, hielten aber viele lange Stunden durch. Es gab – und es gibt immer noch – so viel Mißtrauen, Haß und Unwissen in unseren beiden Gesellschaften. Das alles mußte erst einmal ausgesprochen werden. Am Ende verband uns ein Gefühl der Sorge und Bedrücktheit.
Aber es war ein Anfang, und wir waren bald stolz auf die gemeinsame Arbeit, die wir während der Intifada in die Friedenserziehung investierten …
Im August 1996 haben wir unsere Grundsatzerklärung verabschiedet: »Wir palästinensischen und israelischen Frauen, verbündet im Engagement für einen gerechten und dauerhaften Frieden zwischen unseren Völkern, bestätigen unseren Willen zur Zusammenarbeit im Rahmen von Jerusalem Link.«
Wir Frauen lehnen Gewalt ab und setzen uns für Demokratie und eine Zivilgesellschaft ein. In einer Zeit, in der der Friedensprozeß zum Stillstand gekommen ist, muß ein so ehrgeiziges Vorhaben wie das unsere mit Rückschlägen rechnen. Immer wieder hören wir von Frauen: »Wir weigern uns, mit den anderen zu sprechen! Wir protestieren, und wir wehren uns.« Aber auch das müssen wir respektieren und verstehen. In kritischen Situationen veranstalten wir nach Möglichkeit Sondertreffen, um trotz allem weiter miteinander zu sprechen. Manchmal, wenn zwischen Israel und Palästina gar nichts mehr weiterzugehen scheint, ist es gut, auch die Depressionen miteinander zu teilen.
Beide Seiten, Israelis und Palästinenser, haben Ängste, die angesprochen und verarbeitet – ja, wenn möglich in Vertrauen umgewandelt – werden müssen. Gemeinsam müssen wir die eigene Geschichte und Politik ebenso wie die der anderen erforschen. Dies ist nur möglich durch Umdenken und Mut zum Handeln. Das Überleben der einen Seite ist eng mit dem der anderen Seite verknüpft. Frieden und Sicherheit können nur gewährleistet sein, wenn sie für beide Völker gelten. Dazu muß sich aber auch die internationale Gemeinschaft für einen gerechten Frieden einsetzen. Besonders an Menschen in Europa sei appelliert, denn Europa trägt Mitverantwortung für unsere Situation: Helfen Sie uns, an die Hoffnung zu glauben, denn wir können uns den Luxus der Hoffnungslosigkeit nicht leisten.

Sumaya Farhat-Nasr

MUGHANNAM, RAWAN
1996

*7.3.1977
Ramallah
Bir Zeit University, science
Palestinian delegation

Poems,
Selected by Rawan Mughannam

How to be Happy
Keep your heart free from hate
your mind from worry
live simple
expect little
give much
sing often
pray always
fill your life with love
forget self
do as you would be done by
these are the tied links in contentment's golden chain

The Creation of God
The creation of God is so clear,
but the creation of me,
oh, how did it be?
A mind that can never stop thinking,
feelings that can never be understood
A heart that has millions of paths
A soul that can love, hate, but never kill
Hands and eyes willing to suction everything
they see deeply
Ears that listen, but a mouth that doesn't repeat
A nose that smells, but can never be smelled
Am I the only strange creature created?
Am I a gift or a tragedy given by God to the world
Am I a criminal or a loving person?
Who am I God?

Suad, Rawan, Dima

At the Deheisheh boys school
In der Deheisheh-Knabenschule

NASSER, ZEIN
1996, 1998

*1.8.1977
Bethlehem
Bir Zeit University, engineering, member of St. Joseph scouts
Palestinian delegation

Sharing a personal experience
It was the first time for me to participate in such a kind of programme. My impression of the programme can be summarised through an experience I would like to share with you.
The next day after we went back home I had to go to my university and I thought that everything would go just the way it did the last ten days. I went to the checkpoint with a total confidence that I will pass ... but when I heard the soldiers telling me that I could not pass, I was shocked and stopped talking for some minutes. I wanted to explain to him that the day before I was with a peace group and I've been crossing borders for the last ten days ...
And when I was back with all my thoughts and dreams I found myself far away from him and going back home. That is impossible! It is not fair! All that I wanted to do was to go to my university through Jerusalem to save an hour's drive and I am not allowed to. What has gone wrong with the world? My mind was messed up between the events we experienced the last ten days and between reality. I was disappointed and realised that these days were just a dream and are never to come true.

Eine persönliche Erfahrung
Ich habe zum ersten Mal an einer derartigen Veranstaltung teilgenommen. Ich kann meine Eindrücke zusammenfassen, indem ich euch ein Erlebnis erzähle.
Am Tag nach unserer Rückkehr mußte ich zur Universität, und ich dachte, alles würde so weitergehen wie in den letzten zehn Tagen. Ich kam zum Checkpoint, in der vollen Überzeugung, passieren zu können. Als ich den Soldaten sagen hörte, daß dem nicht so sei, war ich schockiert und einen Moment lang sprachlos. Ich wollte ihm erklären, daß ich noch gestern mit einer Friedensgruppe zehn Tage lang Grenzen überquert hatte ... Als ich aus meinen Gedanken und Träumen erwachte, war ich weit weg von ihm, auf dem Weg zurück nach Hause. Das ist unmöglich! Unfair! Ich wollte doch nur durch Jerusalem zu meiner Universität gehen, um eine Stunde Fahrt zu sparen, und darf es nicht. Was ist mit dieser Welt los? In meinem Kopf herrschte ein Chaos aus dem Erlebten der letzten zehn Tage und meiner Wirklichkeit. Ich war enttäuscht und stellte fest, daß diese Tage nur ein Traum waren, der nie Wirklichkeit werden wird.

ODEH, NAHIDA
1996

*26.4.1980
Jerusalem
Member of YMCA and Palestinian Youth for Peace
Palestinian delegation

Notes from a diary
... In the late afternoon we started the working groups on the topic of "Crossing Borders" with very interesting discussions and touching statements. During the evening plenary, some of the newcomers presented their ideas about their "red lines". They talked about their interior borders, their hopes to live in a world without lines and to cross them without problems ... We were working in an atmosphere of openness and with a feeling of solidarity ...

Tagebuchnotizen
... Am späten Nachmittag begannen wir in den Arbeitsgruppen zum Thema »Crossing Borders« zu diskutieren, mit interessanten Beiträgen und berührenden Statements. Im Abendplenum sprachen einige der Neuen über ihre »roten Linien«, über ihre inneren Grenzen, ihre Hoffnungen, in einer Welt ohne Grenzen zu leben und sie ohne Probleme überwinden zu können. Wir arbeiteten in einer Atmosphäre von Offenheit und mit einem Gefühl der Solidarität ...

Christof, Nahida
At the Undersea Obersvatory
Beim Unterwasserobservatorium

Itsik, Limor

POMERANTZ, LIMOR
1994

*7.12.1975
Haifa
University of Haifa, psychology
Israeli delegation

I truly feel that participating in the forum and being part of the "New Generation" influenced my perceptions of the idea of a real peace in our region. Despite the fact that I have been supportive of the peace process since it began in Madrid, I had my doubts concerning the sincere willingness of the Arab nations to make the necessary compromises in order for peace to prevail. While talking to young people from the Gaza Strip and the West Bank I realised that there's a real desire for peace!

Ich fühle wirklich, wie sehr die Teilnahme am Forum und die Zugehörigkeit zur »Neuen Generation« meine Vorstellung von der Idee des wahren Friedens in unserer Region verändert haben.
Obwohl ich den Friedensprozeß seit seinem Beginn in Madrid 1991 unterstütze, hatte ich Zweifel an der Bereitschaft der arabischen Staaten, die notwendigen Kompromisse zu schließen, um dem Frieden eine Chance zu geben. Im Gespräch mit den Jugendlichen aus dem Gazastreifen und der Westbank zeigte sich mir eine echte Friedenssehnsucht.

QUEDAN, MONTHER
1994

*4.1.1976
Gaza
Al-Azhar University
Palestinian delegation

... What should a man of words do, if he happens to live next door to injustice, to prejudice and to violence? What should this man do, when all he has is a pen, a voice, and sometimes a relatively attentive audience? What do you do when basic decency demands that you try to combat political evil rather than just observe, describe, and decipher? How do you go about making what seems to be an impossible choice between civic decency and artistic integrity? Is it immoral for a writer to turn his pen into a political weapon? Or is it immoral for him not to beat his pen into a polemic thought, at least sometimes?
Well, I do not have a universally valid answer. All I can share with you is my own inconsistent answer and my own inconsistent answer is a compromise. I am a compromiser. And I know the word compromise has a terrible reputation among people with good principles, idealistic people, progressive people, world reformers. Compromise is inconsistency, compromise is opportunism, compromise is lack of a moral backbone. Not to me. To me compromise is life. And the opposite of compromise is not integrity. The opposite of compromise is fanaticism. Life is a compromise. Hear my wisdom. You are speaking to a man who has been married to the same woman for 34 years now. I know a thing or two about compromise.

Amos Oz

Was sollte ein Mann des Wortes tun, wenn sich herausstellt, daß er neben Ungerechtigkeit, Vorurteilen und Gewalt lebt? Was sollte dieser Mann tun, wenn alles, was er besitzt, eine Feder, eine Stimme und manchmal ein halbwegs aufmerksames Publikum ist? Was tut man, wenn der Anstand verlangt, daß man politisches Übel zu bekämpfen versucht und es nicht nur beobachtet, beschreibt und entschlüsselt. Wie schafft man es, eine Entscheidung zwischen ziviler Anständigkeit und künstlerischer Integrität zu treffen? Ist es unmoralisch von einem Schriftsteller, wenn er seine Feder zu einer politischen Waffe macht? Oder ist es unmoralisch von ihm, wenn er seine Feder nicht zu einem politischen Gedanken zwingt – wenigstens zeitweise?
Nun, ich habe keine allgemeingültige Antwort. Alles, was ich mit Ihnen teilen kann, ist meine eigene widersprüchliche Antwort, und diese widersprüchliche Antwort ist ein Kompromiß. Ich bin kompromißbereit. Und ich weiß, das Wort Kompromiß hat einen sehr schlechten Beigeschmack für Menschen mit Prinzipien, für Idealisten, fortschrittliche Menschen und Weltverbesserer. Kompromiß bedeutet Widersprüchlichkeit, Kompromiß ist auch Opportunismus, Kompromiß ist moralische Rückgratlosigkeit. Nicht für mich. Für mich bedeutet Kompromiß Leben. Und das Gegenteil von Kompromiß ist nicht Integrität. Das Gegenteil von Kompromiß ist Fanatismus. Das Leben ist ein Kompromiß. Hören Sie meine Lebensweisheit. Sie reden mit einem Mann, der 34 Jahre mit derselben Frau verheiratet ist. Ich kenne mich bei Kompromissen aus.

Amos Oz

Monther, Maged, Fida, 1994

QUEIDER, KHULOUD

1995, 1996

*8.7.1977
Hebron
University of Bethlehem, language studies
Palestinian delegation

Wadi Rum

... Many people would become great artists if they were not convinced they had to sacrify their abilities to daily political work. But this is not the main thing. The main loss is the loss in wars, in massacres. How many artists have we lost in Sabra and Shatilla for example? Children who would have been born ...

... In politics, one convinces oneself that one sometimes can lie, and does not tell the truth. In literature, in the arts, any lying will be exposed. If you are able to speak the truth about the subjects you are dealing with, then you can write literature.

Emile Habiby

... Viele Menschen würden große Künstler werden, wenn sie nicht überzeugt wären, ihre Fähigkeiten der täglichen politischen Arbeit opfern zu müssen. Aber darum geht es nicht in erster Linie. Der größte Verlust ist der Verlust in Kriegen, in Massakern. Wie viele Künstler haben wir zum Beispiel in Sabra und Shatilla verloren? Kinder, die geboren worden wären ...

... In der Politik ist man überzeugt, daß man manchmal lügen darf, und sagt somit nicht die Wahrheit. In der Literatur, in den Künsten wird jede Lüge enthüllt. Wenn man in der Lage ist, die Wahrheit über die Themen, die man behandelt, auszusprechen, ist man in der Lage, Literatur zu schreiben.

Emile Habiby

RABL, MAXIMILIAN
1996

*24.2.1977
Wien
University of Vienna, Faculty of Law and
Technical University of Vienna, Engeneering
Austrian delegation

I got in contact with the problems in the Middle East by chance. As part of my final exams ... I chose the Middle East Policy of Bruno Kreisky, Austria's long reigning chancellor, who dedicated much of his time and efforts to the peace process in the Middle East and international politics in general. During my research I contacted the Kreisky Forum and I got a lot of information and help from them ... One year later they asked me to take part in the "Crossing Borders" project. For many reasons I was very excited: I theoretically knew so much about the problems in the Middle East, I wanted to see what was really like. Furthermore it was the first chance for me to get in contact with two religions, who had been fascinating me since childhood, mostly because both the Jewish and the Muslim religion played important roles in the history of my country and will do so in the future. I really hope that some day during my life time the people in the Middle East ... will be able to overcome their hatred, distrust and hostility.
The ten days in Israel, Jordan and the Palestinian Autonomy were some of the most interesting days of my life.

Ich kam zufällig mit der Nahost-Problematik in Kontakt. Ich wählte als Teil meiner Schulabschlußarbeit die Nahostpolitik des langjährigen österreichischen Bundeskanzlers Bruno Kreisky, der viel Zeit und Anstrengungen in den Friedensprozeß im Nahen Osten und in die internationale Politik investiert hat. Ich kontaktierte das Bruno Kreisky Forum und bekam viele Informationen und Hilfe ...
Ein Jahr später luden sie mich zur Teilnahme an dem Projekt »Crossing Borders« ein. Es war aus mehreren Gründen aufregend für mich: Ich kannte mich theoretisch in der Nahostproblematik einigermaßen aus und wollte die Wirklichkeit kennenlernen. Außerdem war es eine Chance, mit zwei Religionen in Kontakt zu kommen, die mich seit meiner Kindheit fasziniert hatten, vor allem weil die jüdische und die islamische Religion in der Geschichte meines Landes eine wichtige Rolle gespielt haben und weiterhin spielen werden.
Ich hoffe sehr, daß ich es erleben kann, wie die Völker des Nahen Ostens ... ihren Haß, ihr Mißtrauen und ihre Feindschaft begraben.
Die zehn Tage in Israel, Jordanien und im palästinensischen Autonomiegebiet zählen zu den interessantesten meines Lebens.

Christof, Max

ROHSMANN, KATARINA
1994, 1995, 1996, 1997, 1998

*11.8.1979
Klagenfurt
University of Vienna, political science and history
Austrian delegation

Did the Middle East Youth Peace Forum change my life?
I like to claim that, although I do not know what will happen and what would have happened, had I not taken part in it. But I observed that it opened my mind, made me alert, and turned my criticism into a more positive approach.
It was a change and a challenge to revise the way I looked at the known and the unknown and the presentation of both. It opened my horizon of which I never thought it was narrow and showed me my own prejudice that I never thought I had.
But most important, it made me discover that behind all national, cultural or religious differences, there is a large common, human basis. Differences and the existence of an "other" can either be presented as problems or as values. To get to know the other helps to detect those who abuse stereotyped images and ignorance for blaming the other to cause their problems.

To talk and work together will certainly not erase all problems, but provide a feeling of confidence. But openness and readiness to find a solution is already a first step towards it.

Hat das Nahost-Jugend-Friedensforum mein Leben verändert?
Ich möchte die Frage spontan bejahen, auch wenn ich natürlich nicht weiß, was noch passieren wird und was passiert wäre, wenn ich nicht teilgenommen hätte.
Doch ich habe festgestellt, daß es mich offener, aufmerksamer, positiv kritisch gemacht hat. Das Nahost-Jugend-Friedensforum hat mich herausgefordert, meine Art, Bekanntes und Unbekanntes zu sehen und zu beurteilen, zu verändern. Es hat meinen Horizont geöffnet, den ich als nicht eng eingeschätzt hatte, und mir meine eigenen Vorurteile, die ich nie zu haben geglaubt hatte, vor Augen geführt.
Vor allem aber habe ich entdeckt, daß hinter allen nationalen, kulturellen und religiösen Unterschieden eine breite, gemeinsame menschliche Basis ist. Verschiedenheit und die Existenz »anderer« kann entweder als Problem oder als Wert gesehen werden.
Den anderen kennenzulernen hilft auch jene zu entlarven, die in ihrer Ignoranz und mit ihren stereotypen Vorstellungen anderen die Schuld an ihren eigenen Problemen geben.
Miteinander zu sprechen und zu arbeiten ist sicher nicht die Lösung aller Probleme, bringt aber ein Gefühl des Vertrauens. Und Offenheit und die Bereitschaft, Lösungen zu finden, sind die ersten Schritte in diese Richtung.

SA'AD, ABDUL GHANI
1996

*19.8.1979
Amman
Jordanian delegation

With the Sabelah group in Aqaba
Mit der Sabelah-Gruppe in Aqaba

SAFADY, YAMAAN
1997, 1998

Sabelah supervisor
Studies at Jordanian University, engineering
Jordanian delegation

SALAMEH, DIMA
1996

*2.2.1980
Ramallah
Studies international law in the USA, wants to work for the UN or UNICEF
Palestinian delegation

Rawan, Dima, Mahar in traditional dresses
Rawan, Dima, Mahar in traditionellen Kleidern

Hana'a, Dima, Mahar

Raffi, Tali, Orly, Oded, Burg Schlaining, Burgenland

SANDLER, ODED
1994, 1998

*10.2.1976
Worked with children, studies
Israeli delegation

The Middle East in particular was and is a region shaken by unrest and crises and therefore deserves our utmost attention.
For this reason, the initiatives of the Middle East Youth Peace Forum cannot be praised too highly. This event will definitely make a valuable contribution to mutual understanding and to international co-operation.
Finally, I would like to thank you and the colleagues of the Bruno Kreisky Forum for the efforts undertaken, and would be happy if the "Spirit of the Burgenland" can help to waken, and intensify feelings of understanding and mutual tolerance between the participants.

Karl Stix
Governor of the Province of Burgenland

Gerade der Nahe Osten war und ist eine von Unruhen und Krisen geschüttelte Region und verlangt deshalb unser aller Aufmerksamkeit.
Aus diesem Grund kann die Initiative des Nahost-Jugend-Friedensforums nicht genug gewürdigt werden. Diese Veranstaltung wird bestimmt einen wertvollen Beitrag zum gegenseitigen Verständnis und damit zur Völkerverbindung leisten.
Abschließend darf ich Ihnen und den Mitarbeitern des Bruno Kreisky Forums für Ihre geleistete Arbeit danken, und ich würde mich freuen, wenn das »Burgenländische Klima« mithelfen kann, bei den Teilnehmern Verständnis und gegenseitige Toleranz zu wecken bzw. zu festigen.

Karl Stix,
Landeshauptmann des Burgenlands

SEGAL, KEREN
1994, 1996, 1997, 1998

*13.10.1976
Jerusalem
Studies psychology
Israeli delegation

After her service in the army, Keren travelled to India and wrote this letter:

I am writing to you from Rishikesh – a holy city of the Hindu religion on the banks of the Ganges river in northern India.
India is really exciting and different from anything I have ever seen. There is a large diversity of religions and the culture is very different from the western culture. We have learned a lot from the varied customs and traditions in each place, but the poverty does get us down sometimes.
We have spent three weeks in the desert of Rajasthan (where the Indians experimented with their nuclear bombs recently). We have seen some very impressive forts, ridden on camels in the desert and seen many people living under difficult desert conditions.
In the north we visited the pilgrim centre of the Sikh religion, which was a good opportunity to learn about their religion.
We also went to Oharamsala – the town of the Tibetan government, where the Dalai Lama lives. We spent some time in New Delhi, ... now we are heading east to Calcutta from where I shall fly to Burma.
I will be back in Israel by September and will start my studies at the Hebrew University in Jerusalem.

Nach ihrem Militärdienst bereiste Keren Indien und schrieb diesen Brief:

Ich schreibe euch aus Rishikesh – einer heiligen Stadt der Hindi am Ufer des Ganges in Nordindien.
... Indien ist aufregend und ganz anders. Es gibt viele verschiedene Religionen und eine Kultur, die sich sehr von der westlichen unterscheidet. Wir haben viel über die verschiedenen Bräuche und Traditionen gelernt, aber manchmal deprimiert uns die Armut sehr. Wir waren drei Wochen in der Wüste von Rajasthan, (wo die Inder vor kurzem Atomversuche gemacht haben). Wir haben eindrucksvolle Festungen besucht, sind auf Kamelen geritten und haben Menschen kennengelernt, die unter schwierigen Bedingungen in der Wüste leben.
Im Norden haben wir das Zentrum der Sikhs besucht und etwas über ihre Religion erfahren. Danach waren wir in Oharamsala, der Stadt der tibetanischen (Exil-)Regierung, wo der Dalai Lama lebt, anschließend in Delhi, und jetzt fahren wir Richtung Osten nach Kalkutta, von wo wir nach Burma weiterfliegen. Ich werde im September wieder in Israel sein und mein Studium an der Hebräischen Universität in Jerusalem beginnen.

Keren in Amritsar, India
Karin, Keren

Abeer and Hiba in traditional dresses
Abeer und Hiba in traditionellen Kleidern

SEIKALY, ABEER
1996

Studies arts in the USA
Jordanian delegation

SEPER, SIMONE
1994, 1995, 1996, 1997, 1998

*7.8.1977
Unterwart
University of Vienna, Faculty of Law
Hungarian theatre group
Austrian delegation

I'm one of the "dinosaurs" that saw the Middle East Youth Peace Forum making its first steps in 1994, growing and changing from a formal conference to a creative peace camp, and to a seminar for intellectuals, who are committed not only to the abstract idea of peace, but especially to their Israeli or Palestinian friends.
We always felt a strong responsibility for one goal: the hope for a better future, in a peaceful coexistence of people, who share an enormous love for their home.
We also learned and experienced that the big aim of peaceful coexistence can never be reached for good and is a steady process of listening and talking.
The time we spent together was very intense and I always needed a lot of time to digest my impressions and felt terribly lost after returning home from our meetings, as if I would have left a family for a certain time.
The very dramatic situations we went through, like the decision whether to go to Bethlehem without any official permit from the Israeli security or not, or the terrible accident in Söchau, proved how close we are to each other.
For myself I might say that the spirit of the Middle East Youth Peace Forum formed my personality much more than I would have thought, when filling in the application form in 1994. I don't exaggerate, when I say that my participation completely changed my world and gave me one of the best times in my life.
May the spirit of the Middle East Youth Peace Forum be spread all over the Middle East!

Ich bin einer der »Dinosaurier«, der die ersten Schritte des Nahost-Jugend-Friedensforums 1994 verfolgte und sah, wie es sich von einer formellen Konferenz in ein kreatives Friedenscamp und in ein Seminar für Intellektuelle veränderte, deren Engagement nicht nur einer abstrakten Friedensidee galt, sondern ihren israelischen und palästinensischen Freunden.
Wir waren immer von einer großen Verantwortung für ein großes Ziel getragen: die Hoffnung auf eine bessere Zukunft, auf ein friedliches Zusammenleben von Menschen, die eines gemeinsam haben: die große Liebe für ihre Heimat. Wir haben aber auch gelernt und erfahren, dass dieses Ziel nie ein für allemal erreicht werden kann, sondern ein ständiger Prozeß von einander zuhören und miteinander sprechen ist.
Die Zeit, die wir miteinander verbracht haben, war sehr intensiv, und es dauerte immer sehr lange, bis ich, wieder zu Hause, alle Eindrücke verdauen konnte. Ich fühlte mich total verloren nach unseren Treffen, als hätte ich eine Familie für eine gewisse Zeit verlassen.
Die dramatischen Situationen, die wir erlebten, wie die Entscheidung, ohne offizielles israelisches Clearing nach Bethlehem zu fahren, oder der schreckliche Unfall in Söchau haben uns bewiesen, wie nahe wir einander sind.
Für mich kann ich sagen, daß das Nahost-Jugend-Friedensforum meine Persönlichkeit mehr gebildet hat, als ich es damals 1994 beim Ausfüllen des Anmeldebogens je erahnt hätte. Ohne Übertreibung hat meine Teilnahme am Forum sicher mein Weltbild verändert und mir eine der besten Zeiten meines Lebens geschenkt.
Möge sich der Geist des Nahost-Jugend-Friedensforums über den ganzen Nahen Osten breiten.

Simone at the SOS Children's Village, Bethlehem
Simone im SOS-Kinderdorf, Bethlehem

SHADAH, LINA
1997

Works as a graphic designer
Jordanian delegation

King Hussein's Role in Peace

Jordan had shown great interest in peace in the Middle East and the world in general. Our late King Hussein ibn Talal played a distinguished role in making peace between Jordan, Israel and Palestine. His Majesty always talked about peace, how to make it and how to maintain it, he made a big effort in the peace talks between Palestine and Israel even when he was undergoing treatment in a hospital in the USA in 1998. When President Clinton asked him to help in the talks, he insisted to leave the hospital and joined him in Wye River and he made a big effort so both sides would reach an acceptable agreement. No one in the world can forget His Majesty King Hussein in the ceremony of signing the above mentioned agreement and his sincere speech about peace to the whole world. He was really a brave and noble knight who stood for his principles.

For 51 years, since the year 1948, when the Palestinians were forced to leave their homeland Palestine, hundred thousands of them settled in Jordan and they still live there until now. Many immigration waves crossed the Jordan river after that hour of fear and horror. Since His Majesty the late King Hussein ibn Talal was crowned as a King in 1952, he had always paid a special care and attention to the Holy City (Jerusalem) because this city had a special place in his heart and his soul where his grandfather Sheriff of Mecca Al-Hussein ibn Ali was murdered. When the Israelis occupied the city in 1967 … King Hussein did his best continuously … to find a fair compromise, and he passed away without seeing his dreams come true.

In 1994, he signed the peace treaty between Jordan and Israel … and here we remember him saying:

"I have always believed that the road to peace lies in genuine understanding between people. The more we know about one another, the more we come to realise that, in fact, we are not so different after all."

And he kept saying: »"We are all the grandsons of Abraham."

We all know that he was the king of peace, the king of love, and we will never forget him and what he did for us in Jordan, to the whole world. He is the King of our hearts.

Fares Halasa

König Husseins Rolle im Frieden

Jordanien war immer am Frieden im Nahen Osten und in der Welt interessiert. Unser verstorbener König Hussein ibn Talal spielte eine herausragende Rolle in den Friedensverhandlungen zwischen Israel, Palästina und Jordanien. Er sprach immer über Frieden, wie er zu erreichen und zu bewahren wäre, er unternahm große Anstrengungen in den Gesprächen zwischen Israelis und Palästinensern, sogar als er im letzten Jahr in den USA in Behandlung war. Als Präsident Clinton ihn um Hilfe bat, verließ er das Krankenhaus, fuhr nach Wye River und erreichte eine für beide Seiten ahnnehmbare Vereinbarung. Niemand wird je König Hussein während der Unterzeichnungszeremonie dieses Übereinkommens vergessen, seine ehrlichen Worte über den Frieden, an die ganze Welt gerichtet. Er war ein nobler und tapferer Kämpfer für seine Prinzipien.

In den 51 Jahren, seit 1948, als die Palästinenser gezwungen wurden, ihre Heimat Palästina zu verlassen, ließen sich Hunderttausende in Jordanien nieder. Große Immigrationswellen haben seit diesen Stunden der Angst und des Schreckens den Jordan überquert. Hussein ibn Talal, im Jahre 1952 zum König gekrönt, hatte immer eine besondere Hochachtung vor der Heiligen Stadt (Jerusalem), denn diese Stadt, wo sein Großvater Al-Hussein ibn Ali ermordet worden war, hatte einen besonderen Platz in seinem Herzen. Nach der israelischen Besetzung im Jahre 1967 … tat König Hussein alles, um einen Kompromiß zu finden. Er starb, bevor sein Traum wahr werden konnte.

Wir erinnern uns an seine Worte anläßlich der Unterzeichnung des Friedensvertrages mit Israel im Jahre 1994:

»Ich war immer überzeugt, daß der Weg zum Frieden im gegenseitigen Verstehen der Völker liegt. Je mehr wir voneinander wissen, desto mehr stellen wir fest, wie ähnlich wir einander sind.«

Und er fügte hinzu: »Wir sind alle Enkel Abrahams.«

Wir wissen, daß er der König des Friedens und der Liebe war. Wir werden ihn und das, was er für uns, für unser Land und die ganze Welt getan hat, nie vergessen. Er ist der König unserer Herzen.

Fares Halasa

SHADMI, TOMER
1996

*16.12.1978
Kibbutz Kfar Blum
Counsellor of Hanoar Ha'oved Ve'halomed, active in her kibbutz in different groups
Army service
Israeli delegation

Ramzi, Tomer

Tomer who was invited to Norway together with Natasha Khalidi reports:

Norway

In April I went to Norway. I did not go to see the Fjords, to seek after the roots of the Vikings, nor did I go to watch the aurora borealis.
I went to Norway to tell the Norwegian students how it is to live in a region where daily problems are slightly more difficult and painful than what the weather will be tomorrow. I went to explain how young men and women – not much older than 18 – are already faced with questions of life and death. I went to tell about a small land, special, promised, old, new, a land of milk, honey, guns and blood, a land where Jews and Arabs live together, the land of Israel and Palestine. I did not travel alone; Natasha Khalidi is an Arab speaking Palestinian and a Muslim. I am a Hebrew speaking Israeli and a Jew. We went together, as teenage girls each representing her nation – the two sides of the Israeli-Palestinian conflict.
Prior to the trip I had only met Natasha a few times in the course of the "New Generation" meetings and did not know her very well. In the course of our visit we gave about seven lectures to high school students. Numerous meetings followed these lectures with clergymen, teachers, and public relations people. We were interviewed by several newspapers and visited the house where the secret talks prior to the signing of the Oslo agreement were held and added our modest signatures to the guest book, together with Mr Shimon Peres and Mr Ahmad Qrei (Abu Ala). The Israeli ambassador and the Palestinian representative in Norway held a reception in our honour at the embassy.
Changes in this country are the weather changes, and the people needed to be explained how we live here in Israel.
Watching it from the beautiful and peaceful Norway, the Israeli-Arab conflict seems like a children's game where children fight to death over a single sandbox. It is tremendously difficult to explain how complex and emotional this conflict is. It is difficult to explain that we are not talking about black and white solutions or absolute justice. It is difficult to explain how tragic it is that both sides are just and that there is not one truth. Natasha and I went through a long and strenuous process together. We did not come to Norway as enemies but as two girls representing two nations.
Naturally, each of us wanted to prove to our listeners that she was right. Performing as rivals caused tension between us but it did not last for long. We went through a parallel process at the end of which we became close friends who discuss their private experiences and problems with each other. To our great surprise, the conceptual process we both went through was similar. We both missed our country, its mentality, its food, weather and intensity of the lives we normally live.
We respectively understood that we were not representatives in peace talks nor were we under any international eyes judging who is right and who is wrong. We realised that we must present an overall picture of the situation of our country together. Most of our performances were held in front of the high school students in Fredrikstad near Oslo.
In these lectures we talked about the conflict and its roots but also of our lives, our hopes and of our personal involvement in the Palestinian-Israeli encounters. The Norwegian students did not have many questions but there was always at least one person who was

anxious to know why we were fighting so much for so long and with all the Norwegian naiveté asked: "Why don't you just share the land?"
Unfortunately, there were a few unpleasant incidents in Israel while we were in Norway and people kept asking us about "Har Homa" and Netanyahu's involvement in the incident. My personal opinion was not always similar to the official Israeli standpoint but as a representative of Israel it was important to me to explain it so it could at least be understood. I wanted the Norwegians to understand my people's existential fears and the extreme importance of Jerusalem to the state of Israel.
In all our lectures we repeatedly emphasised that the peace process was the only way out of the conflict, although, we stressed that this peace process would be accompanied by painful compromises for both peoples.
One dilemma accompanied me the whole way: on the one hand, I wanted the people to understand the Israeli-Palestinian reality, On the other hand, however, I still wanted to explain that we live in a democratic and most advanced state. I think that my main gain during this trip was the fact that Natasha and I have reached an understanding. In the course of the eleven days we spent together we had to face each other's faith and beliefs. I learned to know Natasha and her people better.
I realised that a mutual understanding may be achieved in spite of the different languages we speak. We had many loud arguments, which were strange for the ears of the quiet and reserved Norwegians. It was very difficult to explain that the argument in itself was a big achievement.
I want to believe that the Norwegians we met also gained something from our encounters and that we had made them really interested in the problem we presented.
Being young was our greatest key to their open hearts. Through the informal encounters, the jokes and small talk, they came to understand the great difference between their lives and ours, on the one hand, and the surpassing similarity on the other. To our great surprise, we sometimes even noticed that some of the Norwegian kids envied the intensity and maturity demanded from the Israeli and Palestinian youth in comparison with the peaceful lives of the Norwegian youth.
I thank all the people who enabled Natasha and me to go through this rare and important experience.

Tomer war zusammen mit Natasha Khalidi nach Norwegen eingeladen worden. Hier ihr Bericht

Norwegen

Ich bin im April nach Norwegen gefahren. Nicht, um Fjorde zu sehen oder nach den Wurzeln der Wikinger zu suchen, auch nicht, um die Mitternachtssonne zu bewundern. Ich bin gefahren, um norwegischen Studenten über das Leben in einer Region zu erzählen, wo die täglichen Probleme schwerwiegender und schmerzlicher sind als die Wetteraussichten für den nächsten Tag. Ich bin gefahren, um von jungen Männern und Frauen – nicht viel älter als 18 Jahre – zu erzählen, die bereits mit Fragen über Leben und Tod konfrontiert sind. Ich bin gefahren, um von einem kleinen Land zu erzählen, einem besonderen, versprochenen, alten, neuen, einem Land von Milch und Honig, Gewehren und Blut, wo Juden und Araber leben – Palästina und Israel. Ich bin nicht allein gefahren, Natasha Khalidi, eine arabisch sprechende Palästinenserin und Moslemin, ist mit mir gereist. Ich bin eine hebräisch sprechende Israelin und Jüdin. Wir fuhren als zwei Teenager, die ihr Land repräsentieren, die beiden Seiten des israelisch-palästinensischen Konfliktes.
Davor hatte ich Natasha einige Male im Laufe unserer Treffen in der »Neuen Generation« gesehen und kannte sie nicht besonders gut. Im Laufe unseres Aufenthalts hielten wir sieben Vorträge an höheren Schulen. Dazu kamen Treffen mit Beamten, Lehrern und PR-Menschen. Wir wurden von verschiedenen Zeitungen interviewt, besuchten das Haus, in dem die Geheimverhandlungen vor dem Oslo-Abkommen stattgefunden hatten, und setzten unsere bescheidenen Unterschriften im Gästebuch unter jene von Shimon Peres und Ahmad Qrei (Abu Ala).
Der israelische Botschafter und der palästinensische Geschäftsträger in Norwegen gaben Empfänge für uns.
Aus der Perspektive des schönen und friedlichen Norwegen scheint der palästinensisch-israelische Konflikt wie ein Spiel, in dem Kinder bis zum bitteren Ende um einen Sandkasten kämpfen. Es ist sehr schwierig zu erklären, wie komplex und emotional dieser Konflikt ist. Es ist schwierig, jemandem klarzumachen, daß wir nicht von Schwarzweißlösungen und absoluter Gerechtigkeit sprechen. Es ist schwierig zu erklären, wie tragisch es ist, daß beide Seiten recht haben und daß es nicht nur eine einzige Wahrheit gibt. Natasha und ich

sind durch einen langen und anstrengenden Prozeß gegangen. Wir sind nicht als Feindinnen nach Norwegen gekommen, sondern als zwei Mädchen, die ihr Land vertreten.
Natürlich wollte jede von uns die Zuhörer überzeugen, daß sie im Recht war. Diese Rivalität führte zu Spannungen zwischen uns, die aber nicht lange anhielten. Wir machten einen gemeinsamen Prozeß durch, an dessen Ende wir enge Freundinnen wurden, die ihre privaten Probleme und Erfahrungen miteinander diskutierten. Zu unserer großen Überraschung hatten wir ganz ähnliche Gefühle: Beide hatten wir Heimweh nach unserem Land, seiner Mentalität, dem Essen, dem Wetter und der Intensität unseres normalen Lebens. Wir begriffen, daß wir weder Vertreterinnen von Friedensgesprächen waren, noch von einem internationalen Publikum nach Recht oder Unrecht beurteilt wurden. Wir verstanden, daß wir ein Gesamtbild unseres Landes vermitteln sollten. Die meisten Vorträge, in denen wir über den Konflikt und seine Wurzeln, aber auch über unser Leben, unsere Hoffnungen und unser Engagement in palästinensisch-israelischen Initiativen sprachen, hielten wir in Fredrikstad bei Oslo.
Die norwegischen Studenten hatten nicht viele Fragen, aber es war immer wenigstens einer dabei, der wissen wollte, warum wir uns schon so lange bekämpfen, und uns mit all seiner norwegischen Naivität fragte: »Warum teilt ihr das Land nicht einfach?«
Unglücklicherweise gab es während unseres Aufenthalts in Norwegen zu Hause in Israel einige Zwischenfälle, und die Leute fragten uns ständig nach »Har Homa« und Netanyahus Politik. Meine persönliche Meinung war ganz anders als der offizielle israelische Standpunkt, den ich aber als Vertreterin meines Landes wenigstens erklären wollte.
Ich wollte, daß die Norweger die existentielle Angst meines Volkes verstehen und die absolute Bedeutung Jerusalems für den israelischen Staat.
In allen unseren Vorträgen wiesen wir auf die Wichtigkeit des Friedensprozesses hin, betonten aber auch, daß die notwendigen Kompromisse für beide Völker schmerzhaft wären.
Aus einem Dilemma konnte ich mich nie befreien: Ich wollte einerseits die palästinensisch-israelische Realität verständlich machen und andererseits klarstellen, daß wir in einem demokratischen, sehr fortschrittlichen Staat leben.
Mein größter Erfolg war, daß Natasha und ich uns so gut verstanden haben. In den elf gemeinsam verbrachten Tagen wurde jede von uns mit den Überzeugungen der anderen konfrontiert, ich lernte Natasha und ihr Volk besser kennen und begann, sie zu verstehen, trotz unserer unterschiedlichen Sprachen.
Wir hatten viele lautstarke Auseinandersetzungen, die in den Ohren der reservierten Norweger seltsam klingen mußten.
Es war schwierig zu erklären, daß allein diese Streitgespräche ein Fortschritt für uns waren, und ich hoffe, daß es uns trotzdem gelungen ist, unsere Anliegen zu vermitteln.
Unser Jungsein war der Schlüssel zu ihren Herzen, bei informellen Treffen, Gesprächen und Scherzen verstanden sie den Unterschied zwischen ihrem und unserem Leben einerseits und die Ähnlichkeiten andererseits. Manche beneideten uns sogar um unsere Reife und um die Herausforderung, der wir uns stellen müssen, im Unterschied zu ihnen in ihrem ruhigen Leben.
Ich danke allen, die Natasha und mir diese besondere und wichtige Erfahrung ermöglicht haben.

Tomer, Kobi, Adi, Fida

Mohammed, Babsi, Heidi, Amir

SHAIFER, AMIR
1996

*20.3.1979
Natanya
Currently doing his army service, member of the scout movement, teaches first aid at Magen David Adom, volunteer of the civil guard
Israeli delegation

SHAMIR, ERAN
1994, 1995, 1996, 1997

*20.4.1976
Ness Ziona
Graduate Tel Aviv University, Faculty of Law,
Army service as a lawyer
Israeli delegation

Opening statement in Eilat 1996
Today we are starting a new stage in the programme of the "New Generation" for youth from the Middle East, that began three years ago. Through this programme, we overcame many difficulties and barriers, in order to get, where we are today.
Step by step, we have managed to build the foundation for a bridge of coexistence and co-operation between the Israeli and the Arab youth, with the great help of our fellow delegates, the Austrian youth. And now, we hope to be able to continue what we have started.
Our meeting's location is not accidental. The fact that we are here today, different nations, cultures and mentalities, means more, than we can imagine. We can only hope, that in the coming days of our companionship, its meaning will become clearer, and will stand before our eyes, to guide us through our time together.
Since the first conference,many new members joined the programme and we, the Israeli delegation, welcome all of you, newers, with our open hearts. We all went through a very hard, eventful year, that changed our life. One of the main events, especially for my fellow Israeli delegates and myself, was the assassination of our late Prime Minister, Mr Yitzak Rabin, may he rest in peace. His tragic murder made us realise and understand the importance of tolerance, equality and co-operation. I am all hope, that we will be wise enough to fulfil his last wish – to bring peace to our lives. Late Mr Rabin's assassination will not stop the process of peace and co-operation between us. On the contrary, it will only make it stronger. And it will continue to remind us the reason for being here together – understanding, co-operation and seeking common ground.
The members of the Israeli delegation come from different backgrounds and parts of the country, Jews and Arabs, Muslims, Christians and Druzes, religious and secular, from the city, the village and the kibbutz. However, we are all united by the will to meet, talk, and finally, understand those, who, until yesterday, were strangers. Today we are partners in the historical process the Middle East is going through. Tomorrow will depend only on us – the "New Generation".
Remember that we can be part of the problem, or part of the solution. And the solution starts today, in each and every one of us present here. Here is the place to begin to fulfil our dreams for a new Middle East. Obstacles may rise in the future of our process. But every one of us is obligated, by the fact of him being here, to stand up to these obstacles and to continue our path, that we are going for three years now.
We arrived as delegates, who represent their authorities. However, we have to remember that we are also individuals. Each and every-one of us is an individual with dreams, needs and ambitions of his own, and the reason for being here, is to learn more about the little individual in each of us.
As someone, who has lived in this area for 17 years, and had seen the ups and downs of the negotiations and the process, I can tell you, that what you are doing here today is greatly needed and appreciated. Thank you.

Chancellor Franz Vranitzky, Israeli official and Eran at the opening ceremony in Eilat
Bundeskanzler Franz Vranitzky, ein Vertreter Israels und Eran bei der Eröffnungszeremonie in Eilat

Eröffnungsrede in Eilat 1996
Wir starten heute eine neue Phase des Projektes der »New Generation« für die Jugend des Nahen Ostens, das vor drei Jahren begann. Durch dieses Programm haben wir viele Schwierigkeiten und Grenzen

überwunden, um dort anzukommen, wo wir heute sind. Schritt für Schritt haben wir eine Brücke der Koexistenz und Zusammenarbeit zwischen israelischer und arabischer Jugend gebaut, mit der großen Hilfe unserer österreichischen Freunde und Freundinnen. Und jetzt hoffen wir, weitermachen zu können.
Die Wahl des Treffpunktes war kein Zufall. Die Tatsache, daß wir, verschiedene Nationen, Kulturen, Mentalitäten, heute hier sind, bedeutet mehr, als wir uns vorstellen können. Dies wird uns hoffentlich in den kommenden Tagen des Zusammenseins in der ganzen Dimension klar und deutlich werden.
Seit der ersten Konferenz sind viele neue Mitglieder dazugekommen, und wir, die israelische Delegation, heißen euch hier alle herzlich willkommen.
Wir haben ein hartes, ereignisreiches Jahr hinter uns, das unser Leben verändert hat. Eines der erschütterndsten Ereignisse, zumindest für meine israelischen Freunde und mich, war die Ermordung unseres Ministerpräsidenten Yitzhak Rabin, er möge in Frieden ruhen.
Seine tragische Ermordung ließ uns die Bedeutung von Toleranz, Gleichheit und Zusammenarbeit begreifen. Ich bin voller Hoffnung, daß wir klug genug sind, seinen letzten Willen zu erfüllen – Frieden in unser Leben zu bringen.
Der Mord an Rabin kann den Friedensprozeß und die Zusammenarbeit zwischen uns nicht aufhalten. Im Gegenteil, wir werden stärker. Und er wird uns daran erinnern, warum wir hier sind: um gemeinsam Verständnis und Zusammenarbeit zu suchen.
Die Mitglieder der israelischen Delegation kommen aus verschiedenen Realitäten der israelischen Gesellschaft, Juden und Araber, Moslems, Christen und Drusen, Geistliche und Weltliche, Städter, Dorfbewohner und Kibbutzniks. Doch verbindet uns der Wunsch, einander kennenzulernen, miteinander zu sprechen und die zu verstehen, die bis gestern Fremde waren. Heute Partner im Friedensprozeß, morgen Baumeister einer neuen Generation.
Vergeßt nicht, daß ihr Teil des Problems oder Teil der Lösung sein könnt. Und die Lösung beginnt heute, in jedem und jeder von uns. Hier wollen wir beginnen, unsere Träume von einem neuen Nahen Osten wahr werden zu lassen. In der Zukunft werden Hindernisse auftauchen, doch jeder und jede ist verpflichtet – durch seine oder ihre Anwesenheit –, sich diesen Hindernissen entgegenzustellen und den Weg fortzusetzen, den wir vor drei Jahren begonnen haben.
Wir sind als Delegationen gekommen, die ihre Nationen vertreten. Doch wir dürfen nicht vergessen, daß wir auch Individuen sind, mit eigenen Träumen, Bedürfnissen und Wünschen und daß der Grund hier zu sein ist, dieses kleine Individuum in uns näher kennenzulernen.
Als ein junger Mensch, der seit 17 Jahren in dieser Region lebt und das Auf und Ab von Verhandlungen mitverfolgt hat, kann ich euch sagen, daß das, was ihr hier tut, absolut notwendig und von unschätzbarem Wert ist.
Danke.

SHARIR, ZIVAN
1994

*6.11.1976
Even Yehuda
Israeli delegation

... I think there is a huge difference between the political language and the literary one. There is something in the political that is more immediate, that is more general, sometimes more stereotyping; it lacks intimacy, it addresses many, many people. Literature addresses only one, only the writer, only the one who creates the piece of art.

David Grossmann

... Ich glaube, es gibt einen Riesenunterschied zwischen der politischen und der literarischen Sprache. Es gibt etwas in der politischen Sprache, das unmittelbarer ist, etwas allgemeiner, etwas stereotyper: Es mangelt ihr an Intimität, sie spricht viele, viele Menschen an. Literatur spricht nur einen an, den Schriftsteller, nur den einen, der das Kunstwerk schafft.

David Grossmann

Seit ich zu denken begonnen habe, versuche ich, die Sprache meiner Eltern, meiner Lehrer, anderer Schriftsteller und von Journalisten zu verstehen oder zu überprüfen … Irgendwann bemerkte ich plötzlich, daß es um mich herum einen ganzen Zirkus von Klischees gibt, an die ich glaubte, weil ich mit ihnen aufwuchs. In meinen Büchern habe ich versucht – wenn ich zum Beispiel in die besetzten Gebiete reiste –, die Sprache, in der ich spreche oder die dortigen Geschehnisse für mich selbst beschreiben kann, zu erneuern. Ich tat dies, nicht weil ich gegen mein Land oder meine Kultur wäre, im Gegenteil, ich spürte, daß ein Land, das eine falsche Sprache spricht und Worte verwendet, die die Realität nicht richtig beschreiben, irgendwann überrascht sein wird und sich letztlich selbst zerstört …
Wenn wir die Wirklichkeit nicht mit den richtigen Worten beschreiben, werden wir eines Tages erwachen und erkennen, daß sie sich nicht mehr beschreiben läßt. Ich glaube, wir haben nun zum ersten Mal die Chance, eine neue Sprache miteinander zu sprechen.

David Grossmann

Mervat, Oraib, Raimund

SHELBAYA, MERVAT
1994

*29.9.1974
Cairo
American University of Cairo graduate, economics and political science
Egyptian delegation

… What I have tried ever since I started to think is to understand or to check the language that was spoken to me by my parents, by my teachers, by other writers, by journalists … Suddenly I found that there is a whole circus of clichés around me that I believed in because I was brought up on them. What I did in my books, when I went for example to the occupied territories, is really to try to regenerate the language in which I will be able to speak or to describe to myself what happens there. I did it, not because I was against my country or my culture, but on the contrary because I really felt that if a country uses a false language, if it does not use the right words to describe reality, then it will be surprised, it will destroy itself …
If you do not describe reality with the right words, one day you will wake up to a reality that is indescribable. I really think that now, for the first time, there is a chance of talking a new language with each other.

David Grossmann

SHUHABI, MAHAR
1994, 1995, 1996, 1997, 1998

*20.2.1978
Jerusalem
University of Amman, German and English literature
Palestinian delegation

1998
We want to send you our best regards and to tell you that we were very happy last summer and we miss you a lot. Since we came back, we always talk about the great experience we had.

Mahar, Suad and James

1998
Wir möchten euch viele Grüße schicken und sagen, wie glücklich wir letzten Sommer mit euch waren und wie sehr wir euch vermissen. Wir sprechen immer wieder über die großartigen Erfahrungen, die wir gemacht haben ...

Mahar, Suad und James

Mahar, Wafa, Dima

SIMON, MORIAH
1996, 1997, 1998

*5.2.1979
Kdumim Shomron
Bar Illan University, law, Member of Bnai Akiva
Middle East Youth Peace Forum scholar 1998
Israeli delegation

Crossing borders
Wa'el, Moriah

SNIR, ASAF
1996

*31.5.1979
Holon
Currently doing his army service
Israeli delegation

... Ultimately the danger is not politics. It is a very sentimental and in my view even an unhealthy inclination to call politics dirty, and a wish to dissociate oneself completely from this unclean realm of compromises. Politics is healthy in the same sense that life is healthy, and it is unhealthy in the same sense that life itself is unhealthy. It is infected by urges, by ambition, by fear, by double standards, by naive idealism and by stupidity, like the rest of life. The real danger is not politics. The real danger lies somewhere in the province of fanaticism which can exist inside and outside of politics. I say fanaticism and I do not necessarily mean the obvious kinds of fanaticism and chauvinism, religious fanaticism. I have seen fanatics of all faiths and brands and colours. I have seen anti-smokers who would burn me alive for lighting a cigarette in their presence ... I know pacifists who would kill me on the spot just because I happen to have a slight different strategy for peace. So no one is immune. Fanaticism is dangerous because there is a potential, a capacity for fanaticism in everyone of us ... And I think the remedy to fanaticism is a sense of humour because not once in my life have I seen a fanatic with a sense of humour, nor have I seen a person with a sense of humour turning into a fanatic unless he or she lost his or her sense of humour. So if I could only compress sense of humour into capsules and immune entire populations to fanaticism by giving them these capsules I would qualify perhaps for the Nobel Prize not in literature but in medicine. Humour. If I believe in a messiah, a Christian, a Jewish or a Muslim messiah I would say that this messiah would come laughing and telling jokes. Humour is the ability to see that the other story, the other claim, the other complaint has a certain validity, which does not necessarily and automatically devaluate your own complaint, claim or position.

Amos Oz

... Letztlich ist die Gefahr nicht die Politik. Es ist eine sehr sentimentale, und meiner Meinung nach sogar eine ungesunde Neigung, die Politik schmutzig zu nennen und sich zu wünschen, sich ganz von diesem schmutzigen Reich des Kompromisses zu distanzieren. Die Politik ist gesund im selben Sinn, wie das Leben gesund ist, und sie ist ungesund im selben Sinn, wie das Leben ungesund ist. Sie ist infiziert vom Verlangen, vom Ehrgeiz, von der Angst, von der Doppelmoral, vom naiven Idealismus und von der Dummheit wie das übrige Leben auch. Die wirkliche Gefahr ist nicht die Politik. Die wirkliche Gefahr liegt irgendwo auf dem Gebiet des Fanatismus, der inner- und außerhalb der Politik existieren kann. Ich sage Fanatismus und meine damit nicht die offensichtliche Art des Fanatismus und Chauvinismus, den religiösen Fanatismus. Ich habe Fanatiker aller Glaubensrichtungen und Sorten und Farben gesehen. Ich habe Antiraucher gesehen, die mich am liebsten bei lebendigem Leibe verbrannt hätten, weil ich eine Zigarette in ihrer Gegenwart anzündete ... Ich kenne Pazifisten, die mich sofort umbringen würden, nur weil ich eine etwas andere Friedensstrategie verfolge. Niemand ist gefeit. Fanatismus ist gefährlich, weil es ein Potential, eine Anlage für Fanatismus in jedem von uns gibt ... Und ich glaube, daß das Heilmittel gegen Fanatismus der Sinn für Humor ist. Kein einziges Mal in meinem Leben habe ich einen Fanatiker mit Sinn für Humor getroffen, ich habe auch nie einen humorvollen Menschen getroffen, der zum Fanatiker wurde – es sei denn, er oder sie hatte den Humor verloren. Wenn ich den Sinn für Humor in Kapseln füllen könnte und ganze Völker mit diesen Kapseln gegen Fanatismus immunisieren könnte, würde ich mich für den Nobelpreis qualifizieren – nicht für Literatur, sondern für Medizin. Humor. Wenn ich an einen Messias glaube, einen christlichen, einen jüdischen, einen moslemischen Messias, würde ich sagen, daß dieser Messias lacht und Witze erzählt. Humor ist die Fähigkeit zu verstehen, daß die andere Geschichte, die anderen Ansprüche, die anderen Klagen eine gewisse Gültigkeit haben, was nicht unbedingt und automatisch deine eigenen Klagen, Ansprüche oder Positionen entwertet.

Amos Oz

STARNBERGER, SONJA
1994, 1996, 1997

*24.11.1975
Frauenhofen
University of Vienna, international business administration, Erasmus scholar in Athens for one semester, works at the Bruno Kreisky Forum while she is doing her thesis
Austrian delegation

When I was asked to contribute to the book about the Middle East Youth Peace Forum, I didn't know what to write, being convinced that the authors would describe the programme, its development, and its benefits in a much more skilful way than I could ever do it.
So at first, I postponed the task, but finally I decided to at least look for some nice pictures. When I opened the cupboard where I keep all the letters, brochures, documents, souvenirs, newsletters and pictures related to the Middle East Youth Peace Forum and started digging for the photos, many, many memories popped up in my mind ... and many questions:
Would I ever have met all these wonderful, likeable, and interesting people from the Middle East and Austria without the programme, some of which – I hope – will be my friends for life?
Would I have visited Israel, Jordan, and the Palestinian Autonomy so early in my life?
Would I have realised what a complex mass of history, emotions, facts, mutual accusations and sometimes misunderstandings can stand behind those short everyday newspaper articles?
Would I have known about the possibility to work in Jerusalem for one month?
Would I have spent so many hours in heated discussions and also chatting, socialising and having fun with such nice people?
Would I have been as interested in political issues as I am now? Would I have learnt so many things about Arabic and Jewish traditions and culture?
Would my optimism and my feeling that dreams can become true if you believe in them and do not immediately discard them as unrealistic be as strong as they are now?
Maybe I could answer some of these questions with yes, but for sure not all of them. I am convinced that I would be a different person today, had I not been given all those opportunities by the Bruno Kreisky Forum.

Als ich um einen Beitrag für dieses Buch gefragt wurde, wußte ich nicht, was ich schreiben sollte, denn ich war überzeugt, daß die Herausgeberinnen das Projekt, seine Entwicklung und seine Erfolge besser als irgendjemand anderer beschreiben würden. Also schob ich diese Aufgabe auf, beschloß aber dann, zumindest ein paar Fotos herauszusuchen. Als ich den Schrank öffnete, in dem ich alle Briefe, Dokumente, Souvenirs, Newsletter und Bilder aufbewahrte, die zum Nahost-Jugend-Friedensforum gehörten, und die Fotos eines nach dem anderen in die Hand nahm, kamen plötzlich viele Erinnerungen hoch ... und viele Fragen:
Hätte ich ohne das Projekt jemals alle diese wunderbaren, liebenswerten und interessanten Menschen aus dem Nahen Osten und aus Österreich kennengelernt, von denen einige – wie ich hoffe – meine Freunde fürs Leben bleiben werden?
Hätte ich jemals in so jungen Jahren Israel, Jordanien und die palästinensischen Autonomiegebiete besucht?
Hätte ich jemals verstanden, was für eine komplexe Welt von Geschichte, Gefühlen, Tatsachen, Anschuldigungen und auch Mißverständnissen hinter kurzen, banalen Zeitungsartikeln stehen kann?
Hätte ich jemals die Gelegenheit gehabt, einen Monat lang in Jerusalem zu arbeiten?
Hätte ich jemals so viele Stunden mit hitzigen Diskussionen, aber auch mit vertraulichen Gesprächen und unendlich viel Spaß mit so netten Menschen verbracht?
Hätte ich mich jemals so für Politik interessiert, wie jetzt, so viel über arabische und jüdische Tradition und Kultur gelernt?
Wären mein Optimismus und mein Gefühl, daß Träume wahr werden können, wenn du nur daran glaubst und sie nicht sofort in das Reich des Unmöglichen abschiebst, jemals so stark geworden?
Vielleicht kann ich einige Fragen mit Ja beantworten, aber sicher nicht alle. Ich bin überzeugt, daß ich heute ein anderer Mensch wäre, hätte ich vom Bruno Kreisky Forum nicht all diese Möglichkeiten bekommen.

Israeli delegation 1994
Die israelische Delegation 1994

TAMARI, MICHAL
1994, 1996, 1998

*2.5.1977
Jerusalem
Studies psychology
Israeli delegation

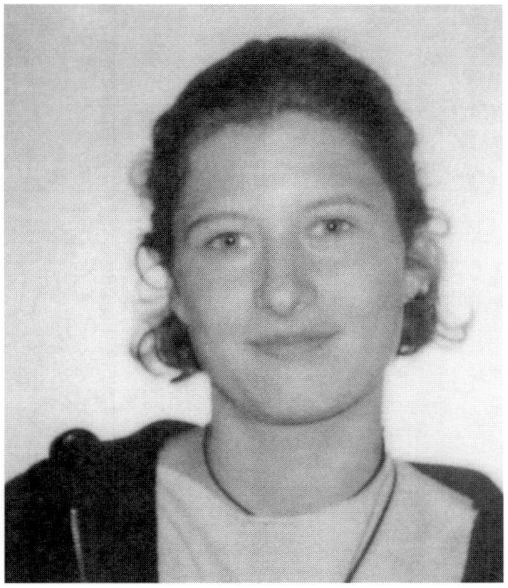

In the garden of the Bruno Kreisky Forum; in the middle Roy
Im Garten des Bruno Kreisky Forums; in der Mitte Roy

TIROSH, ROY
1994

*22.6.1977
Tel Aviv
Israeli delegation

... What will it be like to live without an enemy? I just don't know what it does to our psyche to live without an enemy, because it is so easy to define yourself by having an enemy. So much of our basic ethos was shaped by that, so many of our perceptions – you know dividing reality into an enemy or a friend, black or white – suddenly the world will get so many more nuances.
David Grossmann

...Wie wird es sein, ohne Feind zu leben? Ich weiß nicht, wie es sich auf unsere Psyche auswirkt, ohne Feind zu leben, weil es so einfach ist, sich selbst zu definieren, wenn man einen Feind hat. So viel von unserer Grundethik wurde davon bestimmt, so viele Wahrnehmungen – man teilt die Wirklichkeit ein in Freund und Feind, in Schwarz und Weiß – plötzlich wird die Welt viele neuen Nuancen erhalten.
David Grossmann

TOUKAN, ORAIB
1994

*20.10.1977
Amman
Jordanian delegation

We will have to build a totally new society – not a society of survivors, but of people who lead normal lives. We are just survivors, we and the Palestinians, we forgot how to live, we were caught in a kind of paradox of countries and peoples and leading citizens who survived older history in order to live, and all we know is to live only in order to survive.
It would create a change, and I just hope that this change will happen …

David Grossmann

Wir werden eine völlig neue Gesellschaft aufbauen müssen – nicht eine Gesellschaft der Überlebenden, sondern eine von Menschen, die ein ganz normales Leben führen. Wir sind nur Überlebende, wir und die Palästinenser, wir haben vergessen, wie man lebt. Wir wurden gefangen in einem Paradoxon von Ländern und Völkern und prominenten Bürgern, die die Geschichte überlebten, damit sie lebten. Und alles, was wir kennen, ist leben, um zu überleben.
Es würde Änderungen herbeiführen, und ich hoffe, daß diese Änderungen stattfinden ...

David Grossmann

Oraib, Ali

VORHOFER, HANNES
1994, 1995, 1996, 1997, 1998

*1.10.1975
Mils
University of Innsbruck and University of Frankfurt, political science, peace and conflict research, plans to work as a volunteer in a kibbutz
Austrian delegation

In 1994 I was the students' delegate at the high school for mechanical engineering in Innsbruck (Austria), when I got the invitation for a Middle East Youth Peace Forum from the Bruno Kreisky Froum. After informing the other delegates at our school, I didn't think about it any more for the time being. But when after two weeks no one from my school had applied, I read the brochure once again and became interested in participating myself.
The Middle East Youth Peace Forum was a big experience for me and I got a lot of new friends during those ten days. Also, for the first time I was confronted with the problems of the Middle East conflict, which I had known only through the scarce information in the media. After the Peace Forum I tried to read a lot and to inform myself about the conflict. In 1996 I started to study political science and history at the University of Innsbruck and since then I am intensively interested in the Middle East conflict. I spent the academic year 1998/99 at J. W. Goethe University in Frankfurt. There I studied conflict research and Methods of Research into the causes of war. The Middle East Youth Peace Forum had a very positive and far-reaching influence on my life. The personal continuity throughout the four years was one important aspect for the good and productive work together. We were able to reach a common base for conversations which was characterized by mutual understanding. Through the common work and after all the difficulties we managed together, we changed from a conference with different delegations to one group which plead for a better understanding in the region. The "New Generation" is a very small, but important contribution to the Israeli-Palestinian peace process.

1994 war ich Schulsprecher an der Höheren Technischen Bundeslehr- und Versuchsanstalt für Maschinenbau in Innsbruck, als ich die Ausschreibung für die Teilnahme an der Nahost-Jugend-Konferenz vom Bruno Kreisky Forum zugesandt bekam. Ich informierte die Klassensprecher und machte mir vorerst keine weiteren Gedanken mehr darüber. Als ich allerdings nach zwei Wochen überraschenderweise keine einzige Rückmeldung von der gesamten Schule bekommen hatte, betrachtete ich die Informationsbroschüre nochmals genau. Erst jetzt erweckte die Nahost-Jugend-Friedenskonferenz mein persönliches Interesse, und ich bewarb mich um die Aufnahme in die österreichische Jugenddelegation.
Die Konferenz in der UNO-City in Wien war ein großes Erlebnis für mich. Neben den vielen persönlichen Bekanntschaften wurde ich zum ersten Mal mit der Problematik des Nahostkonflikts konfrontiert. Alles, was ich bisher über den Konflikt gewußt hatte, hatte ich den spärlichen Informationen in den Medien entnommen. Nach dem Ende der Konferenz versuchte ich, so viel wie möglich über den Nahostkonflikt zu lesen, um mein Hintergrundwissen zu erweitern. 1996 begann ich das Studium der Politikwissenschaft und Geschichte an der Universität Innsbruck, und seither beschäftige ich mich intensiv mit diesem Thema. Das Studienjahr 1998/99 verbrachte ich an der J. W.-Goethe Universität in Frankfurt, wo ich Konfliktforschung und Methoden der Kriegsursachenforschung studierte. So gesehen hatte das Nahost-Jugend-Friedensforum einen sehr positiven und weitreichenden Einfluß auf mein Leben.
Die personelle Kontinuität des Forums über die vier Jahre hinweg war ein wichtiger Aspekt für die gute und fruchtbare Zusammenarbeit. Jeder von uns Teilnehmern hat in dieser Zeit sehr emotionale Momente, positive und negative, miterlebt, an die wir uns immer wieder zurückerinnern werden. Es ist uns gelungen, eine gemeinsame Gesprächsbasis aufzubauen, die von Zuhören und gegenseitigem Verständnis geprägt ist.
Durch die mehrjährige Zusammenarbeit und all die gemeinsam bewältigten Schwierigkeiten sind wir von einer Konferenz mit verschiedenen Delegationen zu einer einheitlichen Gruppe geworden, die für eine bessere Verständigung in der Region kämpft. Die »New Generation« ist ein sehr kleiner, aber wichtiger Beitrag zum israelisch-palästinensischen Friedensprozeß.

WEHBEH, EHSAN
1995, 1996

*19.4.1978
Daliat El-Carmel
University of Haifa, Faculty of law
Israeli delegation

We are having very difficult days, since the terror attacks, which, I think, must make us more determined to continue in our co-operation and in our projects as well.
Out of my strong belief that we – the "New Generation" – can try to normalise this peace and out of my faith that we can overcome every barrier, I am very glad to join the group and contribute as much as I can in order to achieve our goals.

Wir haben sehr schwere Tage seit den Terroranschlägen, die uns aber, glaube ich, entschlossener in der Zusammenarbeit und in unserer Projektarbeit machen müssen. Aufgrund meiner tiefen Überzeugung, daß wir – die »Neue Generation« – diesen Frieden auf das normale, tägliche Leben werden übertragen können, aufgrund meines Glaubens, daß wir alle Hindernisse überwinden können, gehöre ich der Gruppe an und möchte so viel wie möglich zur Errreichung der Ziele beitragen.

YASSIN, MAHMOUD
1996, 1997, 1998

*27.9.1975
Ramallah
Bir Zeit University graduate, economics
Palestinian delegation

Muhy, Kareem, Mahmoud

From the Heart

It has been almost a year since the last "Crossing Borders" project took place. This project faced a lot of difficulties, but combined efforts from all the delegations participating helped to overcome them. A major problem that we were able to resolve was the accommodation of the Israeli delegation in Bethlehem. It was the efforts of the Israeli delegation leaders joined with the parents of the participants to allow them to enter Bethlehem, a city under the Palestinian National Authority rule.
Another major obstacle for the Palestinian delegation was to return home. As a group with Austrians, Jordanians and Israelis it was easy to cross borders, but when the project came to an end and we had to go from Bethlehem to Ramallah, it was very difficult, we had to take special cars from Bethlehem and travel around the borders, which separate the Palestinian National Authority areas from Jerusalem. We are banned from entering Arab East Jerusalem, except after obtaining permits, and to obtain a permit you have to present a clean political record ... We are seeking peace, and we know that a lot of Israelis are seeking it as well ... We are still young and we need other things to occupy our minds.

Von ganzem Herzen

Es ist bereits ein Jahr her, daß wir am »Crossing-Borders«-Projekt teilgenommen haben. Wir haben viele Probleme im Laufe des Projektes gehabt, aber die gemeinsamen Bemühungen aller Delegationen haben sie uns überwinden lassen. Eine der größten Schwierigkeiten war die Unterbringung der israelischen Delegation in Bethlehem. Es ist das große Verdienst der israelischen Delegationsleitung und der israelischen Eltern, allen TeilnehmerInnen gemeinsam die Einreise und den Aufenthalt in Bethlehem, einer Stadt unter palästinensischer Verwaltung, möglich gemacht zu haben.
Ein anderes großes Hindernis war die Heimreise der palästinensischen TeilnehmerInnen. Als eine Gruppe von ÖsterreicherInnen, Israelis und JordanierInnen war es leicht, die Grenzen zu überqueren, aber als wir am Ende der Reise von Bethlehem nach Ramallah fahren mußten, war es fast unmöglich; wir mußten in eigenen Autos rund um die Grenzen fahren, die Jerusalem von den Gebieten der palästinensischen Autonomie trennen. Es ist uns verboten, in das arabische Jerusalem zu fahren, außer mit speziellen Genehmigungen, die man nur mit einer reinen politischen Weste bekommt ... Wir wollen Frieden, und wir wissen, daß auch viele Israelis Frieden wollen ... Wir sind jung und sollten uns mit anderen Dingen beschäftigen ...

YVON, YANNIC
1996

*3.6.1978
Wien
University of Vienna, international law and business administration, works at the OPEC Austrian delegation

... Breaking stereotypes is a very painful but also gratifying process – painful because you are suddenly left without any defence mechanism, you just deliberately shutter your defence mechanism if you want to go and meet the other. Gratifying because I think maybe this is the only victory that is available to us human beings – the victory over stereotypes ... It is a sense or a feeling of a victory to the small person that he can suddenly break something that was imposed on him, on his thoughts and on his language.

David Grossmann

Lisa, Orlando, Yannic

... Stereotypen zu zerschlagen kann ein sehr schmerzvoller, aber auch erfreulicher Prozeß sein. Schmerzvoll, weil man plötzlich ohne irgendeinen Verteidigungsmechanismus dasteht, man schaltet den Verteidigungsmechanismus absichtlich aus, wenn man den anderen begegnen will. Erfreulich, weil ich glaube, dies ist der einzige Sieg, den wir Menschen haben können – der Sieg über Stereotypen. Es ist ein Siegesgefühl für den kleinen Mann, plötzlich etwas zerstören zu können, das ihm aufgebürdet wurde, seinen Gedanken und seiner Sprache.

David Grossmann

ZELEZNIKAR, MARIJANA
1994, 1995, 1996

*3.4.1976
Slovenia
University of Vienna, international business administration
Austrian delegation

... I have noticed recently that young Carinthians (the Slovenian minority) are especially very interested in what is going on in Israel and what happened earlier at the conference. I have reported on this in several classes in our schools and written two articles (one especially on the Israel trip) for Slovenian newspapers (Nas Tednik) in Carinthia.

... In der letzten Zeit habe ich bemerkt, daß sich besonders junge Kärntner der slowenischen Minderheit sehr dafür interessieren, was in Israel passiert, aber auch dafür, was früher auf der Konferenz (1994) geschah. Ich habe in einigen Klassen unserer Schule darüber berichtet und zwei Artikel (darunter ein Special über die Israelreise) für slowenische Zeitungen in Kärnten (Nas Tednik) geschrieben.

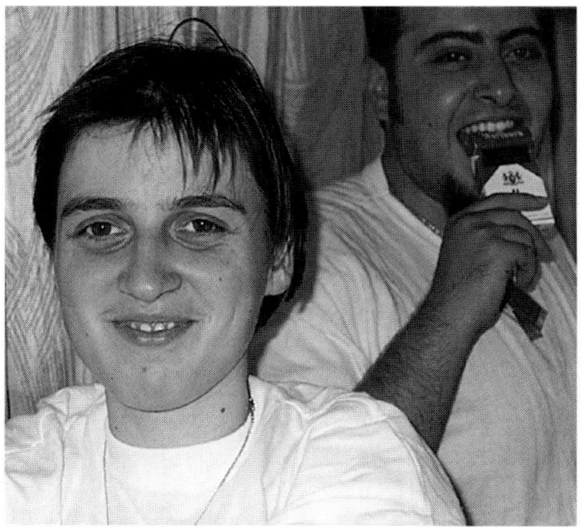

At the Bruno Kreisky Forum
Vor dem Bruno Kreisky Forum

ZELTZER, DAN
1996

*2.1.1980
Tel Mond
Israeli delegation

Hagit, Dan

Yuval, Shirley

ZILBER, YUVAL
1995, 1996

*15.10.1978
Ramat Hasharon
Member of Meretz, currently doing his army service
Israeli delegation

ZIMMERMANN, KARIN

*29.1.1977
Graz
University of Vienna, political science, plans to study for one year at Tel Aviv University, volunteered in Jerusalem for one year as a teacher in an Arab school, member of »Youth Against Violence and Racism«
Austrian delegation

The Peace Conference 1994
A participant's view
... Personal relationships became secondary because we now had to defend our ideas and make our demands. The statements in this context had a remarkably "official" sound; none of the delegations diverged from their demands and barely from their official political opinions.
As the Palestinian youths above all, supported by the Jordanian and Egyptian youths, demanded unconditional recognition of their rights, adherence to UN Resolutions 242 and 338, as well as the right to self-determination, the Israeli youths pointed out repeatedly that in their eyes it was senseless to discuss the demands still to be negotiated, and which hadn't in part yet been clarified among the Israeli society. It would be far more sensible, they argued, to talk about the common future in peace, which lay ahead of us. Since the Israeli youths indeed ignored nearly every political statement on the subjects, which the Palestinians demanded, the Palestinians understandably didn't feel that their demands had been taken seriously. On the other hand, however, the Israeli youths themselves had the impression that all of their constructive proposals for a common future had been immediately rejected.
Although agreement on many things was possible in the various working groups, these fundamental differences of opinion could not be solved.
The final document, in the end, was drawn up after hours of consultation and discussion, in which all agreed that not much had been achieved. Another very essential feeling, however, was that the final document, precisely due to its limitations, was far from being the only important measure and that the time spent together and of getting to know one another was highly appreciated. After a for most of us sleepless night, saying farewell was hard, and the desire to meet again was not a superficial one. Something had indeed changed, but much remained the same. How great the ramifications of this change can and will be, now remains in the stars ...

Karin, Orlando, Katarina

Eindrücke von der Konferenz 1994
... Es wurde deutlich, daß gerade in den Plenarsitzungen die persönlichen Beziehungen zueinander nebensächlich waren, da es um das Verteidigen von Ideen und das Durchsetzen von Forderungen ging. Da die Statements in diesem Rahmen ungemein offiziell wirkten, wich keine der Delegationen von ihren Forderungen und kaum von der offiziellen politischen Meinung ab. Während die palästinensischen Jugendlichen, vor allem von den jordanischen und ägyptischen Jugendlichen unterstützt, eine unbedingte Anerkennung ihrer Rechte, die Einhaltung der UN-Resolutionen 242 und 338 sowie das Recht auf Selbstbestimmung

Suha, Karin

forderten, wiesen die israelischen Jugendlichen wiederholt darauf hin, daß es in ihren Augen sinnlos sei, über die Forderungen zu diskutieren, die ohnedies verhandelt würden und die auch teilweise innerhalb der israelischen Gesellschaft selbst noch nicht geklärt seien. Viel sinnvoller sei es, über das danach Kommende, über die gemeinsame Zukunft im Frieden zu reden. Da die israelischen Jugendlichen ihre politische Stellungnahme zum Thema verweigerten – obwohl von den palästinensischen Jugendlichen dazu aufgefordert –, fühlten sich die palästinensischen Jugendlichen in ihren Forderungen nicht ernst genommen. Auf der anderen Seite wiederum hatten die israelischen Jugendlichen den Eindruck, daß jeder ihrer konstruktiven Vorschläge für eine gemeinsame Zukunft sofort abgelehnt wurde. Obwohl man sich in den verschiedenen Arbeitsgruppen über viele Dinge einigen konnte, war dieser grundsätzliche Auffassungsunterschied nicht zu beseitigen.

Das Schlußdokument wurde letztendlich nach stundenlangen Beratungen und Diskussionen erstellt, wobei alle der Meinung waren, nicht viel erreicht zu haben. Es machte sich aber gerade aus diesem Grund ein anderes, sehr wesentliches Gefühl breit, nämlich daß dem Schlußdokument bei weitem nicht die einzige Bedeutung zukam, sondern daß die gemeinsam verbrachte Zeit und das Kennenlernen von unschätzbarem Wert waren. Nach einer für die meisten von uns schlaflosen Nacht fiel uns allen der Abschied schwer, und der Wunsch, sich wieder zu treffen, war echt. Etwas hat sich wirklich verändert, vieles ist aber gleich geblieben. Wie groß die Auswirkungen der Veränderungen sein können und sein werden, steht in den Sternen ...

ZOMET, YOSSI
1996

*19.7.1979
Karkur
Currently doing his army service, member of Hashomer Hatzair
Israeli delegation

Emad, Anas, Yamaan, Cedar and Ali in traditional dresses
Emad, Anas, Yamaan, Cedar und Ali in traditionellen Gewändern

ZREIKAT, CEDAR
1996

Currently working in women's right NGO
Jordanian delegation

Sometimes I'm discouraged with the world and the way it is. I read in history books how great empires and wars changed history and the face of earth and I smile ..., well the Bruno Kreisky Forum has changed my life.
Words are failing now, for my experience with the Bruno Kreisky Forum can't be described with words. It was so wonderful that my appreciation and gratitude to the Bruno Kreisky Forum can't be expressed with words but by spreading the idea of the "New Generation" and my commitment to the projects. This is the least I can do.
Throughout the wonderful journey I have learned so much to dedicate myself to people and commit myself to projects; and I understood that there are those who dream, and those who do and those who do both. I learned how to join the third group.
They say you can't change the world, it's too hard, too difficult, but we have decided to challenge the world, each one of us has changed his/her life and that is changing a whole world.

Manchmal bin ich entmutigt von der Welt und dem Lauf der Dinge. Ich lese in Büchern, wie große Reiche und Kriege die Geschichte und das Antlitz der Erde verändert haben, und lächle ... Das Kreisky Forum hat mein Leben verändert.
Mir fehlen Worte, um meine Erfahrungen mit dem Bruno Kreisky Forum zu beschreiben. Es war so wunderbar, und ich kann meine Dankbarkeit und Wertschätzung nur ausdrücken, indem ich die Ideen des Bruno Kreisky Forums weitertrage und mich in der Projektarbeit engagiere. Das ist das mindeste, was ich tun kann.
Auf dieser Reise habe ich gelernt, auf Menschen zuzugehen und an Projekten teilzunehmen; und ich habe vor allem begriffen, daß es Menschen gibt, die träumen, andere, die handeln, und solche, die beides tun. Ich habe erfahren, was es heißt, der dritten Gruppe anzugehören.
Man sagt, daß man die Welt nicht verändern kann, daß es zu schwierig, zu mühevoll ist, doch wir haben beschlossen, die Welt herauszufordern, jede/r von uns hat ihr/sein Leben verändert, und das bedeutet, die Welt.

PROGRAMME
PROGRAMM

Crossing borders
Grenzen überschreiten

1994
BUILDING BRIDGES
BRÜCKEN BAUEN
July/Juli 1994

Inaugural Meeting in Vienna and Tyrol

Israeli, Palestinian, Jordanian, Egyptian and Austrian youth met for the first time in Vienna for the Middle East Youth Peace Forum. In emulation of the actual "adult" process of peace negotiations, these teenagers, recognised as opinion leaders in their age groups at home, were to discuss the peace process. Preliminary intercultural workshops and excursions provided a common basis for dialogue and created a relaxed environment that gave participants an opportunity to get to know each other better and facilitated their ability to represent and respect the different points of view at a peace conference held in the Vienna International Centre.
Participants assumed full responsibility for the peace conference. Chairpersons, speakers, and the committee for the articulation of concluding resolutions consisted solely of youth participating in the Middle East Youth Peace Forum. After in part heated debates, the peace conference was concluded successfully, and its resolutions were forwarded to the respective national governments.
• For the first time, the youth who participated in the Middle East Youth Peace Forum had an opportunity to meet their peers from the region. As a result, prejudices were reduced, mutual trust developed, and friendships were made.
• The participants expressed their desire to further develop the newly established relationships.
At the end of the conference, participants and organisers agreed to repeat the meeting of the Middle East Youth Peace Forum in one of the countries of the region in the near future.

Peace Conference/UN-City

The participants agreed to put four general topics on the agenda: the conditions necessary for a just, lasting, and comprehensive peace in the Middle East, security for all parties involved, scenarios for a peaceful development of the region in the future, and the future of the Palestinians. The conference began with opening statements by each of the delegations, the chair persons and rapporteurs for the individual sessions rotated among the respective national delegations in the course of the conference.

Peace Conference at the Vienna International Centre
Friedenskonferenz im Vienna International Centre

Conclusions

A drafting committee met to draw up a series of resolutions on military and political issues and arms control; security in everyday life; economic, social, and environmental issues; education and culture. Individual points in these resolutions included:
• the importance of arms control, non-proliferation, and the limiting of non-conventional weapons in the region;
• the disarmament of radicals on all sides;
• the importance of the development of a sound economic infrastructure, especially in Palestinian regions;
• the establishment of a regional organisation to address social welfare issues;
• the necessity of regional water management and environmental protection;
• proposals for improving cross-cultural understanding and institutionalising educational exchange.

Observers were impressed by the participants'

Hiking in the Tyrolian Alps
Wandern in den Tiroler Alpen

openness, sincerity, capacity for hard work, commitment to the peace process, and comprehension of complex issues, such as refugee rights, the status of Jerusalem, border issues, and the final status of a Palestinian state.

Gründungstreffen in Wien und Tirol

Israelische, palästinensische, jordanische, ägyptische und österreichische Jugendliche trafen in Wien zur Nahost-Jugend-Friedenskonferenz zusammen. Nach dem Modell der Erwachsenen sollten die in ihrer Heimat als »Meinungsbildner« geltenden Teenager über den Friedensprozeß im Nahen Osten diskutieren. In interkulturellen Workshops und auf Ausflügen nach Tirol wurde eine gemeinsame Gesprächsbasis geschaffen und eine entspannte Atmosphäre, in der man einander besser kennenlernte und die es erleichterte, in der anschließenden Friedenskonferenz in der Wiener UNO-City die verschiedenen Standpunkte zu vertreten.
Die jungendlichen TeilnehmerInnen übernahmen die volle Verantwortung für den Ablauf der Konferenz. Vorsitzende, Vortragende und das Komitee für die Veröffentlichung der Schlußresolutionen stellten ausschließlich Mitglieder des Jugend-Friedensforums. Nach zum Teil hitzigen Debatten wurde eine positive Schlußbilanz der Friedenskonferenz gezogen, und die Resolutionen wurden an die nationalen Regierungen weitergeleitet.
• Die Jugendlichen bekamen durch das Forum zum ersten Mal die Gelegenheit, mit gleichaltrigen Vertretern der anderen Konfliktpartei zu sprechen. Es wurden Vorurteile abgebaut, gegenseitiges Vertrauen gefaßt und Freundschaften geschlossen.
• Die TeilnehmerInnen hofften auf eine Weiterentwicklung der neu geknüpften Beziehungen.
Am Ende der Konferenz waren TeilnehmerInnen und OrganisatorInnen dafür, das Treffen in einem der Länder der Nahostregion zu wiederholen.

Friedenskonferenz/UNO-City

Die TeilnehmerInnen einigten sich auf vier Themen: die Bedingungen für einen gerechten, dauerhaften und umfassenden Frieden im Nahen Osten, Sicherheit für alle, Entwurf für eine friedliche Entwicklung der Region, die Zukunft der Palästinenser. Die Konferenz begann mit einem Eröffnungsreferat jeder Delegation. Die Funktion des Vorsitzenden und jene des Berichterstatters wurde im Rotationsverfahren von allen nationalen Delegationen wahrgenommen.

Schlußfolgerungen
Ein Komitee war verantwortlich für den Entwurf der Resolutionen betreffend: militärische und politische Inhalte und Waffenkontrolle; Sicherheit im Alltag; wirtschaftliche, soziale und ökologische Themen; Bildung und Kultur. Im Detail wurde festgehalten:
• die Bedeutung von Waffenkontrolle, Nichtverbreitung und Begrenzung von nichtkonventionellen Waffen in der Region;
• die Entwaffnung aller radikalen Gruppen;
• die Entwicklung der wirtschaftlichen Infrastruktur, besonders in palästinensischen Gebieten;
• die Gründung einer regionalen Organisation zur Entwicklung von sozialen Wohlfahrtsstandards;
• die gemeinsame Verwaltung der Wasserressourcen und des Umweltschutzes;
• interkulturelles Engagement und Bildungsaustausch.

Die Beobachter waren beeindruckt von der Offenheit, Ehrlichkeit und der Bereitschaft der TeilnehmerInnen, hart zu arbeiten. Diese hatten ihr aufrichtiges Engagement für den Friedensprozeß und ihr Verständnis auch von komplexen Themen, wie Rechte der Flüchtlinge, Status von Jerusalem, Grenzprobleme und Gründung eines Palästinenserstaates, unter Beweis gestellt.

Farewell Party
Abschiedsparty

Overcoming Prejudice

During the years of the occupation there has been a growing prejudicial feeling in the Palestinian people's attitude towards the Israelis. For the Jewish people the same is true about the Palestinians. This prejudice is caused by three factors:
The first factor is the brainwashing that both sides go through. From early years of growing up, the Israelis learn that the Palestinians are killers and hostile people, and an Arab youth learns that the Jews are conquerors, that they are evil soldiers without any humanity.
The second factor is that we don't know them and they don't know us, thus each side invents weird ideas about the other side; ideas that in the real world have no basis and are wrong.
The last factor stems from fear. When we see a man with an oriental/eastern appearance, we automatically think that he is a terrorist. When Palestinians see an Israeli soldier, they automatically think that he is against them, that he will strike them or demolish their house. We must remember that prejudice does not stay "just" in thoughts for long, but changes after a while into hatred between the two sides. This hatred is very hard to overcome, but it is possible with efforts from both sides.

Guy Krom

Final evaluation
Abschließende Evaluierung

Überwinden von Vorurteilen

In den letzten Jahren der Besatzung gab es ständig wachsende Vorurteile der Palästinenser gegenüber den Israelis und umgekehrt. Diese Vorurteile werden von drei Faktoren bestimmt: Ersten sind beide Seiten ständig einer Gehirnwäsche ausgesetzt, die uns von klein auf lehrt, daß Palästinenser Mörder und Feinde sind und Juden Eroberer und böse Soldaten ohne Menschlichkeit. Zweitens kennen wir einander überhaupt nicht, und jeder erfindet über den anderen üble Geschichten, die mit der Wirklichkeit nichts zu tun haben. Und drittens haben wir Angst. Wenn wir einen Mann in orientalischer Kleidung sehen, denken wir automatisch, er sei ein Terrorist. Wenn Palästinenser einen israelischen Soldaten sehen, denken sie sofort, er wäre gegen sie, er wolle ihr Haus zerstören und sie schlagen. Wir müssen bedenken, daß Vorurteile nicht einfach in Gedanken bestehen, sondern nach einer gewissen Zeit in gegenseitigen Haß umschlagen. Es ist sehr schwer, diesen Haß zu überwinden, aber gemeinsam können wir es schaffen.

Guy Krom

Dear Bruno Kreisky Forum!

(Excuse this form of address)

After having left the airport and finally slept at home, I pick up my pen to thank you for everything. Thank you for giving me, and all the others, the opportunity to make friends from an entirely different part of the world. Thank you for giving me an insight into the workings of a peace conference and into the amount of work that is hidden behind it. With every new peace agreement in the news, I think of what it takes to reach a sound agreement.
I am thankful that I could get to know you all. I am thankful that my vacation plans for the year after next remain fixed, and for much, much more. The ten days in Vienna and Tirol have brought me more enjoyment, more friends and much more than I can express.

Orlando Mason

Liebes Bruno Kreisky Forum!

(Verzeiht die Form der Anrede)

Nachdem ich vom Flughafen gekommen bin und mich zu Hause endlich ausgeschlafen habe, greife ich zur Feder, um mich bei euch für alles zu bedanken. Danke, daß ihr mir (und allen anderen) die Möglichkeit gegeben habt, Freunde aus einem ganz anderen Teil der Welt zu gewinnen.
Danke, daß ihr mir einen Einblick in den Ablauf einer Friedenskonferenz gewährt habt und in die viele Arbeit, die dahintersteckt. Bei jedem neuen Friedensvertrag in den Nachrichten überlege ich mir, wie man eine vernünftige Übereinkunft finden könnte.
Ich bin dankbar, daß ich euch alle kennenlernen konnte. Ich bin dankbar, daß meine Urlaubspläne für übernächstes Jahr feststehen, und für vieles, vieles mehr. Ich habe in den zehn Tagen in Wien und Tirol viel Spaß gehabt, viele Freundschaften geschlossen und mehr gewonnen, als ich jemals ausdrücken könnte.

Orlando Mason

THE AUSTRIAN DELEGATION ACCOMPANIES FEDERAL PRESIDENT THOMAS KLESTIL ON HIS STATE VISIT TO ISRAEL
DIE ÖSTERREICHISCHE DELEGATION BEGLEITET BUNDESPRÄSIDENT THOMAS KLESTIL AUF STAATSBESUCH NACH ISRAEL
October/Oktober 1994

The Austrian participants were invited by Federal President Thomas Klestil to join him on his state visit to Israel. This gave them the unexpected opportunity to meet each other again.

Die österreichischen TeilnehmerInnen wurden von Bundespräsident Thomas Klestil eingeladen, ihn auf seinem Staatsbesuch nach Israel zu begleiten. Diese symbolische Geste brachte den Jugendlichen die unvorhergesehene Möglichkeit, einander sehr rasch wiederzusehen.

In the Old City of Jerusalem
In der Altstadt von Jerusalem

A Report

On the 13th of November 1994, 13 sleepy Austrians woke up to begin a journey that none of them would ever forget. At 8 o'clock in the morning, we left behind the dismal Austrian weather and three hours later landed in the late summer climate of Tel Aviv. We left the airport in a convoy, without any problems, and headed towards the city on the Mount of Olives. I think we were all pleased to see the Austrian flags that greeted us before the walls of Jerusalem.
As soon as we arrived at the youth hostel, we rushed up to the third floor to greet our Israeli friends. Our pleasure of meeting again was enormous as we had not seen each other for four long months. We were only able to stay there a short time before we started off for Yad Vashem, the holocaust memorial on Theodor Herzlberg. Although it was the president who should have arrived last, in the end it was us who were late. But nobody is perfect.
In the evening we met some members of the Palestinian delegation and, together with the Israelis, walked through Jerusalem by night. After a short night, we rushed through the north of the country, making short stops at Caesarea and Akko. Finally, we found ourselves almost on the border with Lebanon in the kibbutz where Itamar stays.
His father explained the tasks of the kibbutz. Unfortunately, we were all so tired that we were unable to give him our undivided attention. Once we were back at the youth hostel, there was frantic activity, for we were invited to a state reception. Everyone wanted to take a shower, dry their hair and try as much as possible to look their best. We drove to the King David Hotel, together with the Israeli delegation, where we saw people that we would normally only be able to admire on television. After the reception, some of us went to Fink's bar and the rest went back to free themselves from their formal clothing. Finally, we stretched our legs, walked around and fully enjoyed our last night in Jerusalem.

Heidrun Maier

Ein Reisebericht

Am 13. November 1994 standen 13 schläfrige ÖsterreicherInnen auf, um eine Reise anzutreten, die niemand von uns je vergessen wird. Um 8 Uhr morgens verließen wir das triste österreichische Wetter, und drei Stunden später landeten wir im spätsommerlichen Tel-Aviv. Ohne irgendwelche Probleme verließen wir den Flughafen im Konvoi und begaben uns in Richtung der Stadt am Ölberg.
Ich denke, wir alle freuten uns über die österreichischen Fahnen, die uns vor den Mauern Jerusalems begrüßten.

At the Wailing Wall
An der Klagemauer

In der Jugendherberge angekommen, stürmten wir in den dritten Stock, um unsere israelischen Freunde zu begrüßen. Unsere Wiedersehensfreude war enorm, denn schließlich hatten wir einander vier lange Monate nicht gesehen. Nur kurz konnten wir dort bleiben, denn schon bald fuhren wir nach Yad Vashem, zur Holocaust-Gedenkstätte am Theodor-Herzl-Berg.
Am Abend trafen wir noch einige Mitglieder der palästinensischen Delegation, und zusammen mit den Israelis spazierten wir durch das nächtliche Jerusalem.
Nach einer kurzen Nacht düsten wir durch den Norden des Landes, wobei wir in Caesarea und Akko kurz stehenblieben. Schließlich befanden wir uns fast an der Grenze zum Libanon, im Kibbutz, wo Itamar wohnt. Sein Vater erklärte uns dann die Aufgaben des Kibbutz. Leider waren wir alle schon sehr müde, sodaß er sich nicht unserer ungeteilten Aufmerksamkeit erfreuen konnte. Zurück in der Jugendherberge, begann ein hektisches Treiben, denn schließlich waren wir zum Staatsempfang eingeladen. Alle wollten duschen, die Haare fönen und waren bemüht, so gut wie möglich auszusehen.
Zusammen mit der israelischen Delegation fuhren wir dann ins »King David« Hotel, wo wir jene Leute sahen, die wir sonst nur im Fernsehen bewundern konnten.
Nach dem Empfang gingen einige Leute in die Fink's Bar, und der Rest befreite sich von der lästigen formalen Kleidung.
Abschließend schüttelten wir noch unsere Beine im »Underground« aus und genossen unsere letzte Nacht in Jerusalem in vollen Zügen.

Heidrun Maier

1995
FROM COEXISTENCE AND TOLERANCE TO CO-OPERATION AND FRIENDSHIP
VON KOEXISTENZ UND TOLERANZ ZU ZUSAMMENARBEIT UND FREUNDSCHAFT
August 9–15, 1995, Lindabrunn (Austria)

The Middle East Youth Peace Forum goes on

Israeli, Palestinian, and Austrian youth met at a recreational and conference centre in Lindabrunn in order to actively work on confidence building measures and on the popularisation of the peace process in the Middle East. A number of the participants had attended the first Middle East Youth Peace Forum in 1994 and had stayed in touch with each other throughout the intervening year. With the help of these "old hands", youth participating for the first time were quickly integrated into the group of proponents of the idea of constructive change in the Middle East conflict.

The objective of the second Middle East Youth Peace Forum was to articulate concrete projects upon the basis of a fixed procedure. The multinational groups of youth were encouraged to approach tasks commensurate with their everyday realities and ability to influence change. The realisation and continuation of projects was to follow up in the respective homelands of the participants who agreed upon three projects:

- *An Israeli-Palestinian newsletter, "The New Generation": a brochure in English to be circulated among Israeli and Palestinian youth.*
- *A Youth Forum radio programme: a feature produced by members of the Youth Forum to be broadcasted by Israeli and Palestinian radio.*
- *A peace camp in the desert: participants wanted to organise a peace camp in the desert for Israeli and Palestinian children in order to further propagate the ideas of the Middle East Youth Peace Forum.*

Das Nahost-Jugend-Friedensforum geht weiter

Israelische, palästinensische und österreichische Jugendliche kamen im Erholungszentrum Lindabrunn zusammen, um über vertrauensbildende Maßnahmen aktiv an der Popularisierung des Nahostfriedensprozesses mitzuarbeiten. Ein Teil der Jugendlichen hatte bereits am ersten Jugend-Friedensforum, 1994, teilgenommen und die Kontakte untereinander während des gesamten Jahres nicht abreißen lassen. Die Neuhinzugekommenen wurden mit Hilfe der »Routiniers« rasch in die Gruppe der VerfechterInnen der Idee der konstruktiven Veränderung im Nahostkonflikt integriert.

Ziel des zweiten Jugend-Friedensforums war es, auf der Basis eines festgelegten Prozederes konkrete Projekte zu erarbeiten. Abseits von abstrakten Resolutionen sollten die gemischten Jugendgruppen an Aufgaben herangehen, die mit ihren Lebensrealitäten und Einflußmöglichkeiten in Einklang stehen. Umsetzung und Weiterführung der gemeinsam beschlossenen Projekte sollten in der Heimat der TeilnehmerInnen geschehen. Die Gruppe nennt sich von nun an »Die Neue Generation«.

- Israelisch-Palästinensischer Newsletter »The New Generation«: Eine Info-Broschüre, in englischer Sprache verfaßt, soll an israelische und palästinensische Jugendliche verteilt werden.
- Eigene Radiosendung: Ein von Mitgliedern des Jugendforums produziertes Feature soll in einem israelischen und einem palästinensischen Radioprogramm ausgestrahlt werden.
- Friedenscamp in der Wüste: Die Jugendlichen wollen ein Friedenscamp in der Wüste für israelische und palästinensische Kinder und Teenager organisieren, um die Ideen des Nahost-Jugend-Friedensforums weiterzutragen.

Message of Federal Minister Rudolf Scholten

Dear friends,
in this year, 1995, we remember the end of World War II. However, commemoration is not enough. Today we are still witnessing war, aggression and bloodshed throughout the world. We know that peace is not simply absence of war and that everyone of us is responsible for making peace and keeping it. From coexistence and tolerance to co-operation and friendship is a long or a short way, depending on your ideas and your courage. You might change history, you must change history – or rather – you have the chance to change history.

Grußbotschaft von Bundesminister Rudolf Scholten

Liebe Freunde,
in diesem Jahr 1995 begehen wir den 50. Jahrestag seit dem Ende des Zweiten Weltkriegs. Aber erinnern alleine ist nicht genug. Wir sind auch heute Zeugen von Krieg, Aggression und Blutvergießen. Wir wissen, daß Frieden nicht nur die Abwesenheit von Krieg ist und daß es unsere Verantwortung ist, Frieden zu schaffen und zu erhalten. Von Koexistenz und Toleranz zu Zusammenarbeit und Freundschaft ist es ein kurzer oder ein langer Weg, der von euren Ideen und eurem Mut bestimmt wird. Ihr könnt die Geschichte ändern, ihr müßt die Geschichte ändern – oder eher –, ihr habt die Chance, die Geschichte zu ändern.

An open letter to the Youth Peace Forum participants

Dear Friends,
first of all, I'm sorry that I'm not addressing you personally, but since it is important for me to include all of you in my thoughts, I have decided to write and ask Eran to pass them on to you ... You must know that – even though it's impossible for us to come to you and in many cases it's even impossible to contact you during our service in the army – we haven't forgotten you or the wonderful experience we had together, and it cheers us up in our hardest and saddest moments.
In Austria we discovered that there is another way – that it is possible to sit and talk, not always to agree, but to listen and exchange views. Continue, all of you together and each one on his own, to work toward the continuation of the co-operation. It is very important to me personally, despite the limitations to continue keeping contact with you ... I miss you all, and it is very sad that I'm not with you. I'm happy that others are with you, and together you will walk the way we created a year ago.

Guy Krom,
a 1994 participant who could not attend the meeting because he was serving in the Israeli Army

Ein offener Brief an die Teilnehmer des Nahost-Jugend-Friedensforums

... Ich möchte euch nur sagen, auch wenn wir während unserer Militärzeit nicht zu euch kommen können und es oft sogar keine Möglichkeit gibt, euch zu kontaktieren, sollt ihr wissen, daß wir die wunderbare gemeinsame Erfahrung des letzten Jahres nicht vergessen haben und sie uns in schwierigen Momenten nicht verzagen läßt. Wir haben in Österreich einen anderen Weg kennengelernt – die Möglichkeit zusammenzusitzen und zu diskutieren, einander zuzuhören, auch wenn wir nicht immer übereinstimmen, und Ansichten auszutauschen. Macht weiter, ihr alle zusammen und jeder für sich! ... Ich vermisse euch sehr, und ich bin traurig, nicht bei euch zu sein, aber auch froh, daß andere mit euch auf unserem Weg weitergehen.

Guy Krom,
ein Teilnehmer aus dem Jahr 1994, der nicht dabeisein konnte, weil er seinen Militärdienst absolvierte

Fida and Karin at the airport in Vienna
Fida und Karin am Wiener Flughafen

Arrival of the delegations in Vienna
Ankunft der Delegationen in Wien

The idea of coexistence needs great effort to succeed

Impressions from the Coexistence Forum in Vienna, August 1995

It was six o'clock in the afternoon on August 9, 1995, when the participants met in Vienna for the second Forum for Coexistence, Co-operation and Friendship, which was organised by the Bruno Kreisky Forum for International Dialogue.

Hugging, kissing and exchanging flowers expressed the feelings of the Austrian, Palestinian and Israeli delegations. It was a wonderful reception which attracted the attention of many people at the Vienna airport. Then a bus took us to a tourist resort on a small hill near Vienna.

Once we arrived, we were first divided into groups and then entered the residence building for a short welcoming party. It was midnight, when I was lying in bed, thinking of the reasons that had motivated the Austrians to bring us to such a far and quiet area that contains all of nature's beauty.

In this fantastic atmosphere the leaders could really succeed in breaking up the dividings between the participants, during social activities, trips and picnics in the area. The most important and interesting picnic was at a sanctuary area, where the President of the Austrian Parliament hosted us in his wonderful summer house and let us walk around freely in his home.

He was indeed very frank, kind and open minded with us. I had the privilege of having a long conversation with him. He talked to me about the system of democratic elections, the rights and duties of the President of the State, the presidential elections and relations between Austria and its neighbouring countries. We also talked about the phenomenon of suicide and the danger of drinking alcohol at an early age.

The pivot of our discussions during the seminar was the question of "How can we move from coexistence to co-operation and friendship"? To discuss this question the participants of the Peace Forum were divided into four groups. Each group tried to work out the three most important projects to be carried out.

We formed a small committee with one representative from each group and each delegation, to present the ideas. Out of all the proposals the committee adopted three projects:

1. Publication of a monthly newsletter in English that would have the name "The New Generation". Editorial staff and reporters were elected and a deadline for submitting articles, reports, and letters was suggested. We also discussed some technical details, such as a place for our meetings and methods of distributing the newsletter. Once the newsletter will begin to appear regularly, Israeli and Palestinian newspapers will be approached to help with the distribution.
2. Preparation of a regular, weekly or monthly two-hour radio programme that would be broadcasted on Israeli and Palestinian radio stations. The main aim of these programmes will be to transmit the message of Israeli-Palestinian coexistence, co-operation and friendship.
3. Organising joint trips, outings and camps for both Israeli and Palestinian youth. A joint committee will be responsible for organising the first activities in this direction. Such as a trip to Eilat, as well as shorter hikes.
An Israeli and a Palestinian were also elected to look for a suitable place in Jerusalem that could serve as a joint meeting place and as a cultural centre.
The mutual respect and the patience to listen to each other during the discussion were the important achievements of the Peace Forum. It was completed by dancing and laughing, which were the expression of finer feelings and innocent emotions of all delegation members.
The participants of the Peace Forum wrote letters to Arafat and Peres, encouraging them to continue the peace process, not giving the enemies of peace a chance to destroy it.
During the return trip the Israeli and the Palestinian delegations appeared as one. They exchanged addresses and hugged and joked on the flight home. The participants of the 1995 Peace Forum recognised the fact that achieving true peace in friendship and co-operation will require ongoing efforts.
Finally, we all wish to thank again the good people of the Bruno Kreisky Forum, the Israeli Ministry of Education and the Orient House for their fantastic efforts in making this project possible.

Basheer Basheer

Friedliches Zusammenleben setzt große Bemühungen voraus

Eindrücke vom Koexistenz-Forum in Wien, August 1995
Es war der 9. August 1995, sechs Uhr nachmittags, als wir einander wiedersahen zum zweiten Jugend-Friedensforum für Zusammenarbeit, Freundschaft und Koexistenz, das das Bruno Kreisky Forum organisiert hatte. Umarmungen und Blumen zur Begrüßung brachten die Freude der ÖsterreicherInnen, Israelis und PalästinenserInnen zum Ausdruck und erregten die Aufmerksamkeit der anderen Ankommenden am Flughafen Schwechat. Anschließend brachte uns ein Bus in ein kleines Feriendorf in der Nähe von Wien. Nach der Unterbringung in Pavillons trafen wir einander im Hauptgebäude zu einer Willkommensparty. Als ich lange nach Mitternacht im Bett lag und nicht einschlafen konnte, dachte ich darüber nach, was die Österreicher wohl für Motive haben könnten, uns in diese schöne, ruhige Gegend, weit weg von zu Hause, zu bringen. In dieser phantastischen Atmosphäre gelang es den LeiterInnen, die Trennlinien zwischen uns zum Verschwinden zu bringen und in Spielen und Ausflügen das Eis zu brechen. Der interessanteste Ausflug war zur Hohen Wand, wo uns der österreichische Parlamentspräsident Dr. Heinz Fischer in seinem Sommerhaus empfing. Er war freundlich, offen und interessiert, und ich hatte das Privileg, ein langes Gespräch mit ihm zu führen. Er erklärte mir das parlamentarische System, demokratische Wahlen, die Rechte und Pflichten des Bundespräsidenten und die Beziehungen Österreichs zu seinen Nachbarstaaten. Wir sprachen aber auch über Probleme der Jugendlichen, wie Selbstmord und Alkohol.
Unsere Diskussionen während des Seminars drehten sich hauptsächlich um die Frage, wie wir von Zusammenleben zu Zusammenarbeit und Freundschaft kommen können. In vier Arbeitsgruppen versuchten wir, darauf eine Antwort zu finden, und wählten drei wichtige Projekte pro Gruppe aus. Ein Komitee, in dem jede Gruppe und jede Delegation vertreten war, wählte schließlich aus allen Vorschlägen drei zur Realisierung aus, nämlich:
1. Die Veröffentlichung eines gemeinsamen Newsletters in englischer Sprache mit dem Titel »The New Generation«. Wir wählten das Redaktionsteam, die HerausgeberInnen, wir klärten technische Details und besprachen die Möglichkeiten des Vertriebes.
2. Eine wöchentliche oder monatliche

Radiosendung, von israelischen und palästinensischen Sendern ausgestrahlt, um die Botschaft von israelisch-palästinensischer Freundschaft und Zusammenarbeit zu verbreiten.
3. Friedenscamps und gemeinsame Ausflüge für israelische und palästinensische Jugendliche, von einem gemeinsamen Komitee organisiert.
Wir wählten außerdem einen israelischen und einen palästinensischen Vertreter, um in Jerusalem einen geeigneten Ort für gemeinsame Treffen zu finden.
Wir lernten in diesem Forum gegenseitigen Respekt und geduldiges Zuhören, wir lachten und tanzten miteinander und brachten so die Gefühle des Vertrauens und der Nähe zum Ausdruck, die in uns allen gewachsen waren.
Wir schrieben einen Brief an Präsident Arafat und Minister Peres, in dem wir sie zum Weitermachen im Friedensprozeß aufforderten, um den Feinden des Friedens keine Chance zu geben. Auf der Rückreise schienen wir eine einzige Delegation zu sein. Wir tauschten unsere Adressen aus, umarmten einander und scherzten miteinander, wußten aber auch, daß wahrer Frieden viel Engagement und Anstrengung braucht.
Wir möchten all den lieben Menschen im Kreisky Forum, im israelischen Erziehungsministerium und im Orient House danken, daß sie dieses Projekt ermöglicht haben.

Basheer Basheer

A personal message by the Austrian Federal Chancellor Franz Vranitzky

Dear young friends,
at the end of the Middle East Youth Peace Forum in Austria in July 1994 all participants expressed their wish to continue their relationship, and I am very pleased that this desire already has led to a number of follow-up meetings. In spite of many problems, the peace process in the Middle East is making progress and there is genuine hope that your parents will succeed in building the foundations for a just and lasting peace in the region. With your meeting here in Austria you are making a contribution to this important goal. I therefore wish you a pleasant stay and many hours of enlightening discussions in the spirit of mutual understanding.

Persönliche Botschaft von Bundeskanzler Franz Vranitzky

Liebe junge Freunde!
Am Ende des Forums 1994 sprachen sich alle TeilnehmerInnen für eine Fortsetzung ihrer Beziehungen aus, und ich freue mich, daß es bereits zahlreiche Treffen zwischen euch gegeben hat. Trotz vieler Probleme geht der Friedensprozeß weiter, und es besteht berechtigte Hoffnung, daß eure Eltern das Fundament für einen gerechten und dauerhaften Frieden in der Region legen werden. Mit eurer Arbeit hier in Österreich leistet ihr einen wichtigen Beitrag zur Erreichung dieses Zieles. Ich wünsche euch einen guten Aufenthalt und viele anregende Diskussionen im Geiste des gegenseitigen Verstehens.

1996
MARGIT SCHMIDT AND GERTRAUD AUER ON A FACT FINDING TOUR IN THE MIDDLE EAST
REISE VON MARGIT SCHMIDT UND GERTRAUD AUER IN DEN NAHEN OSTEN ZUR VORBEREITUNG VON »CROSSING BORDERS«
***February*/Februar 1996**

Shulamit Aloni *(Minister)*
Mahdi F. Abdul Hadi *(President of PASSIA)*
Naila Sabra *(UN World Food Programme Gaza)*
Uri Savir *(Director General Ministry of Foreign Affairs)*
Haider Abdel Shafi *(Gaza)*
Lea Rabin *(Tel Aviv)*
Teddy Kollek *(Jerusalem Foundation)*
Ziyyad Abu Zayyad *(Palestinian National Council Member)*
Feisal Husseini *(Orient House)*
Prof. Bravermann *(President of Ben Gurion University, Beer Sheva)*
Amos Oz *(writer)*
Doron Shohat *(Central Office of Information, Prime Minister's Office)*
Hanna Nasir *(President of Bir Zeit University)*
Sumaya Farhat-Nasr *(writer)*
Terje Rød Larssen *(UN Coordinator Gaza, Oslo negotiator)*
Yair Hirschfeld *(Oslo negotiator)*

Visit to Israeli and Palestinian Institutions
Besuch von israelischen und palästinensischen Einrichtungen

The trip was meant to prepare the "Crossing Borders" project. Two heavy bomb attacks in Jerusalem and Ashkelon on February 25th killed many people and left the country in a deep shock.

Diese Reise wurde zur Vorbereitung von »Crossing Borders« unternommen. Am 25. Februar wurden zwei Bombenattentate in Jerusalem und Ashkelon verübt, die viele Menschen das Leben kosteten und das Land in einen tiefen Schock versetzten.

Programme/Programm

Meeting with the Israeli and Palestinian youth to discuss the current situation
Meeting with Israeli and Palestinian personalities

Meeting mit den israelischen und palästinensischen Jugendlichen zur aktuellen Situation
Meeting mit israelischen und palästinensischen Persönlichkeiten

Jerusalem:
Knesset,
Ministry of Education
PASSIA (Palestinian Academic Society for the Study of International Affairs)
Al Wasiti-Palestinian Art Center
Municipality of Jerusalem
Jerusalem Foundation
Orient House
Gaza: trip through Gaza Strip accompanied by an UN representative
Haifa: Beit Hagefen Arab-Jewish Centre
Akko: The Sir Charles Clore Jewish Arab Community Centre
Beer Sheva/University
Neve Shalom/Wahat al-Salam
Bir Zeit/University
Nablus and Ramallah

In the garden of the American Colony Hotel, Jerusalem
Im Garten des American Colony Hotels, Jerusalem
In Haifa

DELEGATION LEADERS' CONFERENCE
KONFERENZ DER DELEGATIONSLEITER/INNEN
Aqaba/Jordan
June/Juni 1996

Israeli delegation: Tali Lidar and Orly Fruchter Yagodovsky
Palestinian delegation: Hani Husseini and Wa'el Abu Nemeh
Jordanian delegation: Issam Arida
Austrian delegation: Margit Schmidt, Tove Raiby and Gertraud Auer

Last preparations for "Crossing Borders"
Tove Raiby and Gertraud Auer "rehearse" the crossing of the three borders between Jordan, Israel and Egypt.
Unfortunately Egypt did not send a delegation. As a consequence the Taba crossing was not put on the programme.

Letzte Vorbereitungen für »Crossing Borders«;
Tove Raiby und Gertraud Auer »überqueren probeweise« zu Fuß in einer Tagestour die drei Grenzen zwischen Jordanien, Israel und Ägypten.
Leider schickte Ägypten keine Delegation. Daher wurde der Aufenthalt in Taba aus dem Programm genommen.

Tali Lidar, Wa'el Abu Nemeh

CROSSING BORDERS
GRENZEN ÜBERSCHREITEN
Eilat–Aqaba–Bethlehem
September 1–10, 1996

The initiative travels to the homes of the involved

During the first ten days of September, Israeli, Palestinian, Jordanian and Austrian participants of the Middle East Youth Peace Forum crossed borders at Eilat, Aqaba and Bethlehem in order to discuss together what it means to physically and mentally overcome borders.
Each group involved in the Peace Forum presented their own culture; meetings with local youth of border cities were organised in order to reduce contact anxieties and prejudices; peace trees were planted in each community; and the ideas of "The New Generation" were transmitted in discussions. A new list of multinational projects was worked out and the "New Generation" is still working on these and other projects.
The Austrian Federal Chancellor Franz Vranitzky personally contributed to the realisation of "Crossing Borders" to a great extent by donating the $ 50,000 financial award associated with his receipt of the 1995 J. William Fulbright Prize for International Understanding to the Middle East Youth Peace Forum. Mr Vranitzky came to Eilat to start the programme by addressing the group and discussing the issue of the peace process.

Die Initiative geht in die Heimat der Betroffenen

In den ersten zehn Septembertagen überquerten österreichische, israelische, palästinensische und jordanische TeilnehmerInnen des Jugend-Friedensforums 96 die Grenzen bei Eilat, Aqaba und Bethlehem, um gemeinsam zu erleben, was es heißt, physische und psychologische Grenzen zu überwinden.
Jede Gruppe hatte Gelegenheit, ihr eigenes Land zu präsentieren, in den Grenzstädten wurden Begegnungen mit der lokalen Jugend organisiert, um Berührungsängste und Vorurteile abzubauen, an jedem Ort wurden Friedensbäume gepflanzt und in Diskussionen die Ideen von friedlicher Koexistenz und Zusammenarbeit vermittelt. Die »Neue Generation« erarbeitete eine neue Liste von multilateralen Projekten, die seither konsequent und mit Engagement verfolgt werden. »Crossing Borders« wurde in besonderem Maße durch die persönliche Spende des österreichischen Bundeskanzlers Dr. Franz Vranitzky unterstützt, der den mit $ 50.000 dotierten »Fulbright-Preis für Leistungen um die internationale Verständigung« dem Nahost-Jugend-Friedensforum stiftete. Dr. Vranitzky kam eigens nach Eilath, um das Nahost-Jugend-Friedensforum zu eröffnen und mit den Jugendlichen den Friedenprozeß zu diskutieren.

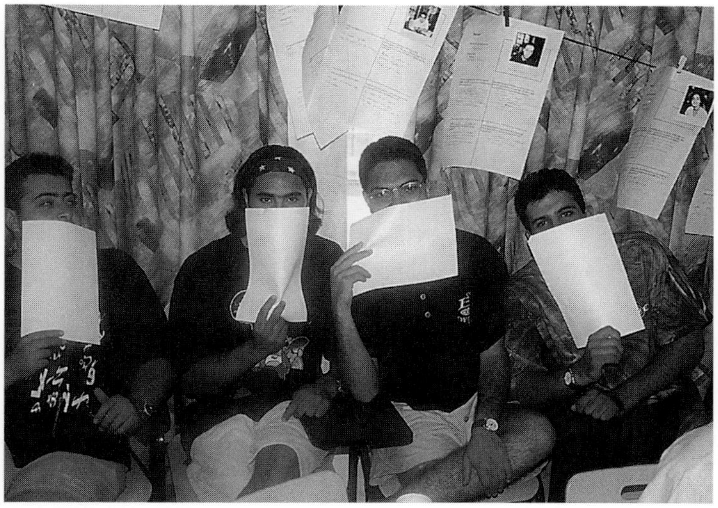

Working / Arbeiten
Crossing borders / Grenzen überschreiten
Joking / Lachen
Discussing /Diskutieren
Cultural presentation / Kulturelle Darbietung

1996

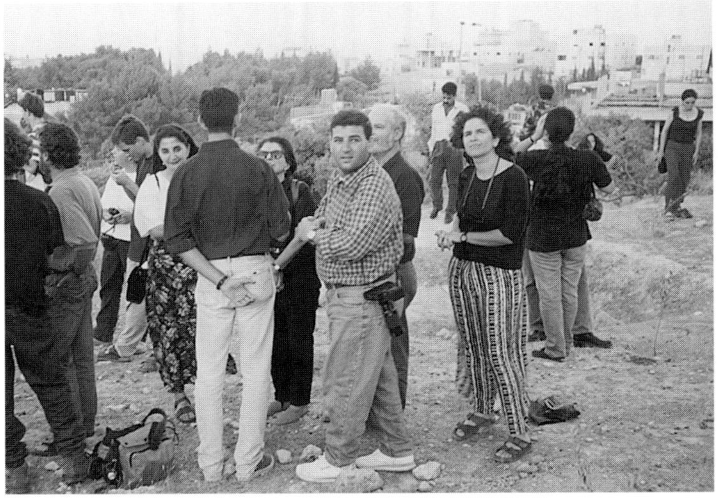

Excursion to Wadi Rum, Jordan
Ausflug nach Wadi Rum, Jordanien
Tree planting in Aqaba, Jordan
Bäumepflanzen in Aqaba, Jordanien

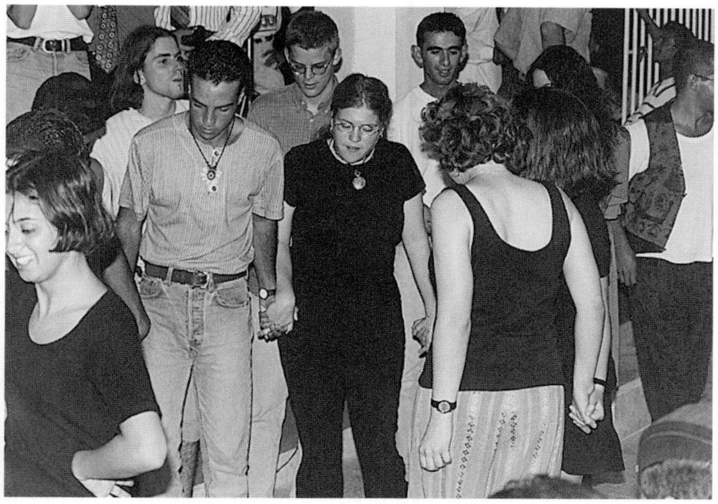

Nativity Church, Bethlehem
Geburtskirche, Bethlehem
SOS Children's Village, Bethlehem
SOS-Kinderdorf, Bethlehem
Dabka dancing
Dabka-Tanzen
Tearful farewell
Tränenreicher Abschied

Crossing Borders, Diary
Crossing Borders, Tagebuch

***Sunday*/Sonntag 01.09.**
Arriving in Eilat;
Reception by the Mayor of Eilat, Mr Gabi Kadosh, in honor of Austrian Federal Chancellor Franz Vranitzky;
Party at the youth hostel

Ankunft aller Delegationen in Eilat, Transfer zur Jugendherberge;
Empfang des Bürgermeisters von Eilat Gabi Kadosh zu Ehren von Bundeskanzler Dr. Franz Vranitzky;
Willkommensparty in der Jugendherberge

***Monday*/Montag, 02.09.**
Lecture by Chancellor Franz Vranitzky
Plenary
- *Introduction*
  Motivation – Expectation – Comments
- *Presentation of the Israeli delegation*
  1. *"My piece of culture"*
  2. *"My country, my home"*
- *Working groups*
  Topic: "Crossing borders"

Kibbutz Yotvata, Planting trees at the International Birdwatching Sanctuary
Party organised by the Palestinians

Vortrag Bundeskanzler Franz Vranitzky und Diskussion mit den Jugendlichen;
Plenum:
- Einführung
  Motivation – Erwartungen – Kommentare
- Präsentation der israelischen Delegation
  1. »Mein Stück Kultur«
  2. »Mein Land, meine Heimat«
- Arbeitsgruppen
  Thema: »Crossing borders«

Kibbutz Yotvata, Bäume pflanzen. Beginn eines Friedenswaldes im International Birdwatching Sanctuary;
Von den Palästinensern organisierte Party

***Tuesday*/Dienstag, 03.09.**
Plenary: Topic: The "New Generation" 1995 projects;
Eilat High School, meeting with students in different working groups;
Undersea Observatory and Eilat surroundings;

Working groups on the topic "Crossing borders";
Evening activities in downtown Eilat with local youth

Plenum
Thema: »The-New-Generation«-1995-Projekte;
Gymnasium von Eilat, Diskussion mit den StudentInnen in verschiedenen Arbeitsgruppen über das Nahost-Jugend-Friedensforum;
Unterwasser-Observatorium und Tour in Eilat und Umgebung;
Arbeitsgruppen zum Thema »Crossing borders«;
Abend im Zentrum von Eilat mit einheimischen Jugendlichen

***Wednesday*/Mittwoch, 04.09.**
Mosaic "New Generation"
A Mosaic, representing the idea of the "New Generation" spirit, was created by all participants to be left behind at the border between Israel and Jordan, in Aqaba and in Bethlehem as a symbol for visitors who cross the border.
Emergency plenary:
• *Problems to continue the programme for Israeli security reasons:*
The Israeli authorities suddenly withdrew the clearance for the Israeli group to stay over night in Bethlehem. Palestinian decision to compromise made the continuation possible.

Mosaik »New Generation«
Ein Mosaik, das die Idee der »Neuen Generation« vermittelt, wird von allen TeilnehmerInnen gestaltet und an der Grenze zwischen Israel und Jordanien, in Aqaba und in Bethlehem, hinterlassen.
Krisenplenum:
• Die Jugendlichen werden informiert, daß das Programm aufgrund von Sicherheitsproblemen möglicherweise abgebrochen werden muß.
Die israelischen Behörden entziehen der israelischen Gruppe die Erlaubnis, in Bethlehem zu übernachten. Die Kompromißbereitschaft auf palästinensischer Seite ermöglichte die Weiterreise.

***Thursday*/Donnerstag, 05.09.**
Crossing the border Eilat–Aqaba by walking.
Hand over the mosaic to the border officer
Arrival in Aqaba –
Welcoming by the Jordanian delegation leader Samar Kildani and the Mayor of Aqaba
Departure to Wadi Rum – Visit to Bedouin tents

Chancellor Franz Vranitzky with the participants in Eilat
Bundeskanzler Franz Vranitzky mit den Teilnehmern in Eilat

Members' welcoming party organised by the Jordanians, Sabelah youth join the group.

Abfahrt nach Aqaba;
Überqueren der Grenze zwischen Israel und Jordanien zu Fuß;
Das Mosaik wird feierlich dem Grenzkommandanten übergeben;
Ankunft in Aqaba – Unterbringung im Youth Camp;
Empfang durch die jordanische Delegationsleiterin Samar Kildani und den Bürgermeister von Aqaba;
Abfahrt zum Wadi Rum;
Willkommensparty der Jordanier; Sabelah-Jugendliche kommen zum gemeinsamen Fest

***Friday*/Freitag, 06.09.**
Lecture by the Governor of the District of Aqaba, HE. Mr Turk;
Presentation of the Jordanian delegation;
Luncheon at the Army Headquarters of Aqaba
with army officials: Traditional food – Mansaf Youth Department;
Tree Planting in the garden of the youth center, hand over the second mosaic

Vortrag des Gouverneurs von Aqaba, HE. Mr. Turk;
Präsentation der jordanischen Delegation;
Mittagessen im Militär Hauptquartier von Aqaba, traditionelles Essen – Mansaf
Aqaba; Bäume pflanzen im Jugendzentrum

Tali and Orly with Jordanian military officials
Tali und Orly mit jordanischen Armeevertretern

***Saturday*/Samstag, 07.09.**
Plenary
Presentation of the Austrian delegation
Working groups;
New projects for the coming year;
Emergency meeting due to message that Israeli authorities withdrew clearance for Israeli group to enter Bethlehem; the Israeli delegation leaders asked the parents to take over responsibility.

Plenum;
Präsentation der österreichischen Delegation
Arbeitsgruppen: die Projekte des kommenden Jahres;
Krisenplenum nach Erhalt der Nachricht, daß den israelischen TeilnehmerInnen die Erlaubnis entzogen wurde, nach Bethlehem zu fahren; die israelischen LeiterInnen bitten die Eltern, die Verantwortung zu übernehmen.

***Sunday*/Sonntag, 08.09.**
Petra – Sightseeing;
Allenby/King Hussein Bridge/Karame Bridge;
Crossing borders;
Arrival in Bethlehem;
Dinner with city officials·

Petra – Sigthseeing;
Allenby/King Hussein/Karame Bridge;
Überqueren der Grenze zwischen Jordanien, Israel und den palästinensischen Gebieten;
Ankunft in Bethlehem;
Abendessen mit Vertretern der Bethlehemer Stadtverwaltung

***Monday*/Montag, 09.09.**
Deheisheh Refugee Camp (UNWRA);
Lecture by the headmaster of the Deheisheh Boys Preparatory School and meeting with students;
Headquarters of Palestinian Police Forces at the "County";
Meeting with the commander and officers of the DCO
Presentation of the Palestinian delegation;
Plenary on the working group proposals;
Selection of projects;
Tree planting in Beit Sahour;
Summing-up Plenary and Farewell Party

Deheisheh Flüchtlingslager (UNWRA);
Vortrag des Direktors der Deheisheh Volksschule für Knaben und Diskussion mit den Schülern;
Hauptquartier der Palestinian Police Forces im »County«;
Diskussion mit dem Kommandanten;
Präsentation der palästinensischen Delegation;
Plenum zu den Projekten der Arbeitsgruppen;
Auswahl der Projekte;
Bäume pflanzen in Beit Sahour;
Abschlußplenum und Abschiedsfest

***Tuesday*/Dienstag, 10.09.**
Early morning tour of Bethlehem;

Hiba and Abeer in traditional dresses
Hiba und Abeer in traditionellen Kleidern

SOS Children's Village – Austrian Initiative;
Departure to Jerusalem;
Luncheon at the Austrian Hospice in the Old City for the Austrian delegation offered by Mr Donatus Köck, Austrian Embassy;
Departure to Vienna

Tour in Bethlehem, Abschied in der Geburtskirche;
Israelische Delegation fährt nach Jerusalem;
Besuch des SOS-Kinderdorfes in Bethlehem;
Abfahrt nach Jerusalem;
Verabschiedung der jordanischen und der palästinensischen Delegation;
Mittagessen im Österreichischen Hospiz in der Altstadt für die österreichische Delegation; Gastgeber: Gesandter Dr. Donatus Köck
Abfahrt zum Ben-Gurion-Flughafen und Rückflug nach Wien

Deheisheh Refugee Camp (UNWRA) in Bethlehem
Das Deheisheh-Flüchtlingslager (UNWRA) in Bethlehem

"Ten days of hope, ten days of dreams, ten days of achievement ..."

The situation in the region had been totally different at the time that this trip was planned. There was a feeling of euphoria after the signing of the peace treaty between Israel and Jordan, the Oslo II Agreement, and the future seemed to be more hopeful. The killing of Prime Minister Yitzhak Rabin, as well as the bombing of buses within Israel and the Israeli actions in Lebanon, both of which involved the killing of civilians, shocked the people and changed the atmosphere completely. The closure of the West Bank and Gaza Strip brought economic disaster to the Palestinians, while the result of the Israeli elections altered the timetable of the peace negotiations.
At a conference of the delegation leaders in Aqaba, in June, we again went over ways of facing the realities of getting permits for the Palestinians, and permission for the Israelis to go into the PA. No obstacles arose until the beginning of our journey. The young people wanted to go ahead and we could see the fruits of our continuous efforts in the relatively easy manner in which newcomers were integrated into the group.
However, the group experienced how difficult it still is to cross borders, while waiting for hours to go through passport controls, but especially when faced with the possibility that the Israeli members of the group would not be allowed to stay in Bethlehem for security reasons. But the emotional interaction among the members of the group and their appeals motivated the delegation leaders to do their utmost to save the project. The will of the Palestinian group leaders to compromise strengthened the feeling of trust and encouraged the Israeli group leaders to propose a transfer of responsibility for permission to stay in Bethlehem, from the government authorities to the parents. Miraculously, at the King Hussein/Allenby/Karame bridge, just before crossing the border, we received permission from 22 Israeli parents (out of 24) for their children to stay in Bethlehem. We were received and looked after by the Palestinian Police Forces who took full responsibility for our security. For the young people, it was the most exciting moment, expressed by Mike, a Palestinian participant, in the last evaluation round before we all parted:
"Ten days of hope, ten days of dreams, ten days of achievement ..., the biggest one is that we are all together here in Bethlehem."
This idea was shared by all the participants who have now developed a real group feeling. Since the return to Vienna, letters and e-mails have reached the Kreisky Forum: words of gratitude, words of concern during the subsequent uprising, words of courage and of hope. A meeting of the Austrian members of the group with the leaders of the other delegations, in Vienna at the end of November, showed that work has already been done on the projects, and that there is a strong will to continue. There have been interviews on the air, the video team has finished a film, the documentary group has started with a photo album, the newsletter team is collecting

articles; lectures at schools will be arranged, and a web page will be created for the "New Generation".
While all these activities will not change the situation, they will affect those who are involved, by helping them to overcome frustrations and to convince others that there are ways and means of interaction without hatred and arms. Politicians can formulate declarations of principles and sign agreements, but people have to carry them through to live in peace.

M.S., G.A., T.R.

»Zehn Tage der Hoffnung, der Träume und des Erfolges«

Als wir die Reise planten, stellte sich die Region in einem ganz anderen Lichte dar. Euphorische Gefühle begleiteten den Friedensvertrag zwischen Israel und Jordanien, und nach dem Oslo-II-Abkommen schien die Zukunft hoffnungsvoller. Die Ermordung von Ministerpräsident Rabin, die Terroranschläge auf israelische Busse, die israelischen Militäraktionen im Libanon, die auf beiden Seiten unschuldige Zivilisten das Leben kosteten, stürzten die Menschen in einen tiefen Schock und veränderten vollständig das politische Klima. Die Sperre der Westbank und des Gazastreifens wirkte sich auf die palästinensische Wirtschaft verheerend aus, und der Ausgang der israelischen Wahlen änderte den Fahrplan der Friedensverhandlungen.
Anläßlich der DelegationsleiterInnenkonferenz in Aqaba im Juni setzten wir uns mit diesen neuen Realitäten auseinander und versuchten trotz allem, Ausreisedokumente für Palästinenser und die Zustimmung für die Israelis zur Einreise in die palästinensischen Gebiete zu bekommen. Bis zum Beginn des Programms tauchten dann keine neuen Schwierigkeiten auf, und wir erkannten die Früchte unserer Bemühungen bereits daran, wie schnell »Neue« in die Gruppe integriert wurden.
Allerdings machte die Gruppe die Erfahrung, wie schwierig es ist, Grenzen zu überqueren, wie viele Stunden Grenzkontrollen dauern können, wie ihren israelischen Freunden die Einreise nach Bethlehem aus »Sicherheitsgründen« beinahe nicht genehmigt worden wäre. Der Zusammenhalt innerhalb der Gruppe ließ die Grenzen zwischen den einzelnen Delegationen verschwinden und bestärkte die DelegationsleiterInnen darin, alles Mögliche zu tun, um das Projekt zu retten. Die Kompromißfähigkeit der palästinensischen Delegationsleitung stärkte das Vertrauen und ermutigte die israelische Leitung, die Verantwortung für den Aufenthalt in Bethlehem von den Ministeriumsbehörden auf die Eltern zu übertragen. Es war wie ein Wunder: Bei unserer Ankunft auf der King-Hussein/Allenby/Karame-Brücke waren 22 Faxe israelischer Eltern (von 24) für ihre Kinder eingetroffen, mit der Erlaubnis, in Bethlehem zu übernachten. Wir wurden von den palästinensischen Sicherheitskräften empfangen und während des gesamten Aufenthalts begleitet.
Für die jungen Leute war das der aufregendste Moment der ganzen Reise, und Mike, ein palästinensischer Teilnehmer, drückte das Gefühl in der Abschlußrunde so aus: »Zehn Tage der Hoffnung, der Träume und des Erfolges; das Größte ist, daß wir alle zusammen in Bethlehem sind.« Dieser Eindruck wurde von der ganzen Gruppe geteilt, und seit unserer Rückkehr nach Wien sind Dutzende von Briefen und E-Mails im Kreisky Forum eingetroffen: Worte der Dankbarkeit, Worte der Sorge während der darauffolgenden Aufstände (Unruhen wegen des Altstadttunnels), Worte der Hoffnung und des Mutes. Ein Treffen der österreichischen TeilnehmerInnen Ende November hat gezeigt, daß bereits an den Projekten gearbeitet wird und ein starker Wille zum Weitermachen da ist. Interviews, Videodokumentationen, Fotoalben, Artikel für den Newsletter, Termine in Schulen, eine »New-Generation«-Webpage sind erst der Anfang. Diese Aktionen verändern sicher nicht die allgemeine Lage, helfen aber, Frustrationen zu überwinden und andere davon zu überzeugen, daß Haß und Gewalt nicht die einzigen Wege sind. Politiker können Erklärungen formulieren und Dokumente unterzeichnen, die Menschen müssen sie umsetzen, um in Frieden zu leben.

M.S., G.A., T.R.

A participant's view

... That the trip was a success became clear to me on the last evening in Eilat, when all the plans for travelling further to Jordan and the PA seemed to come to nothing. The holding together of our group, and the mutual encouragement of the Israelis and Palestinians, showed how mature and sensitive the participants have become since their first meeting in Vienna.
I can only agree with Ala's opinion on the last night when he said that he does not feel

that he is a member of a particular delegation but part of a larger group, almost a family. I felt exactly the same. I think that this spirit of solidarity motivated the delegation leaders to do everything to rescue the project ...

... The meeting was – perhaps especially because of the traumatic circumstances – an unbelievable experience for all the participants that they will never forget in their entire lives. In view of the tragic fighting during the last weeks, it seems even more incredible that we were able to complete our trip. Remembering this gives me hope that, in spite of the gloomy outlook, much progress can be made.

Orlando Mason

Eindrücke eines Teilnehmers

... daß die Reise ein Erfolg war, wurde mir am letzten Abend in Eilat klar, als sich alle Pläne für die Weiterreise nach Jordanien und in die palästinensischen Gebiete scheinbar in Luft auflösten. Der Zusammenhalt unserer Gruppe sowie das gegenseitige Mutmachen der Israelis und Palästinenser haben bewiesen, um wie viel reifer und sensibler die Teilnehmer seit dem ersten Treffen in Wien geworden sind. Ich kann Ala nur zustimmen, wenn er am letzten Abend meinte, daß er sich nicht wie ein Mitglied einer Delegation fühlte, sondern wie ein Teil einer großen Gruppe, fast einer Familie. Genauso ging es mir. Ich denke, daß diese Solidarität, die wir gespürt haben, auch den Delegationsleitern Mut und Motivation gegeben hat, alles zu versuchen, um das Projekt zu retten ...

... Das Treffen war – vielleicht gerade wegen der traumatischen Umstände – ein riesiges Erlebnis, das alle, die teilgenommen haben, ein Leben lang nicht vergessen werden. Angesichts der tragischen Kämpfe der letzten Wochen scheint es noch unglaublicher, daß wir die Reise vollenden konnten. Die Erinnerung daran gibt mir Hoffnung, daß trotz der düsteren Aussichten noch vieles weitergehen kann.

Orlando Mason

Margit and Samar in Petra, Jordan
Margit und Samar in Petra, Jordanien

THE "NEW GENERATION" – PROJECTS
DIE »NEUE GENERATION« – PROJEKTE

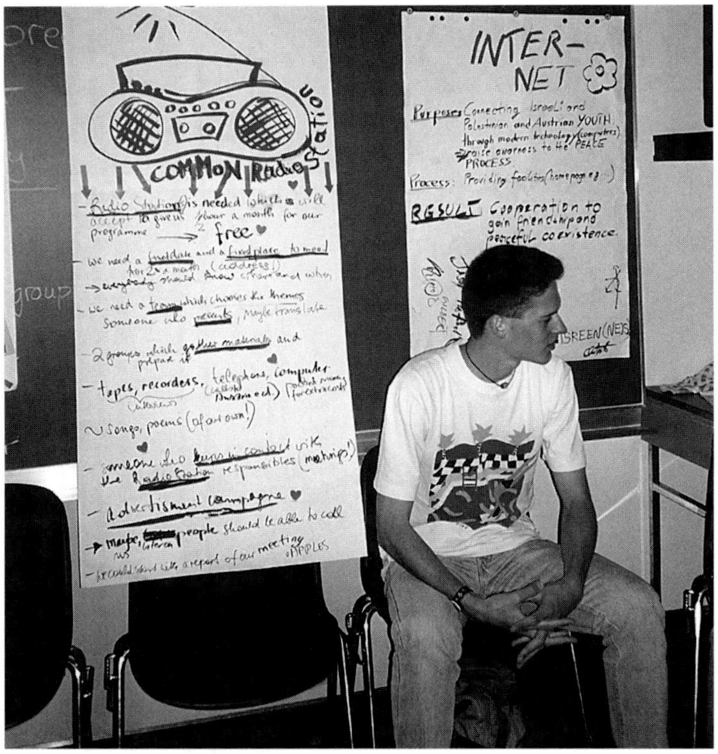

Eran presenting projects
Eran bei der Projektpräsentation

Documentary groups: *Videos from the Middle East Youth Peace Forum 1994, 1996 and 1997 have been produced, as well as a documentation of the programme 1994–1998. A brochure documenting the Middle East Youth Peace Forum 1994 – 1998 has been distributed to all the participants and their delegation leaders.*

External and internal co-ordinators: *Every delegation has appointed one external and one internal co-ordinator, the so-called backbones. The internal co-ordinators are responsible for reporting about the progress of projects and about the meetings within the delegation as well as keeping the list of addresses up-to-date etc. The external co-ordinators are responsible for informing the other delegations about the activities, for co-ordinating joint projects and keeping in contact with the Bruno Kreisky Forum.*

Internet: *This working group has created a web page for the "New Generation" to communicate with each other and with other existing peace initiatives on the Internet.*

Newsletter: *"The New Generation" is issued twice a year. Each edition has a special topic and contains a documentation of the projects. All editions are available at the Bruno Kreisky Forum or through the editors.*

Pen-palship: *Lists with the addresses of interested young Austrians, Israelis, Jordanians and Palestinians are regularly distributed.*

Public relations: *A lot of media/PR work is done in every delegation, for example participation in talk shows, writing of articles, radio interviews etc.*

School and university programme/exchange: *The aim of this project is to establish contacts between Israeli, Jordanian, Austrian and Palestinian schools and universities, in order to inform about the Middle East Youth Peace Forum, to hold discussions with students, and to encourage similar experiences as the "New Generation". Many participants have already held lectures and arranged discussions in their former schools or at their universities. The Austrian students have made the Middle East Youth Peace Forum and the conflict in the region a topic for their papers at school or university.*

Local intercultural workshops: *Encounters between children and youth are organised and discussions are held, in order to involve more people in the peace process.*

Exhibition: *A mobile exhibition presenting the members of the "New Generation", their way of life and their experiences with the Middle East Youth Peace Forum was conceived by the participants and already shown in the Van Leer Institute/Jerusalem and other locations in Israel. It will be shown at Jordanian, Palestinian and Austrian institutions.*

Symbol: *A symbol representing the "New Generation" has been designed by an Austrian art student and has been printed on T-shirts and pins. It is also heading the front page of the newsletter.*

Cookery book: *The members of the "New*

Generation" collected recipes of each region and published a booklet.

Leaders manual: *A reference book with tips and methods for youth leaders, especially for those dealing with conflict groups, will be produced based on the experiences of the training seminar which was organised in 1997/98.*

Cultural book: *The cultural traditions of the different countries and regions will be presented, following the example of the cookery book; it is printed in Jordan.*

Radio project: *One of the Israeli participants has been making her own radio programme for Israeli settlers since 1996. She uses this medium also to present the Middle East Youth Peace Forum and the "New Generation".*

Dokumentationsgruppen: Videos über das Nahost-Jugend-Friedensforum 1994, 1996 und 1997 sowie ein Video über das gesamte Programm 1994–1998 sind im Bruno Kreisky Forum erhältlich. Eine Broschüre dokumentiert ebenfalls das Gesamtprojekt.

Externe und interne KoordinatorInnen: Jede Delegation hat interne und externe KoordinatorInnen. Die internen KoordinatorInnen sind für den Informationsaustausch in der Projektarbeit und für nationale Treffen sowie für den aktuellen Stand von Adressen zuständig. Die externen KoordinatorInnen halten den Kontakt mit den anderen Delegationen und dem Bruno Kreisky Forum.

Internet: Die Gruppe hat eine Webpage realisiert, um untereinander und mit anderen Friedensinitiativen zu kommunizieren.

Newsletter: Alle bisher erschienenen Ausgaben sind im Bruno Kreisky Forum erhältlich. Der Newsletter erscheint zweimal im Jahr, jede Ausgabe hat ein eigenes Thema.

Brieffreundschaft: Eine Liste von interessierten österreichischen, israelischen, jordanischen und palästinensischen Jugendlichen ist jederzeit über die ProjektleiterInnen erhältlich.

Öffentlichkeitsarbeit: Von jeder Delegation wurde Öffentlichkeitsarbeit geleistet in Form von Teilnahme an Talkshows, Veröffentlichung von Artikeln, Radiointerviews usw.

Schul- und Universitätsprogramm: Kontakte zwischen israelischen, palästinensischen, jordanischen und österreichischen Schulen und Universitäten sollen das Nahost-Jugend-Friedensforum anderen Jugendlichen zugänglich machen. Einige österreichische Jugendliche haben das Nahost-Jugend-Friedensforum zum zentralen Thema von Seminararbeiten gemacht.

Ausstellung: Eine Ausstellung präsentiert die Mitglieder der »Neuen Generation«, ihren Lebensstil und ihre Erfahrungen. Sie ist als Wanderausstellung konzipiert und wurde bereits in Jerusalem am Van Leer Institut gezeigt. Anschließend soll sie nach Jordanien, Palästina und Österreich gehen.

Logo: Das Logo für die »Neue Generation« wurde von einem österreichischen Kunststudenten entworfen und bereits auf Briefpapier, T-Shirts und dem Cover des Newsletters abgedruckt.

Kochbuch: Eine Rezeptesammlung aus den verschiedenen Regionen wurde publiziert.

Handbuch für Youth Leaders: Hinweise und Regeln für JugendleiterInnen, Zusammenfassung der Seminare, Ideen für Spiele und Methoden für die Arbeit mit Konfliktgruppen

Buch der verschiedenen Kulturen: Kulturelle Tradition in den verschiedenen Ländern soll in kochbuchähnlicher Form präsentiert und publiziert werden.

Radio: Eine israelische Teilnehmerin betreut seit 1996 ein eigenes Radioprogramm für Siedler und nutzt das Medium, um über das Nahost-Jugend-Friedensforum zu sprechen.

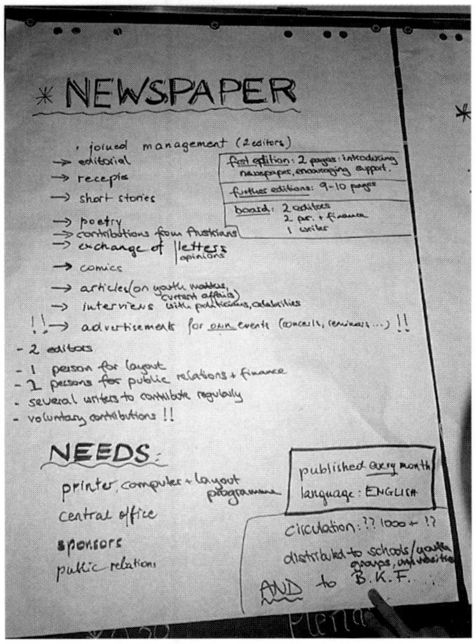

CONFERENCE OF THE DELEGATION LEADERS IN VIENNA
KONFERENZ DER DELEGATIONSLEITER/INNEN IN WIEN
December/**Dezember 1996**

In the garden of the Bruno Kreisky Forum
Im Garten des Bruno Kreisky Forums

Israeli delegation: Tali Lidar, Orly Fruchter Yagodovsky and Shaul Paz
Jordanian delegation: Samar Kildani
Palestinian delegation: Hani Husseini and Wa'el Abu Nemeh
Austrian delegation: Margit Schmidt, Tove Raiby und Gertraud Auer

Programme/Programm

Evaluation of the "Crossing Borders" project
Rückblick auf »Crossing Borders«

Update of the "New Generation" projects
Zur aktuellen Lage der Projektarbeit

Proposals for 1997/98
Vorschläge für 1997/98

1997/1998
CONTINUITY AND RESPONSIBILITY
KONTINUITÄT UND VERANTWORTUNG

In response to the growing desire to heighten awareness and competence in the area of cross-community and intercultural work and to stimulate interest in maintaining and furthering activities in the field of the programme at local, national and international levels, the Austrian, Israeli, Jordanian and Palestinian organisers and delegation leaders have decided to diversify the activities in 1997 and 1998. First of all, a Youth Leader Training Programme, based on special seminars, has been conceived to provide those participants who have participated in the Middle East Youth Peace Forum at least twice with the tools necessary for the development of professional skills as well as a greater sense of civic responsibility.
The second part of the Youth Leader Training Programme was connected with an intercultural workshop involving youth living in Austria and belonging to different minority groups (Croatians, Roma, Hungarians), as preparation for the Bruno Kreisky Youth Peace Forum 98, giving leading roles to the "New Generation" youth leaders.
The Austrian Institute for Conflict Research performed a case study on the MEYPF to evaluate the results of the programme to date and to investigate the possibility of using this concept as a model for conflict resolution in other regions.
Between the training seminars, a field work based on ongoing projects was carried out with the help of the educators and delegation leaders. Travel grants for participants allow them to be directly involved and to move the projects forward.

Als Antwort auf das wachsende Bedürfnis der TeilnehmerInnen, mehr Sensibilität und Kompetenz im Bereich von interkultureller Arbeit zu entwickeln, und auf das wachsende Interesse, die Projektarbeit auf lokaler, nationaler und internationaler Ebene zu intensivieren und zu erweitern, haben die österreichischen, jordanischen, israelischen und palästinensischen DelegationsleiterInnen und Organisatorinnen beschlossen, die Aktivitäten 1997 und 1998 in verschiedene Bereiche aufzufächern:
Zuerst fand ein JugendleiterInnen-Training in Österreich statt für jene, die mindestens zweimal am Nahost-Jugend-Friedensforum teilgenommen haben und die in einem speziellen Seminarprogramm ihre Fähigkeiten und ihre Bereitschaft, mehr Verantwortung zu übernehmen, unter der Leitung von PädagogInnen weiterentwickeln und praktisch anwenden lernen konnten. Der zweite Teil des Seminars beinhaltete auch einen interkulturellen Workshop, an dem Jugendliche verschiedener Minderheitengruppen (Roma, KroatInnen, UngarInnen) aus Österreich teilnahmen, als Vorbereitung und Training für das Bruno Kreisky Jugend-Friedensforum 1998, bei dem die JugendleiterInnen der »Neuen Generation« hauptverantwortlich bestimmte Aufgabenbereiche übernahmen.
Das österreichische Institut für Konfliktforschung und das Institut für interdisziplinäre Forschung und Weiterbildung erarbeiteten eine Studie über das Nahost-Jugend-Friedensforum, um zu untersuchen, wie und mit welchen Ergebnissen die Konfliktregelungen aus der Sicht der daran beteiligten Personen gelingen und wieweit das vorliegende Konzept als ein allgemeingültiges Konfliktregelungsmodell dienen kann.
Zwischen den zwei Trainingsseminaren wurde die Projektarbeit vor Ort – eine Art »Praktikum« mit Unterstützung der DelegationsleiterInnen – weitergeführt. Reisestipendien für die TeilnehmerInnen boten die Möglichkeit der direkten Mitarbeit in der Region.

On top of the roof of the Austrian Hospice, Jerusalem
Am Dach des Österreichischen Hospizes, Jerusalem

CONFERENCE OF THE EDUCATORS AND ORGANISERS
KONFERENZ DER PÄDAGOG/INNEN UND DES LEITUNGSTEAMS
Vienna/Wien
February/Februar 1997

Meeting at the Bruno Kreisky Forum
Treffen im Bruno Kreisky Forum

Israeli delegation: Yael Ben-Ami and Sylvain Biegeleisen
Palestinian delegation: Hani Husseini
Jordanian delegation: Violette Burgan Kildani
Austrian delegation: Diane Hendrick and Hannes Gstir

Programme/Programm

Preparation of the Youth Leader training programme 97/98
Vorbereitung und Programmerstellung des JugendleiterInnen Trainingseminars 97/98

CONFERENCE OF THE DELEGATION LEADERS AND YOUTH DELEGATES
KONFERENZ DER DELEGATIONSLEITER/INNEN UND JUGENDDELEGIERTEN
Rome/Rom
May/Mai 1997

Israeli delegation: Tali Lidar, Orly Fruchter-Yagodovsky, Ori Leibovich and Basheer Basheer
Jordanian delegation: Samar Kildani, Yamaan Safady and Juman Al Nimri
Palestinian delegation: Hani Husseini, Wa'el Abu Nemeh, Hana'a Amin Ibsais and Firas Khalaf
Austrian delegation: Margit Schmidt, Tove Raiby, Gertraud Auer, Heidrun Maier and Thomas Egerer

Programme/Programm

Activities 97/98
Aktivitäten 1997 und 1998

Youth leader training
JugendleiterInnen-Training

Proposals for the Bruno Kreisky Youth Peace Forum 98
Vorschläge für das Bruno-Kreisky-Jugend-Friedensforum 98

Evaluation of the Middle East Youth Peace Forum
Rückblick auf das Nahost-Jugend-Friedensforum

Rome Meeting

Dear Friends, as most of you know we had a meeting in Italy. Two members of each delegation took part in the meeting, which was meant to involve the participants in the leaders' work and to make our projects more flexible and the communication with each delegation and with the Bruno Kreisky Forum better.
In our sessions we talked about next year's programme and decided on a few things that hopefully will help us to go on with the projects.

Ori Leibovich

Treffen in Rom

Wie ihr wißt, hatten wir ein Treffen in Rom, an dem auch je zwei Jugendliche aus jeder Delegation teilgenommen haben. Einerseits sollten wir sehen, wie unsere DelegationsleiterInnen arbeiten, und andererseits wollten wir unserer Projektarbeit mehr Flexibilität geben und zwischen unseren Delegationen und dem Bruno Kreisky Forum eine bessere Kommunikation herstellen. Wir sprachen über die Veranstaltungen des darauffolgenden Jahres und entschieden eine Reihe von Maßnahmen für unsere gemeinsame Arbeit.

Ori Leibovich

TRAVEL GRANT 1997
REISESTIPENDIUM 1997
Orlando Mason
Summer/Sommer 1997

25th June, *15:15: Arrived at Ben-Gurion Airport, picked up by an Israeli friend Eran. Visited the University of Tel Aviv with him and went out that night in Tel Aviv. The place is really alive.*
26th June, *Tel Aviv: Met Kobi for a few hours, who showed me around Tel Aviv. He's about to join the army, after a year of working. Kobi talked of difficulties with the projects: the twins project, he said, got a big no-no from the Foreign Affairs Ministry. The efforts to arrange meetings between classes had run into the obvious security problems. I called Basheer and arranged to go to Jerusalem on Sunday, 29th. Guy wanted to take me to an anti-government demonstration on Saturday night. Nataly, another Israeli friend, too, told of problems with the schools project. The main problem of arranging visits to schools between delegations concerned the issue of security passes. Instead, members of the Israeli delegations have visited schools in Israel, presenting a video on the Middle East Youth Peace Forum project, and speaking about the peace process, questions of identity and their experiences. This has happened about four times during the last year. A larger scale meeting was planned for September, in collaboration with Ala', with whom they were hoping to plan a day together for pupils of various schools.*
27th June, *Kiriat Ono: Went into Tel Aviv, to a market, where Nataly and I bumped into Moriah, who invited me to her settlement in the West Bank for Shabbat. Guy picked me up at around 6 pm. We went to his flat, I met his parents. Guy is very active in Meretz now.*
28th June, *Kfar Saba: Guy drove me up north for the day. Amazing countryside, we were just inland from Haifa, and visited a number of villages in the area, including the town of Carmel. On return we telephoned Hani, before heading into Tel Aviv for two demonstrations, one against the government for its stand in the peace process, the other was a big demonstration against orthodox domination of religious practices and against the orthodox tightening grip on the coalition (note: this was during the outcry over conversion laws).*
29th June, *Bus to Jerusalem. I arrived about 9 am. I got lost on the way to meeting Tali and Orly for lunch. I met Tali and Orly for lunch, and we talked about the delegation meeting in Rome and the current political situation in Israel. We arranged for me to visit the Knesset the next day.*
30th June, *Jerusalem: Went to the Knesset with Basheer and Nataly, who were trying to arrange a meeting for the Israeli delegation. We talked about possible dates for a joint delegation meeting. After a tour of the Knesset and of the Supreme Court, nearby, I visited Hani at the Orient House. We talked about the current situation. Later I talked to Basheer, mainly about the newsletter. He saw the main problems as being the length of the time it takes to lay out and print. Last time, it took four months from the completion of the paper until its distribution.*
1st July, *Jerusalem: Visit to the Old City.*
2nd July, *Jerusalem: Spent the first half of the day reading up on the Middle East, the Palestinians, etc, in the Library. Talked at length with Nisreen about the role of women in Arab society.*
3rd July, *Jerusalem: Israeli delegation meeting in youth hostel. 17 managed to come. They discussed the projects and the Youth Leader Training Course. I visited Hani at the Orient House in the afternoon, where we also talked about the Palestinian participants for the Youth Leader Training.*
4th July, *Last day in Jerusalem. I visited the Old City with Basheer. After lunch I caught a minibus to Ramallah, to meet Kareem.*
5th July, *Ramallah: After breakfast in Ramallah we went to Bir Zeit University with Kareem and Firas. The university is very modern. Kareem needed to work today, so I returned to Jerusalem for the afternoon.*
6th July, *I had a meeting for the Internet Project in Ramat Hasharon, with Yossi and Yaron. We worked out a timetable for progress.*
7th July, *I went to Kibbutz Ga'ash, where Ori lives. I was shown around the kibbutz, which is very interesting. In the evening I chatted to some of the younger members of the kibbutz, who were about to join the army.*
8th July, *Rose early, went back to Jerusalem. It was interesting for me to see how much the participants of the Bruno Kreisky Forum had developed. A lot of effort had been put into the projects.*

***9th July**, We rose early, about 6 am, and set off on a day-long tour of the country. Keren and Guy accompanied us again, like the day before. We visited Jericho, Allenby Bridge, King Hussein Bridge, and then an army base in the north, and finally into the Golan, before returning to Jerusalem, utterly exhausted.*

***10th July**, After brief stay at youth hostel to watch simulated final status negotiations, I met Nisreen and we headed for the Palestinian delegation meeting in Bir Zeit. There we talked about the projects, the future meetings and the possibility of a "New Generation" office to be opened in Ramallah.*

***11th July**, Morning: Bir Zeit to Ramallah, to Jerusalem, to Moriah's Settlement in the West Bank, Kdomim Shomron. I met her family, it was shabbat. I spoke for a long time with her father, who is a barrister, and was one of the first settlers in the West Bank. We visited the synagogue.*

***13th July**, I left at about 10 am for Jerusalem, from where I started for Jordan. I was met at the other side of Hussein Bridge by Anas, with whom I drove slowly to Amman, stopping in a few villages on the way.*

***14th July**, I was taken to the Crown Prince award offices, and met Samar, before meeting Ahmad, who showed me Amman. I met a number of students at the university, most of whom are deeply Islamic, and talked again about peace, etc. I was seeing two opposite sides of the spectrum within 24 hours.*

***15th July**, I left for Irbid, further north, where I met Ali who guided me around.*

***16th July**, Back to Crown Prince Award Office, where I tried to help Samar with her arrangements for the September meeting.*

***17th July**, I met Suha in Haifa, who showed me all the best views of her hometown. We talked a lot about the balance of the Israeli group and the problems she and Basheer faced at the beginning and now. After a great day, I caught a bus to Kibbutz Ramat Hashofet, where I met Marit.*

***18th July**, Kibbutz Ramat Hashofet. I saw the kibbutz, which has a large plastics factory and a wood factory.*

***19th July**, After midday I travelled back to Haifa, and later to Jerusalem. The constant travelling was becoming very wearisome. I needed to tie up some loose ends here before leaving.*

***20th July**, I visited the Tantur, which is on the way to Bethlehem, and a possible location for a "New Generation" office. I left Jerusalem, and caught a bus to Ness Ziona, where Eran met me.*

***20th July**, until departure. Eran took me up north to the Golan. After two days we returned south, and after a long wait at Ben Gurion airport, due to an El Al strike, I returned to Austria*

Kurzfassung

Orlando hat in diesem Monat viele TeilnehmerInnen getroffen und Israel, die palästinensischen Gebiete und Jordanien bereist. Er hat sich über die laufenden Projekte informiert und, wo es ging, geholfen. Mit Hilfe des »New-Generation«-Netzwerkes konnte er viele verschiedene Realitäten des Lebens im Nahen Osten kennenlernen, wurde von Familien eingeladen und übernachtete bei Freunden. Er hat Kontakt mit allen DelegationsleiterInnen gehabt und neue Projekte und Arbeitsschritte besprochen. Mit reicher Erfahrung kam er nach Österreich zurück.

FIRST YOUTH LEADER TRAINING SEMINAR
ERSTES JUGENDLEITER/INNEN-TRAININGSSEMINAR
Söchau/Austria
September 21–28

The initial training phase of the project included:

• reinforcing the new group identity
• gaining trust and experience of working together
• gaining skills and knowledge relating to the role of youth leaders
• reviewing and evaluating ongoing projects
• planning for the implementation of chosen projects
• gaining initial ideas on the content and structure of the February seminar
• provisional planning for the Bruno Kreisky Youth Peace Forum 1998

A tragic accident occured and two participants were heavily injured. The youth revealed a great sense of responsibility and mutual care taking. The programme was interrupted and a psychologist provided individual and group support. The Israeli ambassador in Vienna, Yoel Sher, and Federal Minister Caspar Einem came to see the group.

The aims of the training programme were:

• to achieve greater efficiency and effectiveness in the establishment of groups and networks working on issues of peace and cultural understanding, both within the communities and together with the participants of the other delegations
• to utilise experience of young people already involved in international and cross-community work
• to train young people in the skills of group process, moderation and group leadership
• to heighten awareness and competence in the area of cross-community and intercultural work
• to develop organisational and planning skills
• to develop skills in handling conflicts
• to integrate young people into planning and running the Bruno Kreisky Youth Peace Forum 1998
• to stimulate interest in maintaining and furthering activities in the field of the programme at a local, national and international level

Ziele des Trainingsseminars waren:

• größere Leistungsfähigkeit der beteiligten Personen und Effizienz in der Projektarbeit zu erreichen;
• Erfahrungen junger Menschen, die bereits in internationalen und cross-community-Projekten arbeiten, zu nutzen;
• junge Menschen in Gruppendynamik und Leadership zu qualifizieren;
• das Wahrnehmungsvermögen und das Bewußtsein um Zusammenhänge zu stärken;
• organisatorische und planerische Fähigkeiten zu erwerben;
• Fähigkeiten zur Konfliktbewältigung zu entwickeln;
• junge Menschen in die Planung und Ausführung des Bruno-Kreisky-Jugend-Friedensforums 1998 zu integrieren;
• das Interesse an den bestehenden und neuen Aktivitäten des Programmes auf lokaler, nationaler und internationaler Ebene wachzuhalten.

Ziele der ersten Trainingsphase waren:

- Stärkung der Gruppenidentität
- Bildung von Vertrauen und Sammeln von Erfahrung in Zusammenarbeit
- Vermittlung von Fähigkeiten und Kenntnissen für die Rolle von JugendleiterInnen
- Einschätzung der laufenden Projekte
- Planung der Umsetzung der Projekte
- erste Ideen für Inhalt und Struktur des Februarseminars und des interkulturellen Workshops
- provisorische Planung des Bruno-Kreisky-Jugend-Friedensforums 1998

Bei einem tragischen Unfall wurden zwei Teilnehmer schwer verletzt. Die geschockten Jugendlichen legten in dieser Situation großes Verantwortungsbewußtsein und gegenseitige Fürsorge an den Tag. Das Programm wurde unterbrochen, und eine Psychologin bot Gespräche an. Der israelische Botschafter in Wien, Yoel Sher, und der Bundesminister für Wissenschaft und Verkehr Dr. Caspar Einem besuchten die Gruppe.

Field work in the region

Following the initial training the young people had received a new way of perceiving the work with youth groups. The task during the following months was to actualise that learning by putting the knowledge and skills into practice. The young people required guidance and advice from supervisors who knew what was feasible in that social, economic and political climate. Three basic types of activities were envisaged for the youth leaders during this period:

- *sustaining ongoing projects and actualising previously planned projects*
- *undergoing additional training that they identified as useful for their present work and with the view to working with other groups in the Bruno Kreisky Youth Peace Forum 1998.*
- *creating a "bank of ideas" and undertaking preparatory thinking for planning the 1998 Forum and the February seminar*

The supervisors provided the following services:

- *feedback to the youth leaders*
- *focus on the crucial points of their experience*
- *suggestions on how to carry out the work in an efficient way*

Presentation / **Präsentation**
Evaluation / **Evaluation**

* *aid in the understanding of group dynamics*
* *assistance when problems arose*
* *general support and encouragement*
* *regular contact with the young people*
* *group meetings*

Projektarbeit in der Region

Anschließend an die erste Trainingsphase hatten die Jugendlichen eine neue Sichtweise von Gruppenarbeit kennengelernt. In den folgenden Monaten war es besonders wichtig, diese Fähigkeiten und dieses Wissen in die Praxis umzusetzen. Als Helfer und Supervisoren standen die DelegationsleiterInnen zur Verfügung. In dieser Phase waren für die JugendleiterInnen folgende Aktivitäten vorgesehen:

* Arbeit an den laufenden Projekten und Reaktivieren früherer geplanter Projekte
* Zusätzliches Training, auch im Hinblick auf künftige neue Gruppen im Bruno-Kreisky-Jugend-Friedensforum 1998 – Workshop der österreichischen TeilnehmerInnen in Wien mit Sylvain Biegeleisen über Rassismus und Fremdenfeindlichkeit (Video)
* Schaffung einer »Ideenbörse« für das Forum 1998 und das Februarseminar

Die Supervisors boten folgende Unterstützung an:

* Feedback für die JugendleiterInnen
* Konzentration auf die wesentlichen Problempunkte
* Hilfestellung bei der Ausführung der Projektarbeit
* Interpretation von Gruppenprozessen
* Hilfe bei Problembewältigung
* Ermutigung in schwierigen Situationen
* regelmäßiger Kontakt mit den Jugendlichen
* Organisieren von Gruppentreffen

Some good advice for the future from participants
Einige gute Ratschläge für die Zukunft

Gesammelt von verschiedenen TeilnehmerInnen

Now that most of us have graduated from high school and the new year is already here, we think it's the best time to share with you some good advice for life. We hope it will be useful:

Don't blame others. Be responsible for your actions.
Always try to gain the most out of every situation, even from the worst ones.
Don't refuse help.
Don't be afraid to admit your mistakes.
Laugh with your friends, not at them.
Don't eat too much before you give a speech – especially beans!!!
Be brave, be courageous, be original – just be!
Aim for the sky, but learn to enjoy the little things in life as well.
Always keep your hope!!! Never let it go …
For those of you who are on a diet: Remember even a cucumber has some calories in it …
Don't be afraid of big problems, behind them hide big challenges.
Don't be the one who breaks the strike. And if there's a strike don't stay at home – go to the beach!
Once you have reached a goal take some time off to enjoy your success.
Never underestimate the power of words to overcome gaps.
Hope for the best, but be ready for the worst.
Marry only out of love.
Don't forget to call your mother!!!
Write to the newspaper – you will see how happy it will make you!

I Love Life

When my dreams break down I become hopeless.
I think that nothing in the world deserves laughing or living for.
But after I have seen how suffering people live, how hard they struggle to stay alive, to live under normal human conditions,
I changed my attitude towards life.
Now I love it much.
I am fighting to live like I want.

Recipe for Happiness

Take a cup of kindness
Add a dish of charity
Mix with understanding
And a bit of courtesy
Top it off with patience
Sprinkle liberally with cheer
Serve generously to everyone
You meet throughout the year

DELEGATION LEADERS' AND TRAINERS' CONFERENCE
KONFERENZ DER DELEGATIONSLEITER/INNEN UND PÄDAGOG/INNEN
Jerusalem
***December*/Dezember 1997**

***Delegation leaders and organisers/* OrganisatorInnen und DelegationsleiterInnen**
Margit Schmidt, Tove Raiby, Gertraud Auer, Tali Lidar, Orly Fruchter-Yagodovsky, Samar Kildani, Hani Husseini, Wa'el Abu Nemeh

***Trainers/*PädagogInnen**
Diane Hendrick, Hannes Gstir, Yael Ben Ami, Sylvain Biegeleisen, Helmi Sari, Marwan Darweish

***Location/*Ort**
Orient House and Beit Shmuel

The conference was a feedback to the 1997 activities, in order to plan and prepare the February Seminar, the Intercultural Workshop and the 1998 Bruno Kreisky Youth Peace Forum.

Agenda

- *report on the 1997 activities in general*
- *report on the field work and the on-going projects in particular*
- *preparation of the February seminar and the Intercultural Workshop*
- *discussion of the Case Study*
- *Bruno Kreisky Youth Peace Forum 1998*

Die Organisatorinnen und LeiterInnen der vier am Nahost-Jugend-Friedensforum teilnehmenden Delegationen verbrachten die Tage von 11. bis 14.12. gemeinsam in Jerusalem, um den ersten Teil des Jugend-leiterInnen-Seminars zu reflektieren, den zweiten Teil vorzubereiten und das Programm 98 zu fixieren. Die PädagogInnen hatten ein paralleles Treffen zur Seminarvorbereitung. Beide Gruppen hatten gemeinsame Arbeitsrunden, um das Programm zu koordinieren.

Orient House, Jerusalem

Agenda

- Kalender 98
- Interkultureller Workshop
- Projekte
- Bruno-Kreisky-Jugend-Friedensforum 98
- Evaluation des ersten Seminars und Bericht der PädagogInnen
- Programm des zweiten Seminars und des interkulturellen Workshops

SECOND YOUTH LEADER TRAINING AND INTERCULTURAL WORKSHOP
ZWEITES JUGENDLEITER/INNEN-SEMINAR UND INTERKULTURELLER WORKSHOP

Schlaining/Austria
***February*/Februar 1998**

Diane Hendrick

Aims of the second seminar:

• to train particular skills:
communication
working with conflict groups
feedback
• to provide an opportunity to practise skills from previous training through planning, implementation and evaluation of intercultural workshops
• to plan for the new form of the Middle East Youth Peace Forum at local and regional level
• to begin planning for the Kreisky Youth Peace Forum in August 1998

Intercultural Workshop

In order to actualize the learning of the previous seminar and the inter-seminar experience participants were invited to form teams to run intercultural workshops with representatives of local minority communities (Roma, Croatians, Hungarians). Each group had responsibility to design and plan a four hour programme for an intercultural workshop including the topic, aims, specific exercises, means of evaluation, division of roles and tasks and rehearsal.

Die Ziele des zweiten Seminars waren:

• größere Leistungsfähigkeit der beteiligten Personen und mehr Effizienz bei der Bildung von Gruppen und Netzwerken, die im Bereich von Frieden und kulturellem Dialog arbeiten
• Nutzen von Erfahrungen junger Menschen, die bereits in internationalen und interkulturellen Projekten arbeiten
• Reflexion von Gruppenprozessen
• Stärkung des Wahrnehmungsvermögens und des Bewußtseins um Zusammenhänge
• Reflexion der Erfahrungen mit der Projektarbeit und Analyse der Schwierigkeiten
• Entwicklung von organisatorischen und planerischen Fähigkeiten
• Stärkung der Fähigkeiten zur Konfliktbewältigung
• Anwendung des Know-how in interkulturellen Workshops
• Einbindung der jungen Menschen in die Planung und Ausführung des Bruno-Kreisky-Jugend-Friedensforums 1998
• Interesse an bestehenden und neuen Aktivitäten auf lokaler, nationaler und internationaler Ebene

Interkultureller Workshop

Um das im Seminar Gelernte praktisch anzuwenden, arbeiteten die TeilnehmerInnen einen Tag lang mit VertreterInnen der Roma, der kroatischen und ungarischen Minderheitengruppen in einem Interkulturellen Workshop, für dessen Gestaltung sie verantwortlich waren.

Statements of participants
The essence of the Middle East Youth Peace Forum
Stimmen von TeilnehmerInnen
Die Essenz des Nahost-Jugend-Friedensforums

It is hard to hate the one you can understand ...
Es ist schwer, jemanden zu hassen, den man versteht ...

See different views and bring them closer together.
Verschiedene Sichtweisen kennenlernen und sie einander näherbringen ...

We need to deliver the message of communication between each other, respect each other, listen to each other to the next generation and the people in our communities.
Wir müssen die Botschaft – einander zu respektieren, einander zuzuhören – an die nächste Generation und an die Menschen zu Hause weitergeben ...

I don't know how my life would be without the Middle East Youth Peace Forum, but I'm sure I'd not be on this educated level. It wasn't easy at all. I was faced with personal problems and in discussions I felt as an outsider, but we should be aware of what we reached and not be too critical with ourselves, we should never forget how we learned to talk with the other without prejudice. This is an ability that not many people are able to reach at all, because they never had our opportunity. It is important to go on with our projects, actually it only depends on us. We should not be too lazy, but learn to listen to others and always be aware of the things we achieved. We should try to inform ourselves together with the other side, to stay in touch and stay friends!

Ich weiß nicht, wie mein Leben ohne das Nahost-Jugend-Friedensforum aussehen würde. Es war nicht leicht, ich hatte persönliche Probleme und fühlte mich als Außenseiter. Aber wir sollten das sehen, was wir erreicht haben und nicht zu streng mit uns selber sein. Nun ist es wichtig an den Projekten weiterzuarbeiten, nicht faul zu werden, Kontakt zu halten und Freunde zu bleiben ...

Meeting and co-operation – not without, but despite of differences – gaining people involved, spreading out a "spirit" of conflict-resolution by non-violent means – communication, not only over political issues, but in order to get to know the "other side" – emphasise on similarities ... not on differences.
Einander treffen und zusammenarbeiten nicht ohne Unterschiede, sondern gerade wegen der Unterschiede. Lösungen finden, ohne Gewalt anzuwenden, Gemeinsamkeiten herausstreichen ...

To learn that there is a difference between peoples and cultures and learn about them. You must listen before talking and you can achieve anything if you are clear about your aim and believe in it.
Über verschiedene Völker und Kulturen lernen und sie verstehen. Zuhören, bevor man redet. Du kannst alles erreichen, wenn du dein Ziel kennst und daran glaubst.

The Middle East Youth Peace Forum is meaningful. It gave us this great opportunity to meet, discuss and compromise. We learned to listen and to talk in self-confidence.
Im Nahost-Jugend-Friedensforum haben wir gelernt, offen und vertrauensvoll miteinander umzugehen ...

I learned to be more open and comprehensive to my "neighbours" and learned more about them. The message that I want to spread is tolerance and understanding of different opinions/situations.
Ich habe gelernt, meinen »Nachbarn« zu verstehen, tolerant und offen zu werden ...

Change of our way of thinking in dealing with problems in the future – helping our people (new youth) to widen their possibility of expressing their feelings.
Wir sollten unsere Denkweise bezüglich des Umgangs mit den Problemen der Zukunft ändern ...

To have in your thoughts and feelings an understanding that the same point can mean "white" for one, but "black" for the other, but that in both sides there is also a common concept to understand and accept these differences.
Wir sollten begreifen, daß das, was für den einen »schwarz« ist, für den anderen »weiß« sein kann. Wir sollten diese Unterschiede annehmen.
I learned that people can solve conflicts; I learned it from other people; it really chan-

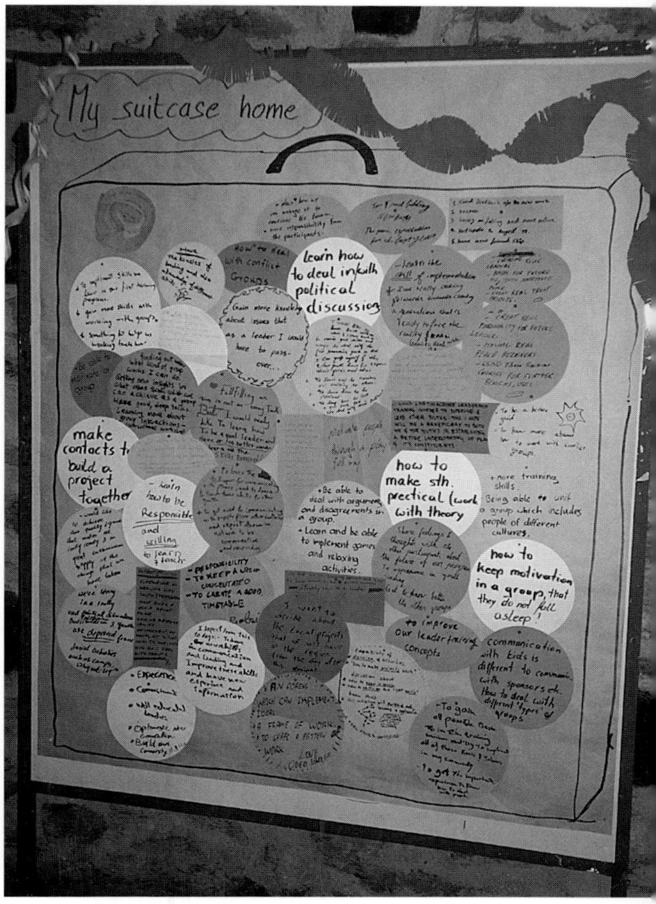

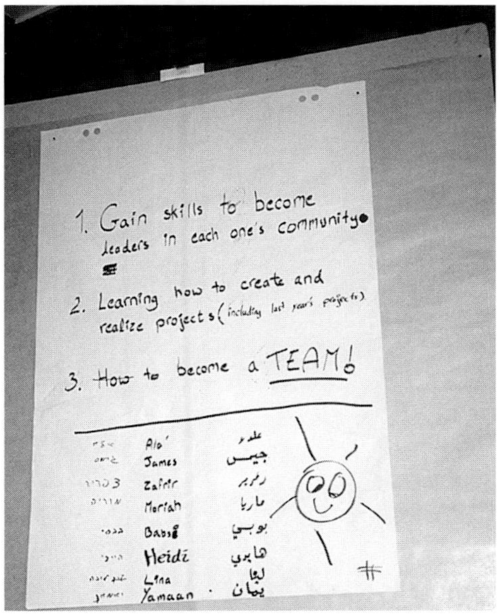

Guy Krom
Interaction /**Interaktion**
Intercultural Workshop
Interkultureller Workshop

ged my life and I wanted that change.
Ich habe von anderen Menschen gelernt, daß man Probleme lösen kann. Das hat mein Leben verändert.

Peace is the aim and it is our duty to spread the concept of the Middle East Youth Peace Forum all over. My question to everybody: Do you know where to go from here?
Frieden ist unser Ziel, und unsere Pflicht ist es, diesen Gedanken weiterzutragen. Meine Frage an alle: Wohin sollen wir jetzt gehen?

The Middle East Youth Peace Forum formed my personality.
Das Nahost-Jugend-Friedensforum hat meine Persönlichkeit geformt.

Behind an enemy there is a face and it gets harder to hate him.
Hinter jedem Feind ist ein Gesicht, und es wird immer schwieriger, ihn zu hassen.

It is a conflict that it is good to be in.
Es ist ein Konflikt, in dem es gut ist, mittendrin zu sein.

Dealing with good values: respect, trust, confidence, co-operation and understanding.
Wir haben mit guten Werten zu tun: Respekt, Vertrauen, Zusammenarbeit und Verständnis.

Speak out loudly what you have learned.
Sprich laut aus, was du gelernt hast.

Do not hurt anybody on purpose.
Niemandem absichtlich weh tun.

Overcome prejudices.
Vorurteile über Bord werfen.

Put yourself in other people's shoes.
In die Schuhe von anderen schlüpfen.

Coexistence as basis, mutual respect.
Koexistenz als Basis, gegenseitiger Respekt.

Recognition of national identity, human rights/personal rights.
Anerkennung von nationaler Identität, Menschenrechten und persönlichen Rechten

We are a team.
Wir sind ein Team.

Dear murderers!

Ladies and gentlemen! Dear friends!
I cannot celebrate this birthday, the birthday of this republic without remembering that people live in this republic who blow other people up. I want to address these bombers, through the only means I have – through words!
Dear murderers!
You cannot be found, but you are next to me, absolutely present. If you were only a couple of idiots, I wouldn't waste a word on you. But, I am afraid that a large number of Austrians are indifferent or in agreement when a few "Gypsies" are found dead in a field. I ask all these silent and semisilent supporters – and I ask you, dear murderers, in the most naive way: "What do you have against these people?" Is it the colour of their skin, the fact that they are "different", that annoys you so much that you reach for explosives? But don't forget: these differences which make them appear so detestable to you, could exist in your own families, could have been passed on to you by your parents or grandparents. It won't decrease in you by hating it in others, by blowing these people up. You, yourselves, are this mixture that you attempt to annihilate.
But, maybe I'm wrong, maybe you have another reason for killing people. Maybe you don't hear the voices of others any more, their whispers, their shouts, their tears, their fun. Maybe, you feel completely deaf, feel that only a loud explosion, can break through this deafness. Maybe, in your opinion, you feel that you have to kill somebody in order to feel alive. But your hopes are deceptive, your longings cannot be stilled. Each death only increases your own inner death. What was meant to be a cry of liberation, will only increase the silence. No joy, no lasting friendship, will come from this deed. Nobody will want to talk to you, not even your accomplices. The only people still close to you will have to remain silent.
Is it not only the hatred for people but also the hatred for this state which has driven you to this? Do you want to replace this fickle democratic institution with something stronger, greater, more unique? If fascism is really your goal just think about the end of the Third Reich. At the end everything was silent, dismembered, dead, on and beneath the ground. Its greatness had become more insignificant than ever.
Or, did you and your companions think that there would be a great fuss made over four dead Roma, when nobody talks about the hundreds of thousands who died in the war? Two of my uncles died as soldiers – my mother's brothers. From time to time, she took their photos, looked at their young faces and shook her head. Her grief was silent, personal. If you decide to honour your dead with monuments and memorial meetings, I will attempt to endure this.
Dear murderers! Are all of my assumptions about you wrong? Are you young and incensed about all those who have made the most of their life, whereas you haven't? Do you hate the sailors who have reached a safe harbour and left you behind without work, without space, without a place to live? If this is true, why then do you kill those who, like you, live on the fringe, on the outskirts of our villages and towns?
This speech, dear murderers, is an attempt to comprehend the incomprehensibility of your deed. I can only do this with words, whereas you take action, and so, I must look rather ridiculous to you. I am sticking to this position. In the end, only words can bring us forwards, talking and not aggression, arguing and not exploding. You won't gain anything by blowing people up – no new people, no new state. With every detonation, part of you will also be destroyed, until you are completely disintegrated, and have disappeared from the earth. It makes no difference if you are in prison or in freedom. I have done the only thing I can. I have spoken to you. Speak back!
Ladies and gentlemen! Dear friends!
Please excuse me for not devoting my time to those who are here, but to those who are absent. I thank you for listening – and if those who are not here also listened, then I thank them too.

Peter Turrini
Speech held on Heldenplatz, Vienna 1995
In memory of the assassination victims in the Roma settlement in Oberwart

Liebe Mörder!

Geschätzte Anwesende! Liebe Freunde!
Ich kann nicht Geburtstag feiern, den Geburtstag einer Republik, ohne daran zu denken, daß in dieser Republik Menschen leben, die andere in die Luft sprengen. Ich wende mich an diese Menschensprenger, mit dem, was mir zur Verfügung steht: mit Worten.
Liebe Mörder!

Learning a Roma love song
Beim Lernen eines Roma-Liebesliedes

Sie sind unauffindbar und doch sind Sie neben mir, ganz und gar gegenwärtig. Wären Sie nur ein paar vereinzelte Verrückte, ich würde kein Wort an Sie verschwenden. Doch ich fürchte, es ist einer großen Anzahl von Österreichern gleichgültig oder recht, wenn wieder einmal ein paar »Zigeuner« tot auf der Erde liegen. Ich frage Ihre vielen stillen und halblauten Zustimmer, und ich frage Sie, liebe Mörder, auf die naivste Art und Weise: Was haben Sie gegen diese Menschen? Ist es die Hautfarbe, das Andersartige, welches Sie so unendlich reizt, daß Sie zu Sprengsätzen greifen? Doch bedenken Sie: das Andersartige, das in Ihren Augen so Hassenswerte, das Fremde, könnte in Ihrer eigenen Familie sein, könnte von Großeltern oder Eltern an Sie weitergegeben worden sein. Es wird nicht weniger in Ihnen, wenn Sie es an anderen Menschen verabscheuen, diese Menschen in die Luft sprengen. Sie selbst sind das Gemisch, das Sie zu vernichten trachten.
Aber vielleicht irre ich mich, vielleicht haben Sie einen anderen Grund, Menschen zu ermorden. Vielleicht hören Sie die Stimmen der anderen Menschen nicht mehr: kein Geflüster, keinen Zuruf, kein Weinen und nicht die Laute der Ausgelassenheit. Vielleicht ist alles in Ihnen taub, und nur ein großer Knall, so denken Sie, kann diese Taubheit lösen. Vielleicht, so denken Sie, müssen Sie jemanden töten, damit Sie sich endlich wieder lebendig fühlen. Aber Ihre Hoffnung ist trügerisch, Ihre Sehnsucht uneinlösbar. Mit jedem Toten vermehrt sich das Tote in Ihnen. Was ein Befreiungsschrei werden sollte, wird zu einer Vermehrung der Stille. Keine Fröhlichkeit, keine bleibenden Freundschaften werden Ihnen aus dieser Tat erwachsen. Niemand wird gerne mit Ihnen reden wollen, selbst Ihre Mitmacher, die einzigen die Ihnen noch nahe sind, müssen mit Ihnen schweigen.
Ist es nicht nur der Haß auf Menschen, ist es auch der Haß auf diesen Staat, der Sie so umtreibt? Wollen Sie anstelle dieser wankelmütigen demokratischen Einrichtungen etwas Starkes, Großes, Einmaliges setzen? Ist der Faschismus tatsächlich Ihr Ziel, dann denken Sie an das Ende des Dritten Reiches. Am Schluß war alles still, zerstückelt, getötet, auf dem Boden und unter der Erde. Das Große war kleiner denn je.
Oder haben Sie und Ihre Anhänger das Gefühl, man würde wegen vier toter Roma ein Riesenaufsehen machen, während niemand mehr von den Hunderttausenden Kriegstoten redet, von Ihren gefallenen Verwandten? Zwei meiner Onkel sind als Soldaten gestorben, die Brüder meiner Mutter. In Zeitabständen nahm sie ihre Fotos zur Hand, betrachtete ihre jungen Gesichter und schüttelte den Kopf. Ihre Trauer war eine stille, private. Sollten Sie es vorziehen, Ihre Toten mit Kriegerdenkmälern und Gedenktreffen zu ehren, dann will ich versuchen, dies auszuhalten.
Liebe Mörder! Irre ich mit allen meinen Mutmaßungen über Sie? Sind Sie jung und voller Wut gegen alle, die sich viele Vorteile zu verschaffen wissen, während Sie keine haben? Hassen Sie die Bootsfahrer, die das andere Ufer erreichen und alles absperren und Sie drüben lassen, ohne Arbeit, ohne Platz , ohne Wohnung? Halten Sie sich für Ausgeschlossene? Wenn das so ist, warum töten Sie jene, die wie Sie am Rande leben, am Rande der Dörfer und der Städte?
Diese Rede, liebe Mörder, ist ein Versuch, das Unfaßbare Ihres Tuns zu fassen. Da ich dies mit Worten tue und Sie auf die Tat setzen, stehe ich ziemlich lächerlich vor Ihnen da. Ich beharre auf dieser Stellung. Letztlich bringen uns nur die Worte weiter, das Reden, und nicht das Zuschlagen, das Streiten, und nicht das Sprengen. Sie werden mit Ihrer Menschensprengerei nichts gewinnen, keinen neuen Menschen und keinen neuen Staat. Mit jedem, den Sie in die Luft sprengen, werden Sie ein Stück von sich selbst mitsprengen, bis Sie aufgelöst sind, verschwunden von der Erde. Egal, ob Sie in einem Gefängnis sitzen oder frei herumlaufen. Ich habe das einzige getan, was ich tun konnte, ich habe eine Rede an Sie gehalten. Reden Sie zurück!
Liebe Freunde! Liebe Anwesende!
Ich bitte Sie um Entschuldigung, daß ich meine Redezeit nicht für Sie verwendet habe, sondern für Abwesende. Ich danke Ihnen fürs Zuhören, und sollten die Abwesenden auch zugehört haben, dann danke ich auch Ihnen.

Peter Turrini
Rede am Wiener Heldenplatz, 1995
Zum Gedenken an die Attentatsopfer der Roma-Siedlung in Oberwart

1998
CO-OPERATION AND DIALOGUE – THE "NEW GENERATION" YOUTH LEADERS AS PARTNERS
ZUSAMMENARBEIT UND DIALOG – DIE »NEUE GENERATION« ALS PARTNER

The Middle East Youth Peace Forum opened up to other young participants from countries in Europe around the Mediterranean Sea as well as North Africa and correspondingly was renamed the Bruno Kreisky Youth Peace Forum.
Youth leaders, who have been trained in the programme of the Bruno Kreisky Forum in recent years and developed specific skills of peer group leadership and project organisation, were included in preparation and execution of the project.

Das Nahost-Jugend-Friedensforum erweiterte sich zu einer neuen Initiative, die nun Bruno-Kreisky-Jugend-Friedensforum heißt, und lud junge Menschen aus dem europäischen, nordafrikanischen und nahöstlichen Mittelmeerraum zur Mitarbeit ein. JugendleiterInnen, die in den vergangenen Jahren bei den Veranstaltungen des Bruno Kreisky Forums dabeigewesen und in einem speziellen Trainingsprogramm ausgebildet worden waren, nahmen als PartnerInnen aktiv an der Vorbereitung und Durchführung des Forums 1998 teil.

Chancellor Viktor Klima with participants and delegation leaders
Bundeskanzler Viktor Kilma mit Teilnehmern und Delegationsleitern

CREATIVE DIVERSITIES – LOOKING FOR COMMON GROUND IN THE MEDITERRANEAN
KREATIVITÄT IN DER VERSCHIEDENHEIT – AUF DER SUCHE NACH GEMEINSAMKEITEN IM MITTELMEERRAUM
Helenental (Austria)
August 11–19, 1998

The Bruno Kreisky Youth Peace Forum 1998

Based on the experience gained since the creation of the Middle East Youth Peace Forum in 1994 and in the spirit of the Euromed Partnership, the Bruno Kreisky Forum for International Dialogue suggested to build a forum of interested countries with young people from Austria, the European Mediterranean region, the Middle East and North Africa to engage in a programme conceived to promote a European-Mediterranean dialogue with Austrian, Egyptian, French, Israeli, Italian, Jordanian, Moroccan, Palestinian, Tunisian and Turkish participants.
The purpose of this encounter was to give participants an opportunity to discover and emphasise similarities in a manner that simultaneously promotes an appreciation for differences. A variety of different activities – working groups, discussions, joint events and excursions – provided participants with an opportunity to get to know each other on a personal level, to discover mutual interests, to fight prejudices and to find common ground. Working groups addressed different and pressing issues young people confront today, such as religion, culture, prejudices, environment, human rights, racism, women's role, migration, integration and democratic rights. With the help of professional trainers, members of the "New Generation" participated actively as tutors. Under the auspices of a four year programme – the Middle East Youth Peace Forum – these youth leaders have gained valuable experience in the promotion of confidence building measures, the resolution of conflicts and the dynamics of cross cultural co-operation. Furthermore each group was encouraged to come up with realistic bilateral projects to be carried out at home in the months following the meeting.

Future consolidated by peace

1994, Dawn of a new era, the year known to be born of peace, a simple handshake weathered away years of hatred and bloodshed. "Peace of brave" gave the olive branch a strength of a bullet bringing love not death, for children born in shelters, dancing to the sounds of gunshots it meant a new era, where prosperity rose in the horizon. For countries sharing border, topography and historical past and destiny, peace meant a united front for the future where generations will exchange knowledge not bullets, sow wheat not mines, to face together the challenging 21st century. Awareness of the future is born today, and a past of the democratisation process, opening up to the outbreaks of years to come, curiosity may deepen and broaden the minds, facing the challenges of technology in a changing world, undercurrents of the parties fighting for the welfare of human beings unite the youth, driving them as a force to determining the future of their country, choosing their representatives, learning from mistakes of the past, fighting for their rights. The youth in a democratic society have their right to choose the political forces formalising the future, building bridges to solve social and human problems, promoting peace not war, forcing economical flourishing into different life aspects. The peace is a message of love that all religions bear. As barriers fall, gaps are reduced; visiting, watching, talking about history, literature, art, politics, etc. thus opinions are exchanged; these challenges formulate an understanding between nations, showing the ultimate example, there is always something to teach. Hand in hand, a future to build, strongly entering the dawn of the 21st century.

Raghda N. Zawideh,
Jordanian delegation

Das Bruno-Kreisky-Jugend-Friedensforum 1998

Das Bruno Kreisky Forum für Internationalen Dialog bildete im Sinne der Euro-Med-Partnerschaft einen Kreis interessierter Länder und lud ägyptische, französische, israelische, italienische, jordanische, marokkanische, österreichische, palästinensische, tunesische und türkische Jugendliche zu einer gemeinsamen Arbeitswoche nach Österreich ein. Sowohl in die Vorbereitungen

als auch in die Durchführung des Projektes wurden JugendleiterInnnen eingebunden, die in den vergangenen vier Jahren mit dem Bruno Kreisky Forum gearbeitet hatten und in verschiedenen Trainingsprogrammen Fähigkeiten zur Gruppenleitung und Projektorganisation erworben hatten.
In Arbeitsgruppen, Diskussionen, gemeinsamen Veranstaltungen und Ausflügen konnten sie Interesse füreinander entwickeln, Vorurteile abbauen, Ähnlichkeiten entdecken, Unterschiede schätzen lernen und Gemeinsamkeiten finden. Verschiedene Themen, die jungen Menschen ein besonderes Anliegen sind, wie Religion, Kultur, Vorurteile, Umwelt, Menschenrechte, Rassismus, Frauen in der Gesellschaft, Migration, Integration, demokratische Rechte, wurden in Arbeitsgruppen von einem sehr persönlichen Standpunkt aus diskutiert.
Die verschiedenen Delegationen wurden eingeladen, an bilateralen Projekten teilzunehmen, die in den folgenden Monaten »zu Hause« weitergeführt werden sollten.

Eine Zukunft auf Frieden gebaut

1994, Dämmerung einer neuen Ära, das Jahr, das uns Frieden brachte, ein einfacher Händedruck wischte Jahre des Hasses und des Blutvergießens weg. »Friede der Mutigen« gab dem Olivenzweig die Kraft einer Kugel, die Liebe statt Tod bringt, für unsere Kinder, die in Lagern geboren wurden und zu Gewehrsalven tanzen, brach eine neue Ära an. Am Horizont schimmert Wohlstand für diese Länder, deren Grenzen, Topographie, Geschichte und Schicksale verwoben sind und in denen Frieden die künftigen Generationen einen soll. Sie werden den Herausforderungen des 21. Jahrhunderts mit Wissen und nicht mit Kugeln begegnen, sie werden Weizen säen, nicht Minen ...
Die Jugend in demokratischen Gesellschaften hat das Recht, ihre politischen Kräfte zu wählen, Brücken der Verständigung zu bauen und die Botschaft des Friedens überallhin zu tragen ... Hand in Hand werden sie in das 21. Jahrhundert schreiten.

Raghda N. Zawideh,
jordanische Delegation

Krainerhütte, Helenental

Letters from participants
Briefe von TeilnehmerInnen

*The week I spent in Austria last summer really changed me, I'm not exaggerating: before coming to Baden I didn't know what was going to happen but well, it has been such an amazing, enriching experience that it would have been impossible for me just to think something similar could take place.
I realised we all have lots of barriers, stereotypes and commonplaces due only to a scarce knowledge of the "others": differences exist, we don't have to deny them, but they're not dividing us; being different doesn't mean being superior or inferior. Very often it's easier to judge something negatively than really try to understand it!*

Valentina,
Italian delegation

Wir kamen nach Wien voll mit Stereotypen und Gemeinplätzen, weil wir wenig wußten ... Es war eine große Erfahrung: Unterschiede bestehen, aber sie dürfen uns nicht trennen ... Oft ist es leichter, etwas zu be- und zu verurteilen, als zu versuchen zu verstehen.

Valentina,
italienische Delegation

Before I came to Austria this year I thought it would be strange for me to spend a week with the youth of ten different countries talking about different matters. Especially when I knew that Israel and Palestine are participating together. I thought it wasn't going to be peaceful at all. But when I came to Austria I found something else. Something I really loved and admired. I found the youth of ten different countries participating together and becoming friends. I found them forgetting all about the differences between their countries, all about the political problems and the old wars, I found "us" becoming friends, very close friends, very true friends. The different languages and religions weren't standing in our way, because we were using the same language and respecting each other's religions. We spent only one week together. Only six days, but I guess that we did something great in this short time. I believe that each of us had his different point of view and his own opinions which (sometimes) didn't go together with other opinions. But that was a very normal thing and it really didn't bother anyone of us because we all came to the same place for the same aim: we are all youth and we all want peace, an everlasting peace. And I guess that we succeeded in doing that. At least between each other we had peace. And let me tell you that most of us became friends, very close friends. Maybe we won't

Projects of the Bruno Kreisky Youth Peace Forum
Projekte des Bruno-Kreisky-Jugend-Friedensforums

Delegation	Newsletter	Family exchanges	Internet	Cultural book	Scholarships exchanges	Pen Pals	National Reporter
Israeli	Galia, Hila	Yousouf	Ayelet, Yousef	Ayelet	Schlomi	Ivgeny	Galia
Palestinian	Amira	Firas	Firas, Layali, Zeina	Amira, Layali, Firas	Firas, Amrira, Layali, Issa, Zeina	Firas, Amira, Layali, Issa, Zeina	Firas
Jordanian	Marwa, Mahmoud		Jameel, Fares	Raghda, Mahmoud			
Egyptian	Ingy			Mohamed, Karim H.	Mohamed, Karim Gh.	Mohamed, Eman	
Tunisian	all		M'hamed S.	M'hamed S.		Haythem	Haythem
Moroccan	Karafi			Amal, Omar		Omar	
French	Chloé	all	Thomas	Natacha	Marion		Aurelie
Italian	all	Valentina, Roberta, Licia, Giuseppe	Roberta, Giuseppe	Licia	Roberta, Ilaria, Valentina, Licia, Giuseppe	Roberta, Ilaria, Valentina, Francesco, Licia	Barbara
Turkish	Orçun, Leyla, Özden	Orçun	Orçun	Peren, Leyla, Orçun	Orçun, Onur, Özden	Leyla, Orçun, Melis, Onur Peren, Farhettin	Orçun, Leyla
Austrian		Niki, Monika, Alexandra, Martina	Odin	Odin, Alexandra	Alexandra, Martina, Niki, Monika	Niki, Monika	Odin, Martina
Contact Youth Leaders	Basheer Basheer		Yamaan Safady	Ali Ababneh Thomas M.	Heidi Maier	Katarina Rohsmann	

Discussing "Human Rights" with Chancellor Viktor Klima
Diskussion über »Menschenrechte« mit Bundeskanzler Viktor Klima

have the chance to meet each other again, but that won't stop our love for each other and our faith in each other.

Eman Gamal,
Egyptian delegation

Bevor ich kam, wußte ich nicht, was ich vorfinden würde. Ich dachte, Israelis und Palästinenser zusammen, das könnte keine friedliche Sache werden. Aber ich wurde eines anderen belehrt: Wir waren Jugendliche aus zehn verschiedenen Ländern und verbrachten eine Woche, die uns alle Unterschiede vergessen, politische Schranken fallen und uns Freunde werden ließ ... Auch wenn wir uns nicht wiedersehen sollten, werden wir unsere Liebe und das Vertrauen zueinander bewahren.

Eman Gamal,
ägyptische Delegation

For what concerns the Italian delegation, we are cultivating the friendship blossomed this summer. We regularly go out together, not only in the weekend but also during the week, especially Valentina, Ilaria and me. We are keeping in touch with some of the participants and are working on the project, finishing some articles for the newsletter.

Ilaria Varese, Valentina Duretto, Licia Pagliaro

Wir von der italienischen Delegation kultivieren die neuen Freundschaften, wir sehen einander regelmäßig, wir schreiben für den nächsten Newsletter und stehen in engem Kontakt mit anderen TeilnehmerInnen.

Ilaria Varese, Valentina Duretto, Licia Pagliaro

It was a very pleasant and meaningful experience. By the way, I would like to tell you that I'm working on peace projects in Tunis and I'm writing an article for the local newspaper ...

Dania Boukadida,
Tunisian delegation

Es war ein wunderbares und wichtiges Erlebnis. Ich arbeite übrigens hier in Tunesien an Friedensprojekten und schreibe einen Artikel für eine lokale Zeitung ...

Dania Boukadida,
tunesische Delegation

Everything we wanted you gave us, and most important is the friendship that we made ... Thanks to you and to everyone that supported the Bruno Kreisky Forum, I have friends from different countries.

Amira Aweidah,
Palestinian delegation

Ihr habt uns alles gegeben, was wir uns wünschen konnten, das Wichtigste ist sicher die Freundschaft zwischen uns. Danke an alle, die das Kreisky Forum unterstützen, ich habe nun Freunde in vielen Ländern.

Amira Aweidah,
palästinensische Delegation

I published an article about the meeting in one of the most famous newspapers and it is the most spread and read all over the country. I'm doing my best to make people know about the activities in the Bruno Kreisky Forum and its efforts of promoting peace.

Karafi Bissam,
Moroccan delegation

Ich habe einen Artikel über das Forum in einer großen, wichtigen Tageszeitung veröffentlicht. Ich tue mein Bestes, um die Tätigkeiten des Bruno Kreisky Forums weiterzutragen und für den Frieden zu arbeiten ...

Karafi Bissam,
marokkanische Delegation

TRAVEL GRANT 1998
REISESTIPENDIUM 1998
Heidrun Maier, Moriah Simon and Nisreen Abu Zayyad
September 1998

Nisreen Abu Zayyad (Palestinian)

My name is Nisreen Abu Zayyad, I am a Palestinian from Jerusalem. I participated in the travel grant project, that offered me a stay in Vienna from the first of September until the first of October. Most of my programme covered some of the Austrian media, my field of interest. I had a tour at the "Wiener Zeitung", I visited the offices of the newspaper and they explained their work to me. I was very interested in the news section, but luckily I got to know more about the production of the newspaper as a whole and its position among other newspapers in Vienna.

I had the chance to visit the European Union building where I met representatives from the EU Commission and the EU Parliament. This visit gave me a deeper understanding of what the EU is. As a Middle East citizen, I only have heard about the EU and its projects in the Middle East through the media, but meeting people at the EU building helped me a lot to understand what it is all about.

I visited the UNO City, where I met the spokesperson for the UNHCR, who explained to me the status of the organisation, their activities and their importance.

I had also a schedule at the ORF, the Austrian Broadcasting and Television and the Blue Danube Radio station to understand the work of Austrian and interrnational media. It was very helpful for me because my aim is to become a journalist.

Last but not least, I visited the Wiener Integrationsfonds, a youth centre for foreigners, and I was amazed by the good activities and chances that this centre offers to young people.

Zusammenfassung

Besuch von österreichischen Tageszeitungen, ORF, EU-Kommission, UNO-City und Wiener Integrationsfonds.

Moriah Simon (Israeli)

More than simply enjoying the magnificent atmosphere of the beautiful city, Vienna, I had the opportunity to meet the people who stand behind the scenes, the people who create what we take so much for granted. The meeting with Erika, at the "Wiener Zeitung" was very interesting. Looking into the everyday work of a small newspaper, which deals with special topics – was unfamiliar to me, I enjoyed every moment of it. Two of the most interesting meetings I had during my stay, were with the UN and the EU institutions. In the EU institution for information I was fascinated by the collaboration between the European Parliament and the European Commission, fascinated by the way of dealing with so many problems for the benefit of so many countries. In the UN-City I was given a lot of information about the commissions, and again, I was fascinated by the power of this organisation and by its sensitivity in every field and aspect of the world. The meeting with ORF Television and Radio were also very

Tommy, Karin, Tove, Nisreen, Moriah, Katarina
Moriah and Heike Hausensteiner from the Wiener Zeitung
Moriah und Heike Hausensteiner von der Wiener Zeitung

nice. I enjoyed making the comparison between my radio station in Israel to this one ... It was also very interesting to meet the people who work with minorities.

Zusammenfassung
Besuch von österreichischen Tageszeitungen und dem ORF, von EU- und UN-Institutionen und von Initiativen, die mit Minderheiten arbeiten.

Heidrun Maier (Austrian)
Middle East Impressions
In September 1998 I got a travel grant from the Bruno Kreisky Forum and so I had the opportunity to go to the Middle East for one month. One of the biggest problems of the Austrians is that they live quite far away from the region. So it is really hard for them to understand the daily life problems there. Secondly, our task was to work upon the common projects the "New Generation" worked out from 1994 till 1998.
One of my aims was to see as much as possible, because for many of my friends it is really hard to travel. Jerusalem, Bethlehem, Ramallah, Tel Aviv, Ness Ziona were just some of my stops. I realised how difficult it is for them to meet, especially for the Israelis and Palestinians.
So, I was carrying information, hopes and desires from one side to the other (Israeli, Palestinian and Jordanian) to strengthen the contact and to work and to update the projects.
My trip broadened my thoughts and when I came back to Austria it was hard getting back to normal life.

Zusammenfassung:
Heidrun Maier bereiste einen Monat lang Israel, die Westbank und Jordanien, traf viele der TeilnehmerInnen wieder und begriff, wie schwer es für ihre Freunde ist, von einem Ort zum anderen zu gelangen. Dieser Aufenthalt hat sie sowohl persönlich als auch hinsichtlich ihrer Studien außerordentlich bereichert.

Nisreen
Moriah
Heidi

Nataly, Shirley, Eran planting trees
Nataly, Shirley, Eran beim Bäumepflanzen
Simone, Tali, Adi, Kirstin after the tree planting
Simone, Tali, Adi, Kirstin nach dem Bäumepflanzen

DELEGATION LEADERS
DELEGATIONSLEITUNG

ABBASI-GHANEM, AHLAM
1994, 1995

Arab Studies Society Jerusalem,
International desk
Palestinian delegation

Orly, Ahlam, Tali
Margit, Nisreen, Ahlam

ABU NEMEH, WA'EL
1995, 1996, 1997, 1998

Works at the Al Quds University and studies law
Palestinian delegation

ARIDA, ISSAM
1994, 1996

Former director of King Hussein Sports City
and Ministry of Youth
Jordanian delegation

Orly, Tali, Issam, Gertraud, Wa'el

Margit, Gertraud

AUER-BOREA D'OLMO, GERTRAUD
1994, 1995, 1996, 1997, 1998

Project leader
Lives in Italy

For Clementina, Marco, Michele, Sara, Sebastian, Cori, Tal, Ido ... and all the children of the "New Generation"

Für Clementina, Marco, Michele, Sara, Sebastian, Cori, Tal, Ido ... und alle Kinder der »Neuen Generation«

DANILOV, SHIRA
1997

Unit for Democracy and Coexistence,
Ministry of Education
Israeli delegation

Shira, Orly

DOSS ADLI DOSS, MERVAT
1994

Professor at the American University of Cairo
Egyptian delegation

Mervat, Margit, Oliver Rathkolb

Orly, Tali

FRUCHTER YAGODOVSKY, ORLY
1995, 1996, 1997, 1998

Unit for Democracy and Coexistence,
Ministry of Education
Israeli delegation

HUSSEINI, HANI
1994, 1996, 1997, 1998

Palestinian delegation

KILDANI, SAMAR
1994, 1996, 1997, 1998

Director of the Al Hassan Youth Award
Jordanian delegation

Wafa, Samar

LIDAR, TALIA
1994, 1995, 1996, 1997, 1998

Unit for Democracy and Coexistence,
Ministry of Education
Israeli delegation

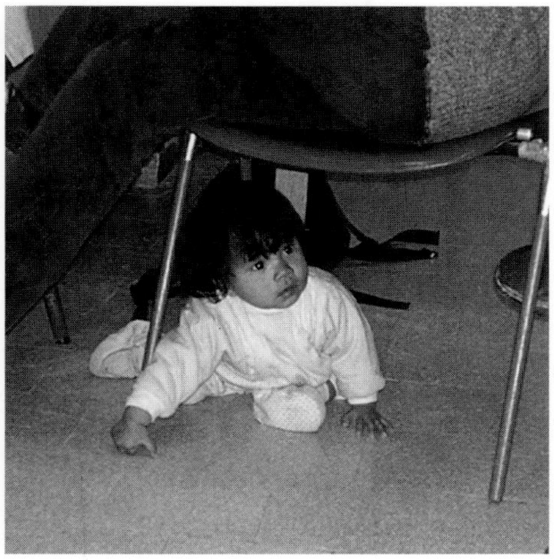

Tali's daughter Cori
Talis Tochter Cori

Shaul, Wa'el, Kareem

PAZ, SHAUL
1996

Director of the Unit for Democracy,
Israeli Ministry of Education
Israeli delegation

RAIBY, TOVE
1994, 1995, 1996, 1997, 1998

Bruno Kreisky Forum, organisation and co-ordination
Austrian delegation leader

Tove's daugther Sara
Toves Tochter Sara

SALEH, HAMDI
1994

Ministry of Foreign Affairs, Cairo
Egyptian delegation

At the Opening Ceremony 1994;
Hamdi Saleh (left) with embassy officials
Bei der Eröffnungsfeier 1994;
Hamdi Saleh (links) mit Botschaftsangehörigen

SCHMIDT, MARGIT
1994, 1995, 1996, 1997, 1998

Bruno Kreisky Forum, Secretary General
Project leader
Collaborator of Bruno Kreisky from
1965–1990

We dedicate the "New Generation" programme to Bruno Kreisky and the legacy for his lifelong vision of a peaceful Middle East for the sake of its peoples.

Wir widmen das Programm der »Neuen Generation« Bruno Kreisky und seinem Vermächtnis einer lebenslangen Vision eines friedlichen Nahen Ostens zum Wohl seiner Völker.

Margit Schmidt and late Chancellor Bruno Kreisky
Margit Schmidt und der frühere Bundeskanzler Bruno Kreisky

SHOHAT, DORON
1994

Israeli delegation

Hannes, Doron

TRAINERS
PÄDAGOG/INNEN

Ben Ami, Yael
1997, 1998
Israeli delegation

Biegeleisen, Sylvain
1997, 1998
Israeli delegation

Burgan Kildani, Violette
1997
Jordanian delegation

Ceplak, Karl
1995
City of Vienna, Youth Department,
Verein Wiener Jugendkreis
Austrian delegation

Darweish, Marwan
1998
IPCRI – Israel/Palestine Centre for Research and Information
Palestinian delegation

Fennes, Helmut
1994
Intercultural Centre
Austrian delegation

Finder, Gudrun
1994
Austrian delegation

Freytag, Ulrike
1994
Austrian delegation

Glatt, Elisabeth
1994
Austrian delegation

Gstir, Hannes
1994, 1997, 1998
Co-leader of the training team with Diane Hendrick; Youth Division of Tyrol
Austrian delegation

Hendrick, Diane
1994, 1997, 1998
Head of the training team
Austrian delegation

Sari, Helmi
1998
Jordanian delegation

Teutsch, Rüdiger
1994
Intercultural Centre
Austrian delegation

Wallner, Michael
1995
Austrian delegation

Karl and his daughter Sara
Karl und seine Tochter Sara
Marwan, Helmi, Samar, Anas
Sylvain, Diane, Ya'el, Violette, Samar

Tyrol – resting pole of the Middle East Youth Peace Forum
Tirol – der ruhende Pol des Nahost-Jugend-Friedensforums

It was not an everyday inquiry when the Kreisky Forum contacted us to ask if we could imagine organising a programme for a cross section of youths from the Middle East. ...
We wanted to create an atmosphere that would make it possible for the participants to deepen their first contacts, reduce prejudices and increase trust. For us, this was the fundamental meaning and lasting value of this event, independent from the peace conference itself.
Young people from very different cultures and states that in some cases were hostile to each other should learn that personal relationships, even friendships are possible, despite profound differences ...

Hannes Gstir

Es war für uns sicher keine alltägliche Anfrage, die wir im September 1993 aus Wien erhielten: Könnt Ihr Euch vorstellen, junge Israelis, Palästinenser, Jordanier, Ägypter, Syrer und Libanesen in Tirol zu empfangen und ein interessantes Programm für sie zu organisieren? Nach kurzer Beratung konnten wir es uns vorstellen – die Herausforderung, bei diesem neuen und sicher auch gewagten Projekt mitzuarbeiten, reizte uns sehr. Außerdem empfanden wir es als eine Ehre, daß aus acht möglichen Bundesländern gerade wir für diese Aufgabe ausgewählt wurden. In der Folge setzten rege Kontakte zwischen Wien und Tirol ein. Es gab jede Menge Sitzungen, um Probleme zu besprechen (z. B. die Absage der Syrer und der Libanesen), das Programm des Nahost-Jugend-Friedensforums zusammenzustellen und die verschiedenen Teile aufeinander abzustimmen ... Es stellte sich bald heraus, daß die ersten Tage in Wien und natürlich auch die Konferenz sehr anstrengend für die TeilnehmerInnen werden würden. Also entschlossen wir uns, das Programm in Tirol eher erholsam zu gestalten ... Ich hatte dann in den ersten Tagen des Nahost-Jugend-Friedensforums selbst Gelegenheit, an der Veranstaltung des Interkulturellen Zentrums teilzunehmen, und war fasziniert von der Offenheit der Jugendlichen. Sie kehrten die unterschiedlichen Meinungen zur Situation in ihrer Heimat nicht einfach unter den Teppich, sondern äußerten sie klar und deutlich und diskutierten sie auch teilweise sehr emotional. Gleichzeitig aber schlossen sie Bekanntschaften über ideologische Grenzen hinweg und erkannten die Menschen hinter den Gegnern. Besonders deutlich wurde das bei den mitternächtlichen Partys im Keller des Jugendgästehauses. Währenddessen liefen die letzten Vorbereitungen in Tirol auf Hochtouren, und als wir in Innsbruck eintrafen, war alles vorbereitet ... Nach der kurzen Eröffnung mit Informationen über das geplante Programm und der Einteilung in Gruppen für den nächsten Tag machte »Maik« Baumgartner mit seinen »Huangartlern« Stimmung mit Tiroler Volksmusik. Es stellte sich heraus, daß die Jugendlichen begabte und begeisterte Volkstänzer waren. Am zweiten Tag sollten sich die Jugendlichen in vier Gruppen mit wichtigen Themen für Tirol vertraut machen. Verpackt in ein abwechslungsreiches Programm mit Wanderungen und Besichtigungen waren die Bereiche Wasser und Energie, Tourismus, Verkehr und Transit sowie Umweltschutz weit interessanter, als es am Anfang den Anschein gehabt hatte. So gewannen die Jugendlichen auf lockere Weise Einblick in Stärken, Schwächen, Probleme und die Schönheit unseres Landes ... Der nächste Tag bot die Gelegenheit einer Fußwanderung vom Heim aus auf den Patscherkofel ... Das schöne Wetter machte diese Wanderung sicher zu einem wunderbaren Erlebnis. Anschließend wurde schon deutlich die Spannung in den Gruppen spürbar, die sich auf die Friedenskonferenz der letzten Tage in Wien vorbereiteten. Dies zeigte auch den Druck auf, unter dem die Jugendlichen durch die Zugehörigkeit zu einer Delegation ihres Landes standen. ...
Für uns blieb ein positiver Eindruck von diesem Ereignis und die Überzeugung, einen kleinen Beitrag zum gegenseitigen Verständnis der beteiligten Jugendlichen geleistet zu haben.

Hannes Gstir

Intercultural Workshop with young people from the Middle East
Interkultureller Workshop mit Jugendlichen aus dem Nahen Osten

"I haven't met any Israeli before I came to the Middle East Youth Peace Forum here in Vienna but I have been informed about the political situation intensively by TV and newspapers in my home country", stated Ramzi (18) from Jordan and expressed what most of

Hannes, Diane

the other participants felt when they arrived … They had neither seen nor talked to each other during their whole life. Considering this fact the Intercultural Workshop which opened the Middle East Youth Peace Forum aimed at the personal encounter in order to contribute to the confidence building between people who were mainly raised in a tradition of mistrust and the unimpeachable certainty of pleading for the right cause.
The concept of the Intercultural Workshop put special emphasis on attempts to overcome culture-centred attitudes and behaviour, to strengthen the sensitivity for complex situations, to develop open-mindedness towards opinions being inconsistent with their own ones and to encourage the young people to continue their personal communication and co-operation in spite of all opposing conflicts. The Intercultural Project continued by exploring Vienna with respect to a specific theme like "Youth", "Media", "Religions", "Food and Drink", "Street Names", "Shopping", "Tourism", "Traffic" and "Housing". The outcome of the project was quite surprising – not only in terms of facts and figures but also regarding the co-operation between the participants: young women and men coming from a region where it is mostly unusual to have peaceful images about each other worked together and developed a basis for the communication and co-operation during the Middle East Youth Peace Conference and hopefully also for a future co-operation in their region …

Dr. Rüdiger Teutsch,
Intercultural Centre

… Der interkulturelle Workshop diente zur Vorbereitung auf die Friedenskonferenz und beinhaltete vertrauensbildende Maßnahmen und Zusammenarbeit in verschiedenen Themenbereichen wie »Jugend«, »Medien«, »Religion«, »Straßennamen«, »Einkaufen und Tourismus« etc.
Das Resultat war überrraschend, da diese jungen Frauen und Männer aus einer sehr unfriedlichen Region zum ersten Mal in ihrem Leben eine gemeinsame Basis der Zusammenarbeit für die Zeit der Konferenz, aber auch für danach herstellten …

Dr. Rüdiger Teutsch,
Interkulturelles Zentrum

OTHER COLLABORATORS
WEITERE MITARBEITER/INNEN

Karin M., Karin P.
Melitta

Our special thanks to the following collaborators:
Besonderer Dank gebührt folgenden MitarbeiterInnen:

Campostrini, Melitta
Bruno Kreisky Forum

Freund, Martina
1994
Austrian delegation

Mendel, Karin
Bruno Kreisky Forum

Paolazzi, Ruth
1994
Youth Division of Tyrol
Austrian delegation

Pramberger, Karin
1994, 1996, 1997
Bruno Kreisky Forum

Schmid, Raimund
1994, 1998
Austrian delegation

Turki, Abdullah
1994
Austrian delegation

EVALUATION OF THE MIDDLE EAST YOUTH PEACE FORUM
EVALUATION DES NAHOST-JUGEND-FRIEDENSFORUMS

The Institute for Conflict Research, Vienna (Austria), evaluated the Middle East Youth Peace Forum in co-operation with the Institute for Interdisciplinary Research and Further Education and concluded:
"Through its continuity over time, through its reluctance simply to accept existing constraints and through its unrelenting efforts to come to grips with external and internal difficulties, the Middle East Peace Forum performs the role of offering political education. By constantly dealing with the other and with divergent opinions, participants are able to learn to deal with conflicts in a constructive manner, which impacts on their attitudes and behaviour patterns (Heintel 1977: Diem-Wille/Wimmer 1988).
Although a project such as this one cannot directly influence the peace process in the Middle East, it has already brought about a lasting change in the everyday lives of participants – it is their task to pass on this idea, and they can build on solid foundations in doing so. (...)
Altogether, this venture has been recognised by everyone involved as highly successful and politically educating. There is full agreement that the form represents a cornerstone for future developments as it supports a new generation of conflicting parties who have learnt that regardless of the many differences friendships can prevail and that there exists a unilateral desire for peace. (...)
Thus, the Youth Peace Forum can be seen as a successful model for political education. The concept has proved suitable for use with young people whose countries of origin or whose ethnic backgrounds are in conflict with each other. Success in the given context implies understanding the other side and being able to talk about differences and similarities."

Research: Dr. Birgitt Haller, Dr. Wolfgang Knopf, directed by: Univ. Prof. Dr. Anton Pelinka

Das Institut für Konfliktforschung in Wien erstellte in Zusammenarbeit mit dem Institut für Interdisziplinäre Forschung und Fortbildung eine Evaluierung des Nahost-Jugend-Friedensforums und kam zu folgendem Schluß:
Das Nahost-Jugend-Friedensforum ist jedenfalls politisch bildend: durch seine zeitliche Kontinuität, durch die Tatsache, daß »Sachzwänge« nicht einfach hingenommen werden, daß die Bewältigung von Schwierigkeiten von außen und von innen immer wieder in Angriff genommen wurde und wird. Die permanent geforderte Auseinandersetzung mit dem anderen ermöglicht es den TeilnehmerInnen zu lernen, sich konstruktiv mit Konflikten auseinanderzusetzen, sie hat Auswirkungen auf Einstellungen und auf das Verhalten (Heintel 197: Diem-Wille/Wimmer 1988). Wenn ein solches Projekt auch keine unmittelbaren Auswirkungen auf den Friedensprozeß im Nahen Osten haben kann, so hat sich doch der Alltag der beteiligten Personen nachhaltig verändert – an ihnen liegt es, diese Idee weiterzutragen, wichtige Grundlagen dafür wurden ihnen vermittelt. (...)
Das gesamte Vorhaben wird von allen beteiligten Personen auf allen Ebenen als erfolgreich und in höchstem Maß politisch bildend betrachtet. Alle sind sich einig, daß das Forum einen wichtigen Baustein für die Zukunft darstellt, weil es eine neue Generation von KonfliktpartnerInnen unterstützt, die gelernt hat, daß Freundschaften trotz Gegensätzen bestehen können und daß auf allen Seiten der Wunsch nach Frieden geteilt wird. (...)
Das Jugend-Friedensforum kann somit als ein Modell der politischen Bildung fungieren. Diese Konzeption erscheint geeignet, um mit Jugendlichen, deren Nationen oder ethnische Herkunftsgruppen miteinander in Konflikt stehen, erfolgreich politische Bildung durchzuführen – wenn als Erfolg das Verstehen der anderen Seite und die Fähigkeit, über Unterschiede und Gemeinsamkeiten zu kommunizieren, gesehen wird.

Wissenschaftliche Durchführung: Dr. Birgitt Haller, Dr. Wolfgang Knopf unter der Leitung von Univ. Prof. Dr. Anton Pelinka

Researchers and trainers with Austrian group
Experten und Trainer mit der österreichischen Gruppe

EPILOGUE
NACHWORT

The idea to open up the programme of peace education, which started in 1994 with the Middle East Youth Peace Forum, to other countries from the Mediterranean region turned out very successfully. It was very healthy for the atmosphere and fruitful for the work to leave the central conflict of the peace process in the Middle East and to concentrate on a cultural dialogue. The participants followed with great interest the confrontation of oriental and western culture, of Jewish, Christian and Moslem religion, of tradition and modernity. Meeting new people offered new possibilities of co-operation and created a feeling of being part of a wider horizon. Federal Chancellor Viktor Klima underlined in his lecture and in the discussion with the youth that such initiatives are the tools for fighting extremism and terrorism. The idea to actively involve the youth leaders of the Middle East Youth Peace Forum showed that it is possible to hand over the torch and to create a new form of co-operation. This potential of young trained people, who have developed methods of conflict resolution by working together as a team, should be used for other initiatives. Public and private institutions, like the Peres Centre for peace (Tel Aviv), the Van Leer Institute in Jerusalem, the European Youth Forum, etc., have already pointed out their interest. The future meetings will be organised in the region in co-operation with the partners and with the help of the youth leaders. The Bruno Kreisky Forum for International Dialogue has proved that the seeds of the last five years have grown and became flourishing trees.

The Project Leaders

Die Idee, den 1994 begonnenen Prozeß der Friedenserziehung und multilateralen Zusammenarbeit auf eine größere Runde von teilnehmenden Ländern auszuweiten und die Mittelmeerregion (Nordafrika und Südeuropa) einzubeziehen, erwies sich als sehr erfolgreich. Es hat sich in allen Programmpunkten gezeigt, daß sich die Herauslösung aus dem Kernkonflikt »Naher Osten« und das Öffnen gegenüber Partnern aus anderen Regionen auf die Atmosphäre entspannend und auf die Ergebnisse extrem befruchtend ausgewirkt haben. Die Auseinandersetzung zwischen westlichem und orientalischem Kulturkreis, zwischen der jüdischen, der christlichen und der moslemischen Weltanschauung, zwischen Traditionsgebundenheit und Modernismus hat großes Interesse hervorgerufen und viele neue Lernprozesse in Gang gebracht. Die direkte Begegnung hat neue Möglichkeiten der Zusammenarbeit eröffnet und das Gefühl, in einen größeren Kontext eingebunden zu sein, entstehen lassen. Wie Bundeskanzler Klima in seiner Rede immer wieder betonte, sind Initiativen wie diese der Weg zu friedlicher Koexistenz und ein Werkzeug zur Bekämpfung von Fanatismus und Terrorismus. Die aktive Einbeziehung unserer jungen PartnerInnen und deren verantwortungsvolles Engagement haben bewiesen, daß es möglich ist, die Staffette weiterzugeben und mit der »Neuen Generation« eine neue Form von Zusammenarbeit herzustellen. Dieses Potential geschulter junger Menschen, die neue Methoden der Konfliktlösung erarbeitet haben, soll in verschiedensten Initiativen eingesetzt werden. Öffentliche und private Institutionen, wie z. B. das Peres Centre for Peace (Tel Aviv), das Van Leer Institut in Jerusalem, das europäische Jugendforum u. a., haben bereits ihr Interesse geäußert. Die zukünftigen Treffen sollen, wie vorläufig geplant, mit österreichischer Unterstützung in der Region stattfinden und mit Hilfe der Youth Leaders organisiert und durchgeführt werden. Damit hat das Bruno Kreisky Forum für Internationalen Dialog gezeigt, daß die vor fünf Jahren in die Erde gesetzte Saat bereits beginnt, erste Früchte zu tragen.

Die Projektleiterinnen

LEADERS, TRAINERS, PARTICIPANTS, PARTNERS AND OFFICIAL REPRESENTATIVES
LEITER/INNEN, PÄDAGOG/INNEN, TEILNEHMER/INNEN, PARTNER/INNEN, OFFIZIELLE

Abbasi, Ahlam (L), 1994, 1995
Abbasi, Mousa (P), 1995, 1996
Abd El-Quader, Ali (P), 1996
Abdul Hadi, Kareem (P), 1994, 1996, 1997, 1998
Abdullah, Nisreen (P), 1995
Abu Ein, Ala' (P), 1995, 1996, 1997, 1998
Abu Karaki, Anas (P), 1997, 1998
Abu Nemeh, Wael (L), 1995, 1996, 1998
Abu Snineh, Sami (P), 1994, 1995
Abu Zayyad, Nisreen (P), 1995, 1996, 1997, 1998
Abu-Nemeh, Nancy (P), 1994
Al-Ababneh, Ali (P), 1994, 1996, 1997, 1998
Alden Rimawi, Muhy (L), 1997
Al-Fuqaha, Emad (P), 1994, 1996, 1997, 1998
Al-Mashat, Rania (P), 1994
Al-Nimri, Juman (P), 1994, 1996, 1997
Al-Sheikh, Fida (P), 1994, 1995, 1996
Amin Ibsais, Hanaa (P) , 1996
Amram, Sima (P), 1994, 1995
Anani, Rawan (P), 1996
Asaf, Zafrir (P), 1996, 1997, 1998
Askria-Dababneh Wafa (P), 1994, 1996, 1997, 1998
Auer-Borea d'Olmo, Gertraud (L), 1994, 1995, 1996, 1997, 1998
Avidan, Shirley (P), 1994, 1996
Aweidah, Mohammad (P), 1995, 1996
Barakat, Abir (P), 1995
Basheer, Basheer (P), 1994, 1995, 1996, 1997, 1998
Ben Ami, Yael (T), 1997, 1998
Ben-Et, Itamar (P), 1994, 1995
Biegeleisen, Sylvain (T), 1997, 1998
Bilia, Itsik (P), 1994
Burgan Kildani, Violette (T), 1997
Campostrini, Melitta (PT), 1994
Caspi, Raffi (P), 1994, 1996, 1998
Ceplak, Karl (T), 1995
Cesnovar, Christof (P) , 1994, 1995, 1996
Christiani, Dr. Alexander (A) , 1994
Cohen, Tal (P), 1996
Daher, Sana (P), 1994, 1995
Danilov, Shira (L), 1997
Darweish, Marwan (T), 1998
Davidai, Nataly (P), 1996, 1997
Doss Adli Doss, Dr. Mervat (L), 1994
Dror, Adi (P), 1995, 1996, 1997
Egerer, Thomas (P), 1994, 1995, 1996, 1997, 1998
El Din Nasrat, Ahmed Nour (P), 1994
El Mikurad, Hesham (P), 1994
Elloulou, Maged (P), 1994, 1995
El-Razzaz, Rania (P), 1994
Erfan, Ihab (P), 1994
Feidi, Adel (P), 1994
Fennes, Dipl.Ing. Helmut (T), 1994
Finder, Gudrun (T), 1994
Fischer, Lisa (P), 1996, 1997, 1998
Freund, Martina (PT), 1994
Freytag, Dr. Ulrike (T), 1994
Fruchter-Yagodovsky, Orly (L) , 1995, 1996, 1997, 1998
Gershtein, Ina (P), 1995, 1996
Gilbert, Jason (P), 1995
Glatt, Elisabeth (T), 1994
Glatz, Philippe (P), 1994, 1996
Grießer, Martin (P), 1996
Gstir, Hannes (T), 1994, 1997, 1998
Habash, Ramzi (P), 1996, 1997, 1998
Halaby, Ramzi (P), 1994
Hameed Al-Hajj, Ahmad (P), 1994, 1996
Hasanat, Salim Mohammed (L), 1996
Helmi, Bassant (P), 1994
Hendrick, Dr. Diane (T), 1994, 1997, 1998
Husseini, Hani (L), 1994, 1996, 1997, 1998
Inmann, Katrin (P), 1996
Inmann, Kirstin (P), 1996
Jalabneh, Hiba (P), 1994, 1996, 1997, 1998
Jarrar, Reem (P), 1996
Jech, Barbara (P), 1994, 1995, 1996, 1997, 1998
Jubran, Suha (P), 1994, 1995, 1996, 1997, 1998
Juha, Elisabeth (P), 1994
Kajjo, James (P), 1994, 1995, 1996, 1997, 1998
Kempel, Dr. Willy (PT), 1994
Khalaf, Firas (P), 1996, 1997, 1998
Khalidi, Natasha (P), 1996
Kheirallah, Amro (P), 1994
Kildani, Samar (L), 1994, 1996, 1997, 1998
Kohler, Bernhard (P), 1996
Koller, Harald (PT), 1994
Krenchel, Mar'it (P), 1996
Krom, Guy (P), 1994, 1996, 1998
Kudsieh, Mike (P), 1994, 1996
Leibovitz, Ori (P), 1995, 1996, 1997, 1998
Leitl, Markus (P), 1994
Levine, Ronit (P), 1996
Lidar, Talia (L), 1994, 1995, 1996, 1998

Ludwin, Kobi (P), 1995, 1996
Maier, Heidrun Liselotte (P), 1994, 1995, 1996, 1997, 1998
Marom, Niv (P), 1996
Marte, Judith (A), 1994
Marx, Yaron (P), 1997
Mason, Orlando (P) , 1994, 1995, 1996
Meir, Hagit (P), 1996
Melichar, Thomas (P) , 1994, 1995, 1996, 1997, 1998
Mendel, Karin (PT), 1994, 1996
Mitwalli, Suad (P), 1996, 1997, 1998
Mughannam, Rawan (P), 1996
Nasser, Zein (P), 1996, 1998
Netzl, Dr.Gerald (PT), 1994
Niv, Eyal (P), 1996
Odeh, Nahida (P) , 1996
Paolazzi, Ruth (PT), 1994
Paz, Shaul (A), 1996
Pomerantz, Limor (P), 1994
Pramberger, Karin (PT), 1994, 1996, 1997
Quedan, Monther (P), 1994
Queider, Khuloud (P), 1994, 1995, 1996
Rabl, Maximilian (P), 1996
Radauer, Leopold (PT), 1994
Raiby, Tove (L), 1994, 1995, 1996, 1997, 1998
Rathkolb, DDr. Oliver (PT), 1994
Rohsmann, Katharina (P), 1994, 1995, 1996, 1997, 1998
Sa'ad, Abdul Ghani (P), 1996
Safady, Yamaan (P), 1997, 1998
Salameh, Dima (P), 1996
Saleh, Dr. Hamdi (L), 1994
Sandler, Oded (P), 1994, 1998
Sari, Helmi (T), 1998
Schmid, Raimund (PT), 1994, 1998
Schmidt, Margit (L), 1994, 1995, 1996, 1997, 1998
Segal, Keren (P), 1994, 1996, 1997, 1998
Seikaly, Abeer (P), 1996
Seper, Simone (P), 1994, 1995, 1996, 1997, 1998
Shadah, Lina (P), 1997
Shadmi, Tomer (P), 1996
Shaifer, Amir (P), 1996
Shamir, Eran (P), 1994, 1995, 1996, 1997
Sharir, Zivan (P), 1994
Shelbaya, Mervat (P) , 1994
Shohat, Doron (L), 1994
Shuhabi, Mahar (P), 1994, 1995, 1996, 1997, 1998
Simon, Moriah (P), 1996, 1997, 1998
Snir, Asaf (P), 1996
Starnberger, Sonja (P), 1994, 1996, 1997
Tamari, Michal (P), 1994, 1996, 1998
Teutsch, Dr. Rüdiger (T), 1994
Tirosh, Roy (P), 1994
Toukan, Oraib (P), 1994
Turki, Abdullah (PT), 1994
Vorhofer, Hannes (P), 1994, 1995, 1996, 1997, 1998,
Wallner, Michael (T), 1995
Wehbeh, Ehsan (P), 1995, 1996
Yassin, Mahmoud (P), 1996, 1997, 1998
Yvon, Yannic (P), 1996
Zeleznikar, Marijana (P) , 1994, 1995, 1996
Zeltzer, Dan (P), 1996
Zilber, Yuval (P), 1995, 1996
Zimmermann, Karin (P) , 1994, 1995, 1996, 1997, 1998
Zomet, Yossi (P), 1996
Zreikat, Cedar (P), 1997, 1998

BRUNO KREISKY FORUM FOR INTERNATIONAL DIALOGUE
BRUNO KREISKY FORUM FÜR INTERNATIONALEN DIALOG

The Bruno Kreisky Forum for International Dialogue was founded as an independent non-for-profit association in May 1991 to promote the exchange of ideas and investigation of political issues that were central concerns of Bruno Kreisky during his career as a politician and statesman, and are still relevant today. Its objectives as a permanent centre of dialogue are to promote international discourse and the joint research and discussion of pressing contemporary issues. The Kreisky Forum brings politicians, scientists, scholars and critical spirits from all countries and continents together on a regular basis to address those problems that only will be able to be solved in a global context in the future. Since 1991 the lectures and discussions at the Kreisky Forum have become an integral component for public discourse and regularly draw a highly qualified audience of decision makers from the private sector, academia, diplomatic circles as well as representatives of domestic and international media.
Its focal points are: unemployment and the global economy, north-south dialogue and development co-operation, human rights, Europe since 1989 and the peace process in the Middle East.

Das Bruno Kreisky Forum für Internationalen Dialog wurde im Mai 1991 als unabhängiger, gemeinnütziger Verein gegründet, der in seiner Aufgabenstellung an die internationalen Aktivitäten des großen österreichischen Staatsmannes Bruno Kreisky anknüpft. Im ständigen und konkreten Dialog zwischen renommierten Persönlichkeiten aus Politik, Wirtschaft, Wissenschaft und Kultur werden reale Lösungsansätze zu den wesentlichen Gestaltungsfragen der Menschheit entwickelt und auch in den internationalen Entscheidungsprozeß eingebracht. Ziel dieses Forums ist es, aus innovativen und zukunftsorientierten Ideen im Dialog realpolitische Strategien zu entwickeln, um einen konkreten Interessensausgleich zu fördern. Seit 1991 sind die Vorträge und Diskussionen im Kreisky Forum integraler Bestandteil des öffentlichen Diskurses, und zum Stammpublikum gehören Entscheidungsträger aus der Wirtschaft, Wissenschaft, Diplomatie und den Medien.
Die Schwerpunktthemen sind: Arbeitslosigkeit und Weltwirtschaft, Nord-Süd-Dialog und Entwicklungszusammenarbeit, Menschenrechte, Europa nach 1989 und der Friedensprozeß im Nahen Osten.

***President*/Präsident**:
Dr. Franz Vranitzky,
former Federal Chancellor of Austria
Bundeskanzler a. D.

***Secretary General*/Generalsekretärin:**
Margit Schmidt

***Address*/Adresse:**
Bruno Kreisky Forum for International Dialogue
Armbrustergasse 15
A-1190 Vienna, Austria
Tel. · +43-1-318 82 60
Fax · +43-1-378 51 11
E-Mail: kreiskyforum@eunet.at
http://members.eunet.at/kreiskyforum/

EDITORS AND WRITERS
HERAUSGEBERINNEN UND SCHRIFTSTELLER/INNEN

Gertraud Auer Borea d'Olmo
Project leader together with Margit Schmidt
Projektverantwortliche gemeinsam mit Margit Schmidt

Tove Raiby
Responsible for organisation and administration
Verantwortliche für Organisation und Administration

Margit Schmidt
Secretary general of the Bruno Kreisky Forum and project leader together with Gertraud Auer Borea d'Olmo
Generalsekretärin des Bruno Kreisky Forums und Projektverantwortliche gemeinsam mit Gertraud Auer Borea d'Olmo

Special thanks to Sonja Starnberger for her kind collaboration
Ein Dankeschön an Sonja Starnberger für ihre engagierte Mitarbeit

Writers
SchriftstellerInnen

Marion Gräfin Dönhoff
Editor of the German newspaper "Die Zeit"
Herausgeberin »Die Zeit«

Freimut Duve
Delegate of the OSCE
Medienbeauftragter der OSZE (Organisation für Sicherheit und Zusammenarbeit in Europa)

Sumaya Farhat-Nasr
Palestinian writer
Palästinensische Essayistin

David Grossmann
Israeli writer
Israelischer Schriftsteller
*Quotations from/*Zitate aus *"A Discussion about Israel Today – Intellectual Mainstreams in Arab and Jewish Communities: Development Towards Fundamentalism on Both Sides" Bruno Kreisky Forum, 26.2.1993*

Emile Habiby
Palestinian writer
Palästinensischer Schriftsteller
*Quotations from/*Zitate aus *"A Discussion about Israel Today – Intellectual Mainstreams in Arab and Jewish Communities: Development Towards Fundamentalism on Both Sides" Bruno Kreisky Forum, 26.2.1993*

Doris Lessing
British writer
Britische Schriftstellerin

Sari Nusseibeh
President of Al Quds University, Jerusalem
Rektor der Al Quds Universität, Jerusalem
*Quotations from the public debate/*Zitate aus der öffentlichen Diskussion *"Arts and Politics – Authors in Dialogue", Bruno Kreisky Forum, 20.6.1995*

Amos Oz
Israeli writer
Israelischer Schriftsteller
*Quotations from the public debate/*Zitate aus der öffentlichen Diskussion *"Arts and Politics – Authors in Dialogue", Bruno Kreisky Forum, 20.6.1995*

Gerhard Roth
Austrian writer
Österreichischer Schriftsteller

Peter Turrini
Austrian writer
Österreichischer Dramatiker und Schriftsteller

FOTOCREDITS
BILDNACHWEIS

Fotostudio Haslinger, 207 (*top*/oben)
Heeresbild- und -filmstelle, 15 (*top right*/rechts oben), 20, 21, 30 (*top*/oben), 38 (*top*/oben), 41, 51, 55, 58 (*top*/oben), 59 (*top right*/rechts oben), 62 (*top*/oben), 63 (*top*/oben), 65 (*top*/oben), 69 (*bottom*/unten), 72, 74 (*top*/oben), 81, 97 (*top*/oben), 100 (*bottom*/unten), 108, 109, 128 (*top*/oben), 133 (*top*/oben), 134, 135, 149, 151, 152, 189, 191 (*bottom*/unten), 193, 203, 209 (*top*/oben), 210, 216 (*bottom*/unten)
Kurier-Foto, Willi Schraml, 156, 157
Kurier-Foto, Gerhard Sokol, 16 (*top left*/links oben), 31 (*top*/oben), 61, 67 (*right*/rechts)
Peter Lehner, 211

SPONSORS
SPONSOREN

Sponsors of this book
Sponsoren dieses Buches

Österreichische Postsparkasse
Amt der Steiermärkischen Landesregierung, Abt. Wissenschaft und Forschung
Karl Kahane Stiftung
Magistrat der Stadt Wien, Kulturabteilung
Bundeskanzleramt Sektion II – Bundespressedienst
Bundeskanzleramt – Kunstsektion

Sponsors and supporters of the Middle East Youth Peace Forum
Sponsoren und Unterstützer des Nahost-Jugend-Friedensforums

Bundeskanzleramt
Bundesministerium für Wissenschaft und Verkehr
Bundesministerium für Unterricht und kulturelle Angelegenheiten
Bundesministerium für Umwelt, Familie und Jugend
Franz Vranitzky (Fulbright Preis)
Bundesministerium für Auswärtige Angelegenheiten
Stadt Wien
Wien xtra
Österreichische Nationalbank
Österreichische Postsparkasse
Karl Kahane Stiftung
Jugendreferat Tirol/JUFF